Melody Maker

Melody Maker

Classic ROCK INTERVIEWS

Compiled by Allan Jones

MANDARIN

Consultant Editor: Allan Jones

Editor: Mike Evans
Design: Ashley Western
Production Controller: Antonia McCardle

First published in 1994 by
Mandarin Paperbacks, an imprint of
Reed Consumer Books Limited,
Michelin House, 81 Fulham Road,
London SW3 6RB
and Auckland, Melbourne, Singapore and Toronto

A Catalogue record for this book is available from the British Library

ISBN 0–749–31885–6

Printed in Great Britain by The Bath Press, Avon

Contents

Introduction   6

1 **John Lennon** *In the studio with Lennon and Spector*   Richard Williams   10

2 **David Bowie** *Oh you pretty thing*   Michael Watts   19

3 **Bob Dylan** *The man called Alias*   Michael Watts   25

4 **Bruce Springsteen** *Lone star*   Michael Watts   42

5 **Rolling Stones** *Exiles on main street*   Michael Watts   57

6 **Bob Marley** *'Don't deal with dark things'*   Ray Coleman   64

7 **Marvin Gaye** *What's going on*   Geoff Brown   71

8 **Sex Pistols** *Rotten!*   Allan Jones   82

9 **Lou Reed** *'Don't make me cry – there's only one Lou Reed'* Allan Jones   94

10 **Eric Clapton** *Portrait of the artist as a working man* Chris Welch   113

11 **Chrissie Hynde** *Say a prayer for the Pretenders*   Mark Williams   129

12 **The Clash** *Banging on the White House door*   Allan Jones   139

13 **Blondie** *Fear of flying*   Harry Doherty   158

14 **Sting** *Can't stand losing*   Allan Jones   171

15 **U2** *The only flame in town*   Adam Sweeting   189

16 **Neil Young** *Legend of a loner*   Adam Sweeting   200

17 **REM** *Welcome to the occupation*   Mat Smith   206

18 **Morrissey** *Viva hate*   Simon Reynolds   216

19 **Public Enemy** *Black Power*   Stud Brothers   223

20 **Elvis Costello** *Songs of love and hate*   Allan Jones   234

21 **Nirvana** *Crucified by success?*   Everett True   247

About the writers   254

Introduction

IT seems like a lifetime ago, and I guess it probably is.

In the murmuring early months of 1974, I was nearly a year out of art school and working in London in the mail order department of a bookshop near Piccadilly Circus. I had never known such teeth-grinding tedium.

It was a season of relentless Dickensian gloom, from which I was thankfully delivered when I saw an ad in Time Out, the London listings magazine. Melody Maker was looking for a new writer. Encouraged by friends, I applied for the job. To my vast and eternal surprise, I was first interviewed and quickly afterwards offered a job as junior reporter/feature writer.

LOOKING back, it is not difficult to recall the strange kind of awe I felt in those first few weeks and months. For a start, MM's offices in those days were in Fleet Street, which seemed rather grand. The gig had its share of glamour, too.

Within a couple of weeks on the staff, I was swanking around the Brompton Road with Bryan Ferry, meeting Leonard Cohen for lunch in Sloane Square, getting drunk with Alice Cooper at the Savoy, where he kept a large plastic dustbin full of beer and ice in his suite.

There was more to my feeling at home than the mere conviviality of my new job, however. I had been reading MM for the best part of ten years and knew it and its writers with a familiarity born of something approaching obsession.

I think the writer who first made an impression upon me in those early years of reading MM was Chris Welch. For a start, he seemed to know everybody, from the Stones to Cream and Jimi Hendrix. But there is nothing especially pally about his 1978 interview with Eric Clapton, whom he had known since the guitarist's days with John Mayall's Bluesbreakers, in which the now-sober guitar legend was cajoled into a spurious defence of his notorious 1976 speech supporting Enoch Powell's anti-immigration policies, which he delivered from a stage in Birmingham in a bout of drunken idiocy.

If MM was central to the shape my life was beginning to take at the end of the Sixties, by the early Seventies it was even more essential. By now, MM's editor Ray Coleman, whose own journalism is represented here by a typically adoring profile of Bob Marley, had a staff of brilliant writers, among them Richard Williams, Michael Watts, Roy Hollingworth and Geoff Brown.

Prior to what was starting to happen at places like Melody Maker in the late Sixties, and a few years later at NME with the introduction of writers like Nick Kent and Charles Shaar Murray, pop writing was bland, superficial, gossipy, uncritical. You often had the impression of press releases being re-written, a dependency on the second-hand. Even the best lacked personality.

Melody Maker began to change things. The paper assumed a new authority. It had always had writers like the legendary Max Jones, who was widely regarded as one of the great jazz critics of the century, now other expert voices were heard - Geoff Brown, for instance, on black music. Even for someone who'd been brought up on the squalling guitars and adolescent whining of white rock'n'roll, his profiles of soul giants like Marvin Gaye, who he interviewed in 1976 when Gaye made his belated UK concert debut, became essential reading.

We were also suddenly in the front line, eye-witnesses, it seemed, to what was going down.

Here, for instance, was Richard Williams - in the studio with John Lennon and Phil Spector, at the sessions that produced "Happy Xmas (War Is Over)". You read things like this and they took your breath away.

Then there was Mick Watts in Mexico, on location with Sam Peckinpah and Bob Dylan on the set of "Pat Garrett & Billy The Kid", on the road in Texas with Bruce Springsteen, for one of the first major pieces that appeared in the UK on the so-called Boss, and in Jamaica with The Rolling Stones. And with a demonstrable eye for a good old fashioned scoop, here was Watts cannily persuading David Bowie to come clean about his bi-sexuality - an interview as famous as Bowie's outrageous and unforgettable first appearance as Ziggy Stardust on Top Of The Pops.

The style of writing he encouraged made him an abiding influence on the future development of Melody Maker; certainly, he helped shaped much of my own writing, including the account that appears here of a 1978 encounter with Lou Reed in New York.

If he was still reading MM in the early Eighties, I'm sure Mick would have found much to admire in Adam Sweeting's notable contributions to the paper, which are represented here by pieces on U2 and Neil Young. With an impeccable sense of timing, Adam struck up a friendship with Bono just as "The Unforgettable Fire" was about to launch U2 into the realms of international mega stardom and his 1985 report from New York is a vivid and dramatic evocation of a group coming to uncertain grips with the inevitability of their success.

A few months later, Sweeting found himself touring America with rock's most legendary maverick, the great Neil Young. The former political radical had come out in support of Ronald Reagan's bullish patriotism. Many of his fans were appalled. So was his record company, who took the unprecedented step of suing Neil for being wilfully uncommercial. You came away from Adam's piece with a brilliantly clear idea of Young's majestic and uncompromising iconoclasm, which is something the so-called grunge bands so admired about him when they re-discovered him some years later.

We were the first music paper to give substantial space to Elvis Costello, and in 1977 carried the first major interview with him - though the piece here is from 1989, when Elvis was talking up his most recent LP, "Spike".

And however slow we were initially to respond to punk, we were certainly in the right place at the right time with The Sex Pistols during Jubilee Week in 1977, when "God Save The Queen" was outraging the nation and the Pistols were being harrassed at every turn. We were also the only UK music paper with The Clash on their unhappy first American tour, which quickly descended into a series of bickering disputes and disenchantment. The same month in 1979, a smitten Mark Williams introduced us to Chrissie Hynde and The Pretenders. From the same period, we also have Harry Doherty on the domestic arrangements of Deborah Harry and Chris Stein, as Blondie began their commercial reign. That September, we were also at home with Sting just as The Police were about to be confirmed as bona fide rock gods.

AND then they made me editor.

When I took over in 1984, MM had been through a couple of lean years. It was time to look for new voices, new opinions, new writers who would champion new bands. What I wanted most for Melody Maker to do was create a climate of enthusiasm. What I guess I meant by that was having the nerve to get behind bands we believed in, to not be shy about our enthusiasms. It was time to start sticking our necks out.

And we did, with The Smiths, Happy Mondays, The Stone Roses, and The Pixies in the Eighties, and more recently with Suede, who were MM cover stars before they'd even released a record, and Pearl Jam, whose first front page anywhere was an MM cover in February 1982. In late 1982, our New York correspondent, David Fricke, who's now the music editor at Rolling Stone, introduced us to a new American band he'd fallen for in a big way. They were called R.E.M. and they were a cover story in MM before even the hippest US rock magazines picked up on them.

We've carried a lot of good pieces on R.E.M. down the years, among the most notable of which is Mat Smith's feature on the making of "Document", which is still regarded by R.E.M. aficianodos as the band's best album. Without wanting to overstate our friendship with R.E.M., it might still be noted that when Michael Stipe broke a long press silence last year, it was with an exclusive interview in Melody Maker. The writer was Mat Smith.

We seem to have a similar sort of relationship with Nirvana. In January, 1989,

Everett True was the first UK rock writer to report from Seattle on the city's Sub Pop label and its emerging grunge scene. As The Legend!, he played a show at Washington State University. Nirvana were the support band. Thus began an enduring friendship with the band.

As MM reinvented itself in the mid-Eighties, we began to recruit new writers, and among the new enlistments were Simon Reynolds and The Stud Brothers. Simon came from Monitor, a provocative and highly articulate fanzine, from which we also shamelessly poached David Stubbs, and together they brought a radical and astringent intelligence and an urivalled breadth of knowledge to our pages. Witness Simon's definitive interview with Morrissey, the former indie godhead of The Smiths, which developed into a fascinating debate on the nature of fame and obsession.

When The Studs first appeared in the MM office, you wondered how they'd got past security. They looked like the survivors of a mercenary commando unit and quickly became notorious for their confrontational noholds-barred outspokenness and controversial views on just about everything.

While most young white rock writers were drooling over the militant black radicalism of Public Enemy, and the spuriously romantic Uzis-with-everything gangbanging imagery of rap, The Studs were tackling PE head-on about the contradictions of their philosophy, particularly their anti-semitism. A year later, New York's Village Voice went through the roof on the same topic.

It was old news, of course, to anyone who regularly read MM.

MAINLY because I didn't speak to any of them, I don't know what the other contributors to this anthology feel about the pieces of theirs we have disinterred and re-printed, some of them many years after they were originally written. Re-reading some of my own pieces made me want to fart with embarrassment. You have to remember that a lot of these articles were written on the hoof, scribbled down in bars, hotel rooms, on tour buses and jets, with dealines usually looming, presses waiting to roll.

So the immediate temptation, looking at them again, was to go back and start re-writing, tidy things up, temper the more fevered outpourings, edit the past with the benefit of hindsight.

But while we may have become wiser with the passing of time, we may not be quite so entertaining. So we left them as they were. I think they can stand up for themselves.

Allan Jones London
January 1994

1

In the studio with Lennon and Spector

November 6 1971

Up on the 17th floor of the St. Regis Hotel in New York City, **John Lennon is learning to type.**
P . . . I . . . M . . . P, he types. I AM A PIMP.

"It's great," he says, "Yoko's teaching me."

John is in his bedroom, surrounded by the detritus of creation: guitars, books, notepads, nylon-tipped pens, and . . . a box full of Elvis Presley singles.

"I asked someone to get all his old singles for me," he says, now down on his hands and knees, opening the box and spilling the bright red RCA labels over the floor.

The next ten minutes are spent sorting them out. "My Baby Left Me," "Hound Dog," "One Night," and the old Sun classics are in one pile, while crap like "Bossa Nova Baby" and "Are You Lonesome Tonight" go on another.

"I'm gonna have a jukebox with just Elvis records on it. Isn't it great?"

In the next room, the living room, is still more tribute to the life and works of a total media freak. There are piles of Yoko's book, Grapefruit, stacks of big film cans, and a hi-fi.

His travelling record collection includes albums by Bo Diddley (three), Chuck Berry (two), Lenny Bruce (six), the Mothers (everything), Paul McCartney ("Ram" – and it's been played at least once), and Link Wray (with cover inscribed "To John and Yoko – thanks for remembering – Peace, Link Wray").

The story behind the Wray inscription is that John and Yoko were getting out of the lift at 1700 Broadway, which houses Allen Klein's office, when they were confronted by Wray, who was going up to Polydor's offices in the same building.

Wray apparently said, "Hey – John and Yoko." John didn't say anything to him, but turned to Yoko and breathed, "Yoko, that's Link Wray. Without him. . . ." Whether it's true or merely apocryphal, it illustrates one of John's most endearing characteristics: he *remembers*.

Back in the bedroom, John's talking about the Plastic Ono Band, and his plans for going on the road early in 1972.

"I've got a lot to learn," he sighs. "It's been seven years, you know . . . . but it's important to get the band on the road, to get tight. It's been fun just turning up at odd gigs like Toronto and the Lyceum and the Fillmore, but I'm sick of having to sing 'Blue Suede Shoes' because we haven't rehearsed anything."

To that end, the band will have a nucleus of John (guitar and vocals), Yoko (vocals), Nicky Hopkins (piano), Klaus Voorman (bass), and Jim Keltner (drums). With luck, there'll also be Phil Spector on guitar and vocals, on stage for the first time since the Teddy Bears (which comes into the Believe-It-When-You-See-It department), and a lead guitarist. John wrote to Eric Clapton, offering him the gig, but Eric isn't too well and didn't reply.

"We'll probably get some kid who just walks in and knocks us out. D'you know anything about a guy called Roy Buchanan? He's supposed to be the greatest, but I've never heard of him. I'll have to find out. I don't want to play lead – I'm just an amateur."

But the flexibility will still be there, and other musicians will be able to come and go as they wish. The nucleus will ensure that they don't have to jam all night on old 12-bars.

John wants to make the whole thing into a travelling circus, sending Yippie leader Jerry Rubin ahead of the troupe to round up local bands and street theatre groups in whatever cities they're playing. As an illustration of the kind of people they want. John mentioned David Peel and the Lower East Side in New York, and the Pink Fairies in London.

He gets to talking about his songs, and how he pinches bits from his favourite rock and roll numbers. There's a new one about Chuck Berry and Bo Diddley, which he sings sitting on his bed, and he shows you how the middle eight is pinched from U.S. Bonds' "Quarter To Three," which he heard on the radio the other day.

Then there's the song he and the Plastic Ono Band will be recording that very night, for their Christmas single. It's called "Happy Christmas (War Is Over)," and he says that when he first played it to Spector, the producer said that the first line is a direct crib from the Paris Sisters' "I Love How You Love Me," which Phil produced back in the pre-Crystals days.

"I like quoting from old songs," John says, "but you get into such trouble with copyrights. It's a drag."

He jams on what looks like a set of earphones, with an antenna protruding from each side. It turns out to be an FM stereo radio, and within seconds he offers it to Yoko.

"Hey, listen Yoko, that's 'Get A Job,' one of the old ones." She listens, and he turns. "I'm having to educate her about rock and roll, you see."

THAT same evening, John is sitting on the fringed carpet of the Record Plant, a studio on West 44th Street. He's surrounded by five young acoustic guitarists, to whom he's teaching the chords of "Happy Christmas."

Why all those rhythm guitars? Listen – just remember who's producing this session, brother.

One of the guitarists is Hugh McCracken, the brilliant session musician who played on "Ram," but John doesn't know that yet.

He asks them for their names. "Chris." "Teddy." "Stu." "Hugh." John turns to Yoko. "Hey, that Hugh looks like Ivan, doesn't he? Hugh, you look just like an old school-mate of mine."

There's a little break, and everybody gets up and walks around. Someone tells John about Hugh.

"Oh, so you were just auditioning on 'Ram,' were you?" John asks. "Yeah, 'e said you were all right." Everyone grins.

They're back to learning the tune, getting the feel. "Just pretend it's Christmas," John tells them. "I'm Jewish," says one. "Well pretend it's your birthday then."

They've all got it down, so John leads them into a jam on "Too Much Monkey Business," "Rock Island Line," and "Slippin' And Slidin'." It's meat and drink to him.

Suddenly there's a little flurry at the entrance. Phil Spector's arrived, in big shades, wearing a red and white button saying "Back To Mono," which breaks everyone up. But he's serious, you know.

Immediately, the session is working. Within seconds of getting behind the huge board, Spector is thinking in terms not just of sound, but of arrangement, drama, *production*. It takes him about ten seconds to get a sound which transforms the guitars from a happy rabble into a brilliant cutting wash of colour, and they aren't even miked properly yet.

"Play that back to 'em," Phil tells the engineer. "Get 'em relaxed." It does just that, and during the playback Phil goes into the studio and dances around with John.

They run through the changes again, with Nicky Hopkins on piano this time. Immediately, Phil tells him: "Nicky, I'd like to hear more of that in octaves in the right hand . . . . makes it more dramatic." John leans down to the guitar mike and shouts: "Don't dictate on them yet, Phil. Let's get comfortable first."

Already, you see, Spector is into the groove, moulding and blending and transforming in the tradition of "Be My Baby," "Then He Kissed Me," and "River Deep." Right now, well ahead of anyone (even Lennon), he's hearing what it's going to sound like when it's coming out of a million transistors.

At this point, they add bass and drums. Jim Keltner settles behind his kit, and one of the rhythm guitarists is moved over to the bass because Klaus's flight from Germany has been delayed and he's going to miss the session. They can't wait.

They run it down a few times, and Keltner's expression while playing is like that of a man whose toes are slowly being eaten away by a shoal of piranhas. It's sounding very good, the tape is spinning all the time, and after each run they come back and listen."

John: "I like ones that sound like records . . . ."

". . . . before you've made 'em." Phil finishes the sentence for him.

Without even seeming to notice, they're doing takes. During the second or third, it really begins to lift off. Phil is sitting at the board, staring through the sound-proofed window into the studio, spitting out comments at the engineer: "More echo on the piano, Roy . . . . more echo . . . . more . . . . more . . . . more echo, c'mon! More! That's it!"

He stands up during the second chorus, arms wind-milling, looking at Keltner, signalling and willing him to lay into his tom-toms, urging him to explode like Hel Blaine did almost ten years ago. Keltner strains to oblige, and the take ends in a blaze of glory with Phil shouting "F*****g great! great!"

Now, as the overdubs start, the Spector magic is again overwhelmingly apparent. At John's suggestion, the acoustic guitars play a mandolin-like riff, strongly reminiscent of Ronnie Spector's "Try Some, Buy Some," and all sorts of percussive effects are tried.

Nicky plays chimes and glockenspiel, which have been hastily hired, and Keltner adds a jangling four-on-the-bar on a handy pair of sleigh bells.

"How can you make a song called 'Happy Christmas' without bells?" Phil had asked, rhetorically, earlier. Now he's smiling and mutters from the corner of his mouth: "I know something about Christmas records, you know."

Instantly, minds float back to Philles LP 4005, "A Christmas Gift To You," several months in the making back there in the Sixties, and now a rare classic to those who know it. After that, Phil probably knew more about making Christmas records than anyone in the world.

The instrumental dubs over, time comes for the vocal track to be cut. The song itself is really in three parts: the verse, sung by John; the chorus, sung by Yoko; and a secondary chorus, sung under the lead vocal, for which they'll be getting in a bunch of kids the next day.

John says that he wrote it "because I was sick of 'White Christmas'," and it could well take over as the annual Yuletide anthem. It's terrifically singable, in the tradition of "All You Need Is Love" or "Give Peace A Chance," and it's very pretty too. The words are simple and direct, with the chorus going "War is over/if you want it/war is over now," while John and Yoko express appropriate good wishes to all mankind.

The pair of them enter the studio, clap on the cans, and start singing over the track. John sounds wheezy, unable to hit the high notes, and Phil shouts through the talk back: "Yoko's out-singing you, John." He tells everyone in the booth: "He's smoking his ass off while he's singing," and shakes his head in disapproval.

John finally gets Yoko to come in at all the right places, with the aid of tactful prods in the back, and when Phil's got the right echo on the voices they finally lay it down right, and come back to listen to the rough mix.

It's right, and they start talking about what they're going to do with the strings, which they'll overdub in a couple of days. Phil has the idea of getting them to play "Silent Night" over the fade, and after falling about they all agree that it's exactly right.

Nicky is worrying about the piano part, which he's already overdubbed, and wants to do it again. They listen back once more, tell him it's perfectly all right as it is, and John adds: "Did you know that George wanted to redo his guitar solos on 'Gimme Some Truth' and 'How Do You Sleep'? That's the best he's ever played in his life, and he'd never get that feeling again, but he'd go on for ever if you let him."

Once again they remix what they have. By this time it's four o'clock, and after a few more listens everyone goes home. Three hours later, I wake up singing "War is over . . . . if you want it . . . . war is over now."

JIM KELTNER is the kind of musician all too few drummers are. His experience comes from long days and nights in the studios of Los Angeles, and from years of listening to the best.

His musical interests are wide. He talks with equal pleasure of going to see Ornette Coleman years ago, when the altoist had drummer Ed Blackwell in his band and of living near Hal Blaine, who himself created a whole style of drumming, partly on the early Philles records.

Keltner talks softly, but wields a big talent. His playing is tight, precise, and funky, and Lennon says of him: "He's a drummer who leads you, instead of dragging, and there aren't too many of those." That's why he's in the Plastic Ono Band, instead of all the other names you could mention.

He knows a hell of a lot more about more musicians than most of his contemporaries bother to learn. He particularly reveres the late Benny Benjamin, whose work gave the early-Sixties Motown records their unstoppable drive, and for tightness, he says, you can't beat Jabbo, James Brown's veteran percussionist.

Drinking an orange juice on 8th Avenue just before dawn, he pricks his ears to the sound of Diana Ross's "Surrender," on the jukebox. It's all music – he's all music.

IT'S the following night, and the band is running through the song which is going to be the single's B-side, Yoko's "Snow Is Falling," the first of her songs that she ever showed John, when they first got together five years ago. At last, she's getting a chance to record it.

But there's an argument. John and Yoko can't agree about the tempo. "I'm not gonna play on this," says John, who was picking out lines on heavy-reverb guitar. "I asked you to play the organ," says Yoko. "I've been asking you to do that all along."

John decides to go back into the booth, where Phil greets him with "I thought this was supposed to be a light thing." It was, John agrees, but "she says 'faster' and they all get to rocking like —."

Yoko is telling Nicky to play lighter on the intro. "Pretend that it's snowing. . . . that snow is melting on your fingertips. Not that banging."

Nicky gets it right, while Klaus and Hugh McCracken (who's been invited back after his performance the previous night, and on the strength of his reputation) work out little runs and licks which turn out like early Curtis Mayfield.

They all try it, and Yoko and Klaus get into a shouting match about where the chords go at the end of the song. Klaus gets up, unstraps his bass, and appears ready to walk about. But John placates both him and Yoko, and they try it again – with successful results.

They take it, get a good one, and come back to the booth.

John: "Fantastic . . . ."

Phil: "Great, great tape echo. . . ."

Yoko: "How was my voice?"

Phil: "Great . . . . lots of tape echo . . . ."

It sounds simple and pretty, but within five minutes they're talking about adding organ, chimes, more guitar, and even sound effects.

What they want is the sound of a celeste, but there isn't one available, so the engineers get to work to make the electric piano sound like one.

While they discuss it, Phil pronounces the name "cheleste." Everybody else starts by calling it "Seleste," But within minutes, it's "cheleste" all round. Phil is the musical heavy, you see, and if that's how he says it, that's how it is.

As the engineers work, Nicky and Hugh and Jim start to play the blues.

"Oh-oh," says Phil. "They've started jamming, and we'll never get anything done. Let's put a stop to that." He moves to the connecting door.

"STOP JAMMING" screams Yoko, neatly bursting the talkback speakers. They stop as one man, in mid-semiquaver, leaving John to add, almost apologetically: "Well, you've got to do something while they're trying to make the piano sound like a celeste." His pronunciation has slipped back to the "s."

Yoko is obviously tense, and confides that she believes the musicians don't take her songs as seriously as they might, but this is a very good song, no doubt about it; very attractive and extremely commercial, and by the time the overdubs have been done it sounds like a potential A-side, much stronger than her current single, "Mrs Lennon."

Only one thing remains, and that's to put on the sound effects. Someone digs out the effects album that all studios keep for such occasions, and they decide to open and close the track with the sound of "Feet In The Snow," superimposed on "Strong Wind."

The engineers begin splicing the tapes, and Phil asks John: "Have you heard Paul's new album?"

"No."

"It's really bad . . . . just four musicians, and it's awful."

"Don't talk about it. It depresses me.

"Don't worry, John. 'Imagine' is number one, and this will be number one too. That's all that matters."

"No, it's not that. It's just that whenever anybody mentions his name, I don't think about the music – I think about all the business crap. Don't talk about him."

Splicing over, the lights are turned off for the final playback, and it's magical. "Listen . . . . the snow is falling everywhere."

Leaving the studio, it's a shock to realise that those soft, white flakes aren't drifting down through cold night air. Actually, it's quite warm out.

JOHN and Yoko are being talked about as the new Burton and Taylor, but really they're closer to Douglas Fairbanks and Mary Pickford, in the way that they're at the centre of an artistic maelstrom.

They've been in New York since the middle of August, and they're likely to stay there a long time. John's recent statement, in the MM, that they're not appreciated in Britain, is entirely understandable when one sees them in New York.

There, they're in a creative milieu which understands and embraces them, and, what's more, moves at their phenomenal pace. Everybody travelled to Syracuse, in upstate New York, for Yoko's recent exhibition, whereas if they'd held something similar in, say, Coventry, it would have been virtually ignored.

It's a never-ending furore, and to zone in on it even harder, they've moved out of the St. Regis Hotel and into the Village, where they've bought one loft and are renting another, from ex-Spoonful drummer, Joe Butler.

Butler's loft where they're presently living while the other is being readied, has two huge rooms with a wrought-iron spiral staircase up to a small roof garden. The walls are painted brick, the furnishings and fitting immaculate and mostly interesting antiques.

The Lennons have both bought push-bikes, which is the way to travel around the Village. John's is English, Yoko's is Japanese. Coincidence, they say, and John's has got a nice shiny chromed bell on the conservative sit-up-and-beg handlebars.

"Everybody cycles around the Village," John says. "Dylan goes about on his all the time, chaining it to the railings when he stops, and nobody ever recognises him. I can't wait to get out on mine."

But the main beauty of the Village is the company they can keep. In the next loft to the Lennons is John Cage, whom they haven't seen yet (although

Yoko keeps trying to rouse him by banging on the windows), and round the corner are Dylan, Jerry Rubin, and a host of other superstars.

"It's the best place in the world," John states flatly. "Every time the car leaves the Village, I feel sick. Going back to England is like going to Denmark – and I don't want to live in Denmark."

SUNDAY afternoon at the Record Plant, and they're starting early because the choir is there, and the choir has to be in bed soon.

The choir is 30 black kids, aged from about four to 12, with a quartet of nubile young teens whom John instantly dubs "The Supremes." A few mothers are there, too, generally shushing and finger-wagging and making sure that ribbon-bows aren't crooked.

John and Yoko teach the kids the song and the words to "Happy Christmas" from a blackboard, and after only a few tries they've got it, superimposed on the already-mixed track.

"F——g great!" shouts Phil afterwards, leaping around, and the engineer quickly checks that the talkback is off.

It's all finished now, apart from the strings, so the Lennons, the band, the kids, the engineers, the secretaries, Phil, and Phil's brother-in-law Joe gather round to pose for a picture for the cover of the single.

A plastic Christmas tree, with lights, has been erected, and towers above the group. The photographer is being a little slow, having trouble getting everyone into the frame, so Phil takes over: "C'mon Ian . . . . when I shout 'ONE TWO THREE,' everybody shout 'HAPPY CHRISTMAS' and you take the picture. ONE TWO THREE (HAPPY CHRISTMAS) ONE TWO THREE (HAPPY CHRISTMAS) ONE TWO THREE (HAPPY CHRISTMAS). Okay Ian, you got it."

I'll bet he even produces his breakfasts.

Richard Williams

2

Oh you pretty thing

DAVID BOWIE
January 22 1972

EVEN **though he wasn't wearing silken gowns right out of Liberty's, and his long blond hair no longer fell wavily past his shoulders David Bowie was looking yummy.**

He'd slipped into an elegant-patterned type of combat suit, very tight around the legs, with the shirt unbuttoned to reveal a full expanse of white torso. The trousers were turned up at the calves to allow a better glimpse of a huge pair of red plastic boots with at least three-inch rubber soles; and the hair was Vidal Sassooned into such impeccable shape that one held one's breath in case the slight breeze from the open window dared to ruffle it. I wish you could have been there to varda him; he was so super.

David uses words like "verda" and "super" quite a lot. He's gay, he says. Mmmmmm. A few months back, when he played Hampstead's Country Club, a small, greasy club in north London which has seen all sorts of exciting occasions, about half the gay population of the city turned up to see him in his massive floppy velvet hat, which he twirled around at the end of each number.

According to Stuart Lyon, the club's manager, a little gay brother sat right up close to the stage throughout the whole evening, absolutely spellbound with admiration.

As it happens, David doesn't have much time for Gay Liberation, however. That's a particular movement he doesn't want to lead. He despises all these tribal qualifications. Flower power he enjoyed, but it's individuality that he's really trying to preserve. The paradox is that he still has what he describes as "a good relationship" with his wife. And his baby son, Zowie. He supposes he's what people call bisexual.

They call David a lot of things. In the States he's been referred to as the English Bob Dylan and an avant garde outrage, all rolled up together. The New York Times talks of his "coherent and brilliant vision." They like him a lot there. Back home, in the very stiff upper lip UK, where people are outraged by Alice Cooper even, there ain't too many who have picked up on him. His last but one album, "The Man Who Sold The World," cleared 50,000 copies in the States; here it sold about five copies, and Bowie bought them.

Yes, but before this year is out all those of you who puked up on Alice are going to be focusing your passions on Mr. Bowie, and those who know where it's at will be thrilling to a voice that seemingly undergoes brilliant metamorphosis from song to song, a songwriting ability that will enslave the heart, and a sense of theatrics that will make the ablest thespians gnaw on their sticks of eyeliner in envy. All this, and an amazingly accomplished band, featuring super-lead guitarist Mick Ronson, that can smack you round the skull with their heaviness and soothe the savage breast with their delicacy. Oh, to be young again.

THE REASON is Bowie's new album, "Hunky Dory," which combines a gift for irresistible melody lines with lyrics that work on several levels – as straightforward narrative, philosophy or allegory, depending how deep you wish to plumb the depths. He has a knack of suffusing strong, simple pop melodies with words and arrangements full of mystery and darkling hints.

Thus "Oh! You Pretty Things," the Peter Noone hit, is on one strata, particularly the chorus, about the feelings of a father-to-be; on a deeper level it concerns Bowie's belief in a superhuman race – homo superior – to which he refers obliquely: "I think about a world to come/ where the books were found by The Golden Ones/ Written in pain, written in awe/ by a puzzled man who questioned what we were here for/ Oh, The Strangers Came Today, and it looks as though they're here to stay." The idea of Peter Noone singing such a heavy number fills me with considerable amusement. That's truly outrageous, as David says himself.

But then Bowie has an instinct for incongruities. On "The Man" album there's a bit at the end of "Black Country Rock" where he superbly parodies his friend Marc Bolan's vibrato warblings. On "Hunky Dory" he devotes a track called "Queen Bitch" to the Velvets, wherein he takes off to a tee the Lou Reed vocal and arrangement, as well as parodying, with a storyline about the singer's boyfriend being seduced by another queen, the whole Velvet Underground genre.

Then again, at various times on his albums he resorts to a very broad Cockney accent, as on "Saviour Machine" ("The Man") and here with "The Bewley Brothers." He says he copped it off Tony Newley, because he was mad about "Stop The World" and "Gurney Slade": He used to make his points with this broad Cockney accent and I decided that I'd use that now and again to drive a point home."

The fact that David Bowie has an acute ear for parody doubtless stems from an innate sense of theatre. He says he's more of an actor and entertainer than a musician; that he may, in fact, only be an actor and nothing else: "Inside this invincible frame there might be an invincible man." You kidding? "Not at all. I'm not particularly taken with life. I'd probably be very good as just an astral spirit."

BOWIE is talking in an office at Gem Music, from where his management operates. A tape machine is playing his next album, "The Rise And Fall of Ziggy Stardust And The Spiders From Mars," which is about this fictitious pop group. The music has got a very hard-edged sound, like "The Man Who Sold The World." They're releasing it shortly, even though "Hunky Dory" has only just come out.

Everyone just knows that David is going to be a lollapalooza of a superstar throughout the entire world this year, David more than most. His songs are always ten years ahead of their time, he says, but this year he has anticipated the trends: "I'm going to be huge, and it's quite frightening in a way," he says, his big red boots stabbing the air in time to the music. "Because I know that when I reach my peak and it's time for me to be brought down it will be with a bump."

The man who's sold the world this prediction has had a winner before, of course. Remember "Space Oddity," which chronicled Major Tom's dilemma, aside from boosting the sales of the stylophone? That was a top ten hit in '68, but since then Bowie has hardly performed at all in public. He appeared for a while at an arts lab he cofounded in Beckenham, Kent, where he lives, but when he realised that people were going there on a Friday night to see Bowie the hit singer working out, rather than for an idea of experimental art, he seems to have become disillusioned. That project foundered, and he wasn't up to going out on one-nighters throughout the country at that particular time.

So in the past three years he has devoted his time to the production of three albums, "David Bowie" (which contains "Space Oddity") and "The Man" for Philips, and "Hunky Dory" for RCA. His first album, "Love You Till Tuesday," was released in 1968 on the new Deram label but it didn't sell outstandingly, and Decca, it seems, lost interest in him.

It all began for him, though, when he was 15 and his brother gave him a copy of "The Subterraneans" by Jack Kerouac; when he decided he wanted to play an instrument he took up sax because that was the main instrument featured in the book (Gerry Mulligan, right?). So in '63 he was playing tenor in a London R & B band before going on to found a semi-pro progressive blues group, called David Jones and The Lower Third (later changing his name in '66 when Davy Jones of The Monkees became famous). He left this band in 1967 and became a performer in the folk clubs.

Since he was 14, however, he had been interested in Buddhism and Tibet, and after the failure of his first LP he dropped out of music completely and devoted his time to the Tibet Society, whose aim was to help the lamas driven out of that country in the Tibetan/Chinese war. He was instrumental in setting up the Scottish monastery in Dumfries in this period. He says, in fact, that he would have liked to have been a Tibetan monk, and would have done if he hadn't met Lindsay Kemp, who ran a mime company in London: "It was as magical as Buddhism, and I completely sold out and became a city creature. I suppose that's when my interest in image really blossomed."

DAVID'S present image is to come on like a swishy queen, a gorgeously effeminate boy. He's as camp as a row of tents, with his limp hand and trolling vocabulary. "I'm gay," he says, "and always have been, even when I was David Jones." But there's a sly jollity about how he says it, a secret smile at the corners of his mouth. He knows that in these times it's permissible to act like a male tart, and that to shock and outrage, which pop has always striven to do throughout its history, is a balls-breaking process.

And if he's not an outrage, he is, at the least, an amusement. The expression of his sexual ambivalence establishes a fascinating game: is he, or isn't he? In a period of conflicting sexual identity he shrewdly exploits the confusion surrounding the male and female roles. "Why aren't you wearing your girl's dress today?" I said to him (he has no monopoly on tongue-in-cheek humour). "Oh dear," he replied, "you must understand that it's not a woman's. It's a man's dress."

He began wearing dresses of whatever gender, two years ago, but he says he had done outrageous things before that were just not accepted by society. It's just so happened, he remarks, that in the past two years people have loosened up to the fact that there are bisexuals in the world – "and – horrible fact – homosexuals." He smiles, enjoying his piece of addenda.

"The important fact is that I don't have to drag up. I want to go on like this for long after the fashion has finished. I'm just a cosmic yob, I suppose. I've always worn my own style of clothes. I design them. I designed this." He broke off to indicate with his arm what he was wearing. "I just don't like the clothes that you buy in shops. I don't wear dresses all the time, either. I change every day. I'm not outrageous. I'm David Bowie."

How does dear Alice go down with him, I asked, and he shook his head disdainfully: "Not at all. I bought his first album, but it didn't excite me or shock me. I think he's trying to be outrageous. You can see him poor dear, with his red eyes sticking out and his temples straining. He tries so hard. That bit he does with the boa constrictor, a friend of mine, Rudy Valentino, was doing ages before. The next thing I see is Miss C. with her boa. I find him very demeaning. It's very premeditated, but quite fitting with our era. He's probably more successful than I am at present, but I've invented a new category of artist, with my chiffon and taff. They call it pantomime rock in the States."

Despite his flouncing, however, it would be sadly amiss to think of David merely as a kind of glorious drag act. An image, once strained and stretched unnaturally, will ultimately diminish an artist. And Bowie is just that. He foresees this potential dilemma, too, when he says he doesn't want to emphasise his external self much more. He has enough image. This year he is devoting most of his time to stage work and records. As he says, that's what counts at the death. He will stand or fall on his music.

As a songwriter he doesn't strike me as an intellectual, as he does some. Rather, his ability to express a theme from all aspects seems intuitive. His songs are less carefully structured thoughts than the outpourings of the unconscious. He says he rarely tries to communicate to himself, to think an idea out.

"If I see a star and it's red I wouldn't try to say why it's red. I would think how shall I best describe to X that that star is such a colour. I don't question much; I just relate. I see my answers in other people's writings. My own work can be compared to talking to a psychoanalyst. My act is my couch."

It's because his music is rooted in this lack of consciousness that he admires Syd Barrett so much. He believes that Syd's freewheeling approach to lyrics opened the gates for him; both of them, he thinks, are the creation of their own songs. And if Barrett made that initial breakthrough, it's Lou Reed and Iggy Pop who have since kept him going and helped him to expand his unconsciousness.

"

He and Lou and Iggy, he says, are going to take over the whole world. They're the songwriters he admires.

His other great inspiration is mythology. He has a great need to believe in the legends of the past, particularly those of Atlantis; and for the same need he has created a myth of the future, a belief in an imminent race of supermen called homo superior. It's his only glimpse of hope, he says-"all the things that we can't do they will."

It's a belief created out of resignation with the way society in general has moved. He's not very hopeful about the future of the world. A year ago he was saying that he gave mankind another 40 years. A track on his next album, outlining his conviction, is called "Five Years." He's a fatalist, a confirmed pessimist, as you can see.

"Pretty Things," that breezy Herman song, links this fatalistic attitude with the glimmer of hope that he sees in the birth of his son, a sort of poetic equation of homo superior. "I think," he says, "that we have created a new kind of person in a way. We have created a child who will be so exposed to the media that he will be lost to his parents by the time he is 12."

That's exactly the sort of techological vision that Stanley Kubrick foresees for the near future in "A Clockwork Orange." Strong stuff. And a long, long way away from camp carry-ons.

Don't dismiss David Bowie as a serious musician just because he likes to put us all on a little.

Michael Watts

The man called Alias

BOB DYLAN
February 3 1973

UNDER any other circumstances the remark wouldn't have been unusual. But today, riding this plane 20,000 feet above the Mexican desert, with these people, wow, the normality of it struck a freaky note.

The little guy with the pale, wispy beard and the worn black stovepipe hat, who had not spoken much to anybody these past few weeks, had sidled cautiously down the aisle of the aircraft and nudged me abruptly in the shoulder.

The distant view of the mesas, like red, swollen welts, lying thousands of feet below, switched suddenly to a close-up of blue, almost translucent eyes.

"You with Melody Maker?" he demanded. Surprised nod. "Is Max Jones still working there?" Max Jones? Yes, sure he was, but . . . you remember!

A slight, unsmiling inclination of the fuzzy, black-topped head leaning over the seat. It stretched back all of ten years now to the time when this young folkie played the Royal Festival Hall.

He was only a kid then, but he'd stayed at the swanky Mayfair Hotel. He drank Beaujolais, wore jeans, boots and a leather jacket. He told everyone he wrote "finger-pointing" songs. He told Max Jones.

As a matter of fact, it had been the first time Bob Dylan was ever interviewed in Britain.

RODOLFO The Glasses knew all about Durango.

He had carried my bags to the room on the fourth floor of the Camino Real Hotel, the most space-age in Mexico City, where the swarthy porters wore black capes printed with gold lozenges. Rodolfo was fussing with the curtains whilst waiting for his tip.

"Durango? Si, si." He pushed his dark glasses further back on his nose, a short, stocky Mexican, eager to please as always the Americanos.

"Very, very hot, very dry." His hands moved like butterflies. "Make lots of films there." A pause. He brightens. "You go for film?" His face split into two rows of white teeth.

Sam Peckinpah, I muttered.

"Sam Peckinpah!" he burst out. "Sam, he my friend!" It was as if the name of his own father had been invoked.

"He stay here. Great man – he drinks, drinks mucho." He put one hand to his lips and tilted back an imaginary glass, then shook his head in pure delight. I slipped the coins into his free hand.

"Thank you, senor, mucho gracias." He moved away.

"Tell him, when you see him," he said, closing the door, "you saw Rodolfo." He pointed to his eyes.

"He remember the glasses." I could hear his faint chuckle as he disappeared down the corridor.

Sam Peckinpah! The terrible if no longer the enfant, of Hollywood, the apostle of ultra-violence, even before Kubrick, the director of The Wild Bunch and Straw Dogs, the boozer, the wildman, the misogynist – that devil! (heavy-set).

In these times of spoof Westerns, comedy Westerns, black Westerns, fag Westerns a la Warhol, neo-Realism Westerns, anything-to-be-different Westerns, Peckinpah remained a hardliner in his attitude towards how cowboy movies should be made.

He believed in physicality and hard-core action, adhering to the myth of the Western but intent at the same time to dirty it up, to show some of the scabby underbelly. His pictures were made for men, just as surely as he was a man's man, and his tough outlook on both life and movies had spun a cult around him that had not been achieved without mishaps along the way.

After his first two pictures, The Deadly Companions and Ride The High Country, he had made Major Dundee in 1964 with Charlton Heston but the producer, Jerry Wexler (of Atlantic Records fame) had it re-edited.

He then went through a period of disillusionment. The producer of The Cincinnati Kid, Martin Ransohoff, sacked him, he lost a lot of dough, went in for hard-drinking, and had wife-trouble (he's twice married and divorced his Mexican wife, Begonia, and wedded the middle of last year a 29-year-old blonde, English secretary, Joie, whom he met in Twickenham whilst in England for the shooting of Straw Dogs).

Then, after a period in television, he made The Wild Bunch with William Holden, which capitalised in a tremendously successful fashion on the atmosphere of acceptable violence that was permeating motion pictures.

It turned around his ailing reputation at the same time that his slow-motion depiction of carnage made him the controversial eye of a critical whirlpool surrounding his bloody permissiveness.

"I want to rub their noses in violence," he told Time magazine. "I regard all men as violent, including myself." He had gone on to direct Dogs with Dustin Hoffman and Junior Bonner and The Getaway with Steve McQueen, all of which delineated further his buckets-of-blood approach to movie-making.

But now! No film of his had whipped up such pre-release speculation as the present one, Pat Garret And Billy The Kid, not so much because of him this time or his celluloid theories but because of a certain "actor."

I mean, James Coburn had done scores of films, like The Magnificent Seven, and Jason Robards Jnr was in Peckinpah's The Ballad Of Cable Hogue, and Kris Kristofferson might be a famous folksinger but he'd also acted already in two movies, Cisco Pike and Bloom In Love (with George Segal, which is to be released in May).

But Bob Dylan! Bob Dylan and Sam Peckinpah! At first glance it was old America meeting the new, the traditionalist values of the West encountering the pop surrealism of the East. It was a symbolic meeting of two vastly different generations, of two attitudes to life. It was all this, but more. Beneath the skin depth lay other meanings.

FOR Peckinpah, the inclusion in his movie of Dylan and, to a lesser extent, Kristofferson (whose lifestyle may be rock but who has much of the traditional about him), represents a mellowed acceptance of the youth culture and its totems, a phenomenon to which he has been totally deaf in his past work.

Doubtless he has been somewhat persuaded by their box-office appeal to the rock generation, which MGM studios, his financiers, will have pointed out.

But to Dylan the role is of much more momentous importance. He is the ageing and long-appointed prophet, who has grown old and increasingly distant in a role which for years has held for him no relevance yet which seems effectively to have constrained his talents.

It is more than two years since he made his last album, "New Morning," and there are apparently no plans for another solo venture; his contract with Columbia records has run out, although he can't deliver an album to another company unless he wishes to forego huge royalties CBS are holding.

He has consistently intimated to friends that he is tired of the music business, that he has no desire to play live anymore, and he takes little active part in it, except on a casual basis when he appears on the albums of friends like Doug Sahm and Steve Goodman.

Moreover, he has been away too long now to return to the heart of the action with the same pertinence as before, even if he wished to. And, as Grossman astutely realised, his past performances were so often uneven, anyway, as to necessitate them being infrequent.

He is Bob Dylan. But who is Bob Dylan? As the myth of the musician and the generational symbol rises like creeping fog he casts about for some direction, for a new purpose to it all.

He sees other pre-eminent musicians, like Lennon and Jagger, involved in movies. An old mentor is Andy Warhol. While down in Mexico a newer friend, Kris Kristofferson, is making a film. About Billy The Kid.

Billy The Kid! Whatever the nature of fact, Billy The Kid is part of American legend. As was John Wesley Hardin(g), and him he knows about, from the past, from an idea he once used. Down in Durango, Mexico, visiting Kristofferson on the set, he writes this song about Billy and plays it to the cast. It only follows that he should get a role in his first full feature film.

He got the part, in fact, through a combination of circumstances precipitated by Bert Block, Kristofferson's manager. Block, an old music pro who at one time managed Billie Holiday, was the guy who looked after the arrangements when he played the Isle of Wight. He's the nearest thing Dylan has had to a business manager since he let his contract to Grossman expire (Grossman and Block were partners for a while, indeed, and handled Janis Joplin together).

Block mentioned to Dylan that Kristofferson was in a movie and suggested it to him as well. He also spoke to Gordon Carroll, the producer, who was delighted at the proposition.

Dylan had talks with Rudy Wurlitzer, the screenplay writer, and went to a private screening of The Wild Bunch. He was sceptical of the project at first. He only intended to see one reel. But then it stretched to three, to four . . . Dylan came out of MGM's theatre with a celluloid monkey riding on his back.

He was fascinated with the idea of a movie part as much as he was daunted by his feeling of inadequacy towards doing it. Before there had only been documentaries. And Peckinpah was a frightening genius!

But he went down with Bert to Mexico to exorcise his doubts. The first night they dined at Peckinpah's house on a meal of roast goat. Then he was shown around the set. He was particularly captivated by the wardrobe of Western clothes, trying on the hats and costumes like a kid dressing for a fancy dress party.

He looked around for a while, and then, on that second day, quietly picked up a guitar and sang to Kris and Coburn and Peckinpah this song he'd made up called "Billy The Kid." Peckinpah offered him a part there and then.

It's a small part as one of Billy's sidekicks but it would have been expanded any time he wished. The fact that he hasn't asked illustrates his tentativeness. He plays, with the most fitting of poetic justices, the part of Alias.

In the public life of the musician he is the man of uncertain identity. In the movies he is the man with no name. He continues to play the game of "famious-ity," as he once called it. But he may well have found that new direction which has been eluding him. People on the film say he would like to continue the part of Alias in succeeding movies, jokily preserving that anonymity.

In a sense Dylan is like Brando. The one is to the sixties what the other was to the fifties: a representation of their style and mood. In the late sixties, however, the charisma of both of them began to erode a little.

They began to go out of fashion and the criticisms increased about their performances, the one in films, the other on records.

The difference is that Brando has recently sought, and successfully achieved, his rejuvenation, with The Godfather and now Last Tango in Paris. Dylan is still in the process.

This movie is an enormous step in switching media to test the viability of his talent, not necessarily in transforming him into an actor but more in enabling him to ascertain for himself his filmic sense. It's a training ground for a possible directorial debut.

When I arrived in Durango he had been there for three months, since November 23. He had with him his wife, Sara, five kids and Rover the dog.

She had taken the children to Yucatan, a neighbouring state whose inhabitants, direct descendants of the Maya Indians, like to think of themselves as a separate entity from the rest of Mexico. They have a daughter, Maria, aged 11, and their eldest son is Jesse Byron, who's seven and reputedly something of a wild kid.

Maggie Netter, an MGM publicist, said she went riding with the boy on Sundays. "He's so intelligent! They all are. But they let them run wild, they don't look after them especially. They just let them do what they want. If they're going home they tell someone to bring the kids back with them, so they're always around people."

"

Wandering around Durango, in fact, and finding myself in one of the many banks, I came upon a Texan schoolmaster who was teaching at an American school there. Jesse was one of his pupils for a month.

This Texan was large-boned, wore a red, V-necked sweater and horn rims, and had an accent like the twang of a plucked bow-string.

"You must've taken the wrong turning somewhere," he smiled pleasantly after the introductions, and waved his hand generally at the town. The movie was mentioned. "I s'pose you're out here then for Bob Die-lan," he twanged, and then remarked about teaching Dylan's kid. The way he said it reminded me of ten years ago when no one in England seemed to know how to pronounce the name correctly.

I asked about the kid. He just gave a slow, Texan smile and muttered something inconsequential. Then I changed the subject and asked how people amused themselves in this place at night. Dull wasn't a strong enough word for my initial impression of Durango.

He looked at his companion, another schoolteacher, a Mexican woman in glasses, and said, "How do we amuse ourselves, Juanita?" and she shrugged her shoulders and smiled, and he smiled again. I couldn't guess what there was to smile about so much in this one-hoss city.

DURANGO is, indeed, a city, the capital of the state of Durango. It has the highest homicide rate in Mexico. A hundred and sixty thousand people live there digging out gold, silver or iron (particularly) from the mines, or else working in the numerous small stores that serve the community.

It seems incredible that there can be so many human beings cast out into this arid wilderness, 600 miles nor' nor' west of Mexico City, fringed by the Sierra Madre range that from the only plane flying daily from the capital, the 6.45 am, is like a series of grey-red hummocks under a thin blanket of mist.

But beautiful, yes. You step out onto the tarmac from the plane, which is always full, and the pale red stripes of dawn have now dissolved into the horizon, and the spicy January air is like a cold douche, and you become suddenly aware of all these people, these kids; with eyes that are eating up this huge metal thing which has dropped once again out of the skies, and you know it's a cliche but you find yourself wondering about their thoughts. *What's it like out there, beyond the mountains?*

An odd feeling for the traveller, because if you believe the books, something like this happened before, aeons ago, when the gods descended from spaceships among the Mayas and the other primitive Indian tribes and told them to build pyramids and roads, to be the cradle of civilisation, and . . . hell, if God was an astronaut and felt as bleary as me this January morning he'd get his blue ass back onto that thing and light out for Los Angeles, a thousand miles north, because in the year of our Lord 1973 there seemed precious little here to do.

The city of Durango is a wide, two-lane highway, shimmering metallically in a haze of heat and dust as the sun winches upwards, with numerous smaller roads intersecting off it. It is pale, stucco churches, and banks, and a huge square flanked by finely-clipped yews. It is the Old World and it is the New.

The little shoe-shine boy at the pavement's edge puts spirit on the toecap of his customer's shoe and lights a match, pausing an instant while the flame spurts before applying his rag.

While next door, almost, there is a massive supermarket, the Soriana, larger than any I've seen in the States, which could supply the whole populace. The wire shopping trolleys outside the window are serried ranks, poised to trundle into action.

But most of all it is Hollywood – it is the myth of the Western movie made flesh there amidst the vista of cacti, scrub, old lava stones and brown, rolling plains. Today in these parts God is not an astronaut, he is a cowboy, who rides into town on that plane for a couple of months and shoots his motion pitcher, for which you're paid so many pesos a day as an extra.

In the office of the best hotel in town, the Campo Mexico, one of the three there, which consists of a number of one-storey rooms slung together in a wide, semi-circle, are hung signed portraits of the stars who've made movies in this area. "Hasta la vista – Glenn Ford"; "Many thanks – Kirk Douglas"; "Best Wishes – John Wayne."

Wayne, he even has his own spread outside of town where he makes films. In fact, he'd only just left. It would have made a great picture for that wall, him and Sam, and Jim Coburn, and Kris, and . . . Bobby Dylan.

Dylan and the other leading figures in the movie have their own houses close to each other in Durango. Maggie tells me this as we drive out this Saturday morning for the location site, El Sauz, which is about 20 to 30 minutes from the Campo Mexico.

She also informs me that Dylan is "very strange" and if I'm looking to speak to him . . . she smiles very prettily but adamantly. It seems there are strict instructions that his privacy be not so much as tampered with.

Expressly no cameras, except for the stills photographer and John Bryson, a former Life picture editor and old friend of Sam's, who was given a chunky role in The Getaway.

Maggie says Dylan talks to no-one, unless he wishes to. Like, he's a big friend of Kristofferson, they share a trailer together on the site, but some days he won't speak to him at all. He's the same with everyone.

"It's not just that he's picking on you, but he's . . ." she searches for the right adjective . . . "he's just *rude*." Ah! The mucho mysterioso quality.

They all tell me the same. "Dylan? Forget it? He won't talk." Casually mention his name in a conversation and a veil of protectiveness descends. He's like an ever-present wisp of ectoplasm floating in the consciousness of all these assembled people, a thing intangible which needs to be preserved from the prying outside in case it blows away.

But it's not simply that no one wants to be the person to reveal anything. No one is sure if they have anything to reveal! They're uncertain about their own reactions to him, and even more, what their reactions *should* be.

One minute he's the breathless myth, set down exotically in the land of Quetzalcoatl, the next he's just a guy, working on a movie like the rest of us, isn't he? *Isn't he?* About the only thing they are sure of is they're not gonna say too much, just in case.

IT WAS eerie, those first few moments of arriving on the set.

The car pulls into a large open space in front of the preserves of a big, crumbling stone building, which was constructed as a cavalry fort some hundred years ago and now renamed Fort Sumner.

Dotted around are a few smaller ruins – walls, mostly, that have long since ceased to support houses. The skull of a dead cow shines bone-white by a gate. And a Mexican is propping up a long pole with a red flag hanging stiffly at its mast and a white one trailing in the dirt. Red meant shooting was in progress.

It was extraordinary the effect this pole had on people. As soon as that red rag poked up into the cloudless sky everyone's conversation fell to a dead whisper, mouths were in suction with ears, and footsteps were as timid as if the slightest noise would precipitate a wrathful earthquake – which it would, as we shall see.

There must have been 200 or more people – actors, Mexican extras, film people, men, women and kids – wrapped up in these mute, stony poses, or else gliding in concentrated slow-motion in and around the old lumps of stone that once rang to the sounds of army life.

A silent frieze, while the birds twittered, horses snuffled in the pens inside the fort, and a couple of vultures wheeled obscenely in the sky.

Here was the true conspiracy of silence. It was broken by the only man who held the right.

In one of the fort buildings, its blank windows shielded in black back-drops,

Peckinpah was shooting and rehearsing his actors. He was out of sight, but the authority in the voice left no doubt as to its identity.

Coburn appeared, a lean, handsome face with greying hair. He was wearing a Mexican coat in coloured patterns over a black vest and pants, and a black hat was perched on his head. He walked out the door three times, on each occasion using the same movements and talking behind his shoulder as he did so.

"Right, like this, you say. Like this?"

And then Kristofferson. His face orange-brown with make-up and, minus his beard, looking about ten years younger. He was rangy in his dark, faded pin-stripes with the gun hanging off his hip. Sheriff Pat Garret and Billy the Kid. Meet the stars of the show.

And finally Sam Peckinpah came out. Not as tall or as big as you might have expected, but fierce, like an old, bristling lion, with a thick, white moustache and hair of the same colour wrapped round at the forehead with a green bandana.

He was the ferocious Anglo-Indian major of all those Kipling stories, leading his men over the Khyber Pass, sword in hand and a curse on his lips. It was easy to see why he scares the shit out of all and sundry.

He walked out the door and spat dramatically in the dirt. There was a loud phut! as the spittle hit and settled.

Later, when the scene was over and the white flag was up, I met Rudy Wurlitzer. He was the 36-year-old author of three novels, one of which, Nog, has achieved cult status in England and America.

He was also the writer of the screenplay for the James Taylor vehicle, Two-Lane Blacktop, never shown in Britain.

And now this movie. Wurlitzer was involved in this one as an actor, as well. He played another of Billy's gang. To this end his tall body was dressed in cruddy clothes and leather chaps, he had make-up like Clearasil smeared all over his face, and a battered top hat sat on his head. In his hand he twirled a Colt. He looked a real mean dude.

In reality he wasn't too happy, I learned, as weren't a good many on this film. It was two weeks overdue and a million dollars over budget, largely through technical problems; almost a fortnight's filming had been spoiled because the cameras were found to be out of focus.

Peckinpah was always in a huddle with the producer, Gordon Carroll, a tall, thin, snappy-looking man with light glasses. They were worried. And MGM was worried. The studios had sent down three executives already from Culver City to investigate the reasons for the late schedule. Peckinpah hated the studios with as much venom but more realistic cause than was contained in that gob of spit. He felt betrayed by them.

And then, as if that wasn't enough, there was always Durango. Godddddd, Durango! The soullessness of the place, the boredom! The frustration of nothing to do, nothing to occupy the mind beyond memorising lines and that day's shooting, lay like an implacable, heavy hand over the set.

"Durango . . . it's a strange, dark place to make a film," Wurlitzer said. "Everyone gets so exposed." He whispered the last sentence.

We were sitting in one of the outhouses, which had been roughly converted into a canteen for the crew. Outside they were shooting again. The voices came softly on the afternoon breeze.

This and Two-Lane Black-top, he muttered morosely, were both horrible movies to work on, but in different ways. At the memory of the one he shook his head.

"James Taylor wasn't given a chance, no chance at all. He got no direction from Monte Hellman (the director) at all, which was what he desperately needed. Two-Lane Blacktop was a better movie than people thought but it forgot about two essentials: the road and speed. Monte didn't have too much strength to get it on. The original script was a little too original in a way.

"There's no doubt this is a better film, even if it turns out to be one of Sam's worst, because it has energy. What Sam does to language, for instance . . . he makes it more theatrical because he's innately theatrical. It's like he's almost old-fashioned in what is the most effective. He imposed three scenes in the beginning on my script so that it works better from a film point of view. In my version, Pat and Billy never meet until the end. Here they do so at the beginning and the end."

To him, he explained, Pat and Billy were two gunmen who essentially felt a kinship but had chosen two diametrically opposed roles in life, the former as a sheriff, the latter as an outlaw. Thus they were symbols of a changing America in the last century: the one a roving free spirit, symbolising the pioneer nature of the Old West; the other selling out to the Establishment for a steady-job and security, representing, therefore, the solidifying respectability of the new America.

And Dylan?

"Dylan is great," Wurlitzer whispered without any hesitation. "He's come down here to learn, he's turning in stuff, and it's been really impressive. I think he's completely authentic. No, I don't know what he really wants to do but I would hope he would do his own film because he's an artist and he can't help it. He's just finding out about films."

Dylan and Peckinpah? He cocked an eye at me. "That's the really interesting thing," he replied thoughtfully, "what's going on between Peckinpah and

Dylan. Sam is really Western, like an outlaw, looking to the wide-open spaces, and he didn't know about Dylan before.

"Dylan, you could say, was Eastern. He brings a different point of view, especially to a Western. The part is small but it's important in a funny sort of way. Do the two of them have any common ground to meet on – *that's* the big question."

Dylan, I'd been told, played the part with a stutter. "Yes, but it will have to be taken out. It becomes too much of a big thing if you only have a small part, and . . ."

Outside, where there had been almost total silence except for faint, inaudible words, there now came a sudden, angry bark and a command like a grating snarl.

"Get outa that truck," it rapped with terrifying evenness. And then higher. "Get out! All of you!! Over there, behind the wall!!" There was a pause and then the rapid sound of many feet, and then quiet again.

A crew-member tip-toed into the canteen with a ferocious grin on his face.

"He's the only person that can clear all the people outa one country just to make a f. . .ing pitcher," he breathed gleefully. There had been too much noise for Peckinpah.

They love Sam and they hate him. One bit player proclaimed proudly, as if he'd been granted his flying colours, "I bin 16 weeks with him on The Wild Bunch." But he can be as mean as snake juice when that devil bubbles to the surface.

Kristofferson spoke more fondly of him. "He's always gentle with his actors. He only bawls out one or two who know him well and have worked a lot with him before."

We were talking on the nightly plane from Durango back to Mexico City. He and all the other leading actors and members of his band were flying out for the rest of the weekend. It was Saturday evening. The final of the American World Series football championship was being televised on Sunday afternoon – there were no televisions in Durango. And Dylan was going to record with Kris' band that night at Columbia's studios in Mexico City.

I sat across the aisle from Kristofferson and we cradled a bottle of Jamieson's between us. On his other side was Rita Coolidge, who plays one of Billy's ladies in the film, as in real life. Her black hair was still pulled back into twin braids and she wore the rough, grey-patterned wool coat that costumes had given her, while Kristofferson was still in his movie duds; everyone had had to make a dash for the plane.

Leaning across the gangway, shouting above the noise of the engines, I was

35

close enough to observe his pale, blue eyes, which seem oddly sightless, swim a little with the effect of the whisky.

And there, in the seat right behind him, was a little guy from Minnesota named Bob Dylan.

I had seen him fleetingly on the set that day. He had been wearing a serape and an old grey top hat, but as he wasn't filming he flitted occasionally around the outskirts of the location, saying a few words to the odd people he knew well enough, but generally mute-faced and unsmiling.

He'd looked skittery and ill-at-ease, and people seemed to avoid confronting him, as if the moment might be too charged with electricity.

But it was so obviously him! That face the colour of sour milk, and the full, sensuous nose, now pronouncedly Jewish, and the whole appearance of him that was nondescript at the same time that it was illuminated with the magnitude of him and our experiences of him.

He was a whole era of youth coiled into one man and now slowly winding down into the years past 30, and the consciousness of this had escaped no-one, least of all him, with his eyes set straight and stonily to the front lest he be forced to pick up those curious sidelong glances, as a magnet does iron filings.

Even on this plane his inviolacy was to be preserved to the full. He'd boarded with James Coburn and as they walked down the aisle together a seated passenger had asked for an autograph . . . from Coburn.

He hadn't been recognised in his rimless glasses, baggy, beige parka and straw hat. But then, as the plane was taking off and I began to speak to Kristofferson, he got up jumpily from his seat and went to sit at the back.

We had begun to climb as he reluctantly dumped himself down again behind Kristofferson and next to Wurlitzer. He pulled his hat down right over the front of his face, which was odd because his body was rigidly upright in the seat, cocked and attentive.

We were touching down into Mexico City, with the Irish stuff two-thirds gone, and had had all the stories about his last English tour, his old landlady in Oxford, and his ups and downs with Rita at the time, when Kristofferson's head came halfway across the gangway again and motioned behind him. He had just offered the bottle to Dylan, who had waved it away.

"Listen," he said, "this guy can do anything. In the script he has to throw a knife. It's real difficult. After ten minutes or so he could do it perfect."

He leaned over further. "Listen, he does things you never thought was in him. He can play Spanish-style, bossa nova, flamenco . . . one night he was playing flamenco and his old lady, Sara, had never known him do it at all before."

I looked back at the crown of the straw hat in uncompromising full-frontal. I said I was too scared to talk to the man right now.

"Sheeeeit! man," Kristofferson roared. "You're scared. I'm scared, and I'm making a pitcher with him!!"

I began to feel more than ever like the lead in "Ballad Of A Thin Man."

THEY recorded until seven the following morning on Dylan's "Billy The Kid" and some other stuff he'd written down there in Durango.

Nobody knew if the material would be the basis of the movie soundtrack, or if Kristofferson's own song, "Pat Garret," would be included, but a good deal of it was instrumental and it featured some local trumpet men to give a Mexican flavour.

Yet Jesus! It was so awkward with all those people in there, all those Mexican studio men come to see Bob Dylan play and sing. It began to be apparent that the stuff would have to be re-done, maybe in LA after the movie.

The following day, though, it was Sunday, and in the afternoon practically everybody went over to the Fiesta Palace Hotel, where a suite had been booked, to see the Miami Dolphins beat up the Washington Redskins.

The Sheraton Hotel, where they were all staying, hadn't got television, either. The hotel was always full of Americans and they never usually wanted to see Mexican television, which was filled out with the starch of Yankee series, like "The FBI" and "McCloud," only in Spanish, and soccer. Soccer for God's sake!

In room 734 Dylan slept deeply. He was still asleep when the maid came to the door and said it was ten o'clock. Ten o'clock! No, it couldn't be! He'd missed that plane back to Durango and, it was his big scene today, where he got to throw the knife he'd been practising with!

He slung all his stuff in a carpet bag and flung himself down to the lobby, his eyes still popping like a camera shutter, just adjusting to being awake, to all these people down at reception, to the actual time it was! And then they tell him it's okay anyway, and it's really ten at night, and he needn't have worried after all. He shook his head in relief.

There was no problem in making that plane the next Monday morning. He passed through gate four, the exit for Durango, and again nobody showed any sign of recognition. At least, they didn't ask for his autograph. But then, nobody wanted to talk too much at 6.30 am, except, it seemed, Coburn and Wurlitzer, who were deep in conversation about the former's part.

Kristofferson was looking a little groggy. He'd been ill over the weekend. Probably that damned Irish whisky. He'd been smashed when he left the airport that Saturday evening. Hadn't stayed for the whole session, either.

Bobby got on the plane when they called the flight and sat towards the back where there were a few empty seats around him. Kris and Rita were right down the other end on the very front row.

About three-quarters of an hour out from Mexico City he saw the newspaper guy get up out of his seat, walk down to Kristofferson and crouch down to him talking.

This is part of what Kristofferson was saying. ". . . I was just disgusted with him. He'd start a song and then keep changing it around. He had horn players, trumpets, and they didn't know a damn thing what they had to do 'cause he couldn't make up his mind. I left about three." He said this very tiredly, then answered the question he'd been asked. "No, we haven't spoken today."

Dylan saw all this, he saw the guy go back to his seat, and then he spoke to Bert Block about the newspaper he worked for.

That was when he spoke to me. I guess you could say I was startled.

DYLAN talks in this light, soft voice with a husk to it, and he has this disconcerting habit of forcing you to lead the conversation.

He takes another person's sentence, chops it up in his mind, tosses it into the air and examines it when it falls, all before replying, so there are often a long couple of seconds before the answer comes; it's an unnatural limbo. It's not that he's unfriendly, but he's guarded and watchful to the point where conversation with strangers appears onerous for him.

He is also terribly shy, which he largely masks by an air of alienation he throws around him, like an enveloping cloak with a built-in burglar alarm.

It's because, beneath all the layers of the onion, there lurks a deep vulnerability that people instinctively feel protective towards him and are inspired to unsolicited loyalty, as if to say anything out of turn would not only betray a confidence, however unspoken but would be bruising for him.

He doesn't smile too much and publicly he laughs even more rarely. His public persona never falters. Even those who could be considered friends are not privileged to many intimacies.

He may be the loneliest man in the world or he may be the happiest. There is no way of telling. Those who have known him since his early New York folk days say he has mellowed, but in so becoming he now holds the world at a distance and treats with it from a detached position on his terms.

All that may fairly be said is that those who count themselves among his friends, or even good acquaintances, prize their situation dearly.

Dylan talked to Playboy about his desire for anonymity back in 1966.

"People have one great blessing," he said, "obscurity, and not really too many people are thankful for it. You can't take everything you don't like as a personal insult. I guess you should go where your wants are bare, where you're invisible and not needed."

Considering all this attitudinising, our conversation was prosaic enough. He did say, most interestingly, that he had been in England quite recently for a few days ("The clothes are different since last time"). We spoke for five minutes. Then I glanced out the window briefly, turned back, and he was gone.

But debarking from the plane, while everyone waited at tiny Durango airport for their baggage to be taken off, I found him at the bar, sipping a cup of coffee and engrossed with a camera belonging to CBS records executive, Michael O'Mahoney, asking normal stuff like what lens it had. This was almost eight in the morning.

"It's not happening in London," I said, apropos a remark made on the plane.

"New York's the place."

"That's what John Lennon says." Focusing the lens.

"I saw Eat The Document there at the Whitney."

Pauses, returns the camera to O'Mahoney, and looks directly at me.

"Do you know Howard (Alk, who co-edited the film with Dylan)?"

"No. Was it originally like Don't Look Back before it was re-edited?"

"No, it couldn't be. We didn't have enough good footage. There was 40 hours of it, but the camera was jumping around all the time. That was the only stuff we could salvage."

"Would you go back and play in England ever?"

Silence. He turned three-quarters and carefully placed his cup on the counter. There was no answer. Instead, taking off at a sudden tangent, "did you see Fly?"

"You mean the one about the fly crawling up the wall for half an hour? No." All three of us laughed, the first time I'd seen him do so.

"Did you see Hard On," he asked suddenly.

"Huh?"

"Hard On."

"No, but I saw Rape. You know, the one with that girl being chased."

He nodded.

"Andy Warhol was making movies like that years ago. The Empire State Building, all those shadows. I prefer the stuff with Morrissey, actually." I was trying not to sound smug.

He nodded again, then, "did you see Lonesome Cowboys?"

"No, but I saw Heat." It was getting to be quite funny. Every time he asked me he looked so intense. "Sylvia Miles."

"Yeah." Silence once more.

"Tell me, how can you stand it down here?"

"It's not too bad because I'm making a film. If I wasn't . . ." The sentence was chopped off because the producer, who was fidgeting all this time like an old hen over her chick, had come up and told him he could get into the car.

The next time I saw Dylan was on the set later that day and he was locked tight once more behind his stoniness.

I WENT OUT to El Sauz around one that afternoon, when the sun was cutting through the thinness of the desert air and the horizons were as sharp and concentrated as if focused through a lens.

This time nerves on the set were so jagged you could run a finger along their psychic edge. There was the same pregnant hush as two days ago, but it was even more intensified, as if everyone were holding in their breath in some giant expectation. It was the fascination of peering through a microscope, of seeing Dylan put through his paces in a crucial scene.

The shooting was out in the open, with six huge silver reflectors tilted on high above the scene. Peckinpah sat in his canvas director's chair by the camera. Emilio Fernandez, the famous Mexican director, was an onlooker. Before each take there was an abrupt cry of "silenzio," repeated twice to cut dead any lingering conversation.

As the scene was shot again and again the tension was alternately cranked up and then relaxed momentarily, so that with each successive time it became tighter and increasingly insufferable. I wanted to snap it violently, like severing a taut string, to let out all that constricted breath in a great explosion of air.

As the cameras rolled Dylan was sitting on a chair surrounded by half a dozen ragged Mexican kids. He was strumming an acoustic, wearing a brown shirt, black pants and a grey top hat.

On the far right of the scene a cowboy was leaning on his horse. Billy the Kid and half a dozen of his gang were around a campfire on the left, nearest the camera.

One of this gang, Harry D. Stanton, dressed in black with an old, greasy hat of the same colour, sat on a fence and shouted out, "hey Chita, bring some beans, soup and tortillas, and be quick about it," and out from left comes this young Mexican serving wench carrying the chow, accompanied by Rita as another peasant chick. There's a lot of laughing and tom-foolery, with Kristofferson's voice striking a resonant bass note.

It's then that Dylan rises. He's playing nervously with a knife, turning it round in his hand. The jitters seem genuine. He walks a dozen paces towards the campfire as the cowboy on the horse shouts after him, "hey, boy, what's your name?" like he was a piece of dirt, and then he stops and faces round with the knife in his hand.

"Alias," he replies shortly. His body twitches a little. The knife taps against his leg.

"Alias *what?*" barks the horseman, the second word like the snake of a whiplash.

"Alias whatever you want" comes the rejoinder. Tough punk stuff. The gang laughs.

"They just call him Alias," says one. His interrogator grunts.

There's the sound of muttering – and then suddenly, in a flash-point that takes you by surprise, Dylan's right arm arcs back with the knife, and not the horseman but a seated outlaw gargles in the back of his throat and is knocked on his side with the force of the knife supposedly sticking through his neck. The moment still seems unexpected even after the sixth take.

"Cut," says Peckinpah. "Aaaaaaah!" goes all that escaping air, in relief. "Print it," grins Bert Block. The tableau of watchers and watched dissolves for another five minutes.

Print it! This is Bob Dylan, throwing a knife in a Sam Peckinpah movie, would you believe!

It's ironic. He leaves society at large as some kind of generational leader, a musical Messiah, and returns years later as an actor playing a small role in a movie – yet already the film, before it's been finished even, sets us agog with speculation.

The questions mount. Will Dylan really turn away from music to concentrate more on films? Will he start making records again on a more regular basis now he's been drawn once more into a kind of public performance?

Could he ever return to doing concerts? The only answer that is really ascertainable is his acting ability, which will be on the line when this movie comes out some time after May. But even then there will be arguments about his performance, about its *meaning*.

He's unwavering, however, in his refusal to relinquish any part of his private self to his public, and this seems destined to continue.

You ask who is Bob Dylan? He is Alias, Alias whatever you want.

Michael Watts

4

Lone star

BRUCE SPRINGSTEEN
September 30 1974

IT RAINED torrents that week in Texas, but the outlook never seemed less than fine. We were down there for a christening, anyway, albeit a little late in the day.

The baby, you see, has long been bawling for our attentions, and most of us have been a little slow to notice. And then, it's a very HUNGRY baby we have here.

So Texas it was, though it could have been anywhere, because Bruce Springsteen is some baby, all of 25 years old and pretty seasoned as far as these things go; you figure he'll have the crowds on top of their seats anyplace he turns up.

He wants a shot at the big title, as they say, and in turn a growing number of people would like to see him take that crown which has been bobbing from head to head of every rock and roll champ in the past two decades.

In their minds he's the logical contender, the new golden boy of rock 'n' roll, who's finally emerged from the fastnesses of New Jersey bars and campus halls to bid for the public's heart.

You talk to almost anybody in New York now and what do they say? "Bruce Springsteen! Oh, sure, he's great. But, sugar, you've seen NUTHIN'. You shoulda been there TWO YEARS AGO when he was playing at the Student Prince in Asbury Park. THAT was really somethin'."

And so on, blah, blah blah, New Yorkers always being like that after the event.

But in Texas, that big, lone star state brooding southwest on the map, where the news takes a while to filter down, it's hard to be blasé, especially when the rain is falling in gut-buckets.

"Springsteen, you say? Jewish fella?" We-ell, no. Of Dutch origin, actually, a Catholic, but we'll let it pass.

It's not their fault. Bruce Springsteen has only just begun to break big anywhere, to touch that vital psychic nerve of a mass audience which sets the ball rolling, and no one can be absolutely sure why it's happening now, though those who've seen him lately instinctively feel his rapport with the goddess of fortune.

Two years ago however, when that benign spirit John Hammond signed him to Columbia records, the press mostly snickered up their sleeves about the "new Bob Dylan." Springsteen replied with his manic-euphoric grin, and then they wrote him off as some kind of Dr. Demento.

"Madman drummers bummers and Indians in the summer with a teenage diplomat" – they always picked up on that first, and wildly off, line from his first album, "Greetings from Asbury Park, N.J.," and dismissed the rest as junk in some sort of summary tribunal.

After all, surely you had to be a nut, gobbling bennies, or some misdirected/ informed Dylan disciple to write like that didn't you?

To his credit – or perhaps he was just oblivious – Springsteen hung on in, sustained by kind words from worshippers who had seen him in his long-haired, bar-band days back in Asbury and thereabouts, plus new fans who were jolted back by the fierce, jumping current of his personality, with its foggy mumblings and inpenetrabilia, the feisty stance of the street punk, and those lyrics that leaped at the inner ear with their role-call of weird, vibrant characters – Wild Billy, Crazy Janey, Rosalita, Weak Knee Willie and the whole steamy essence of Latin street-life that has wafted out from the kitchen of his imagination.

He stuck to it the only way a musician can – he kept on playing even though other bands took fright at him and wouldn't, increasingly, use him as a support in case they were blown away – and a double difficulty here, because he was opposed anyway to gigs with heavy rock sets and their attendant zombie audiences.

Finally, he had a job getting booked anywhere outside New York and New Jersey. But he didn't seem unduly bothered because, as he often said, he'd as soon play to 15 people as 1,500 if the music was right.

Although the second album, "The Wild, The Innocent And The E Street Shuffle," sold more than the first, Springsteen had still not really registered as the major artist Columbia and John Hammond had prophesied, and Hammond

– everybody always brought this up – had been the guy who brought Dylan to the label a decade before.

The presence of the Minnesota Kid did seem in all truth to loom uncomfortably over any young unfortunate who had aspiration, even circumstantially, to the crown.

Just because he was new, and he had the beard and the hair . . . it was too bad, it really was, and him not even Jewish. Springsteen, in fact, only owned a few Dylan singles – being too shy to ask his record company for the catalogue – and he'd never even seen Dylan perform, since Bobby hadn't made it to Asbury before the motorcycle disaster.

They still said he'd been influenced by him – well, if you were healthy at all, he reasoned you'd better be influenced by him!

And then, in the middle of this year, the numbers appeared to click in a perfect combination. No longer playing to chick peas and shell steaks at Max's Kansas City, that downtown pitch for wide-eyed tourists, he and his E Street Band were booked in July into the posh Bottom Line club, Greenwich Village's finest and the kind of place where CBS president Goddard Lieberson might feel more at home.

In the space of a couple of nights the boast of his manager, Mike Appel, that this scruffy kid with the perpetual grin was the "finest actor/artist in the history of rock 'n' roll" could no longer be laughed off on the rock gossip circuit, but had to be fed for analysis into the critical computer.

A top-notch American rock critic had already come out with his own strip of ticker-tape proclaiming Springsteen as "the future of rock 'n' roll."

In New York, at least nobody laughed after that, nobody said it was "Bellevue rock" anymore. At concerts girls threw red roses to him in a Spanish love tryst, stages buckled from too many vociferous feet.

And a lot of people began remarking, "do you remember that time we went out to New Jersey, and there was that band . . . . ?"

TO BE fair, it was certainly true that Springsteen's performance had developed in a year since he was Upstairs at Max's.

At New York's Avery Fisher Hall in October what once were mannerisms had flowered into a perfect synchromesh of rock 'n' roll ballet – theatrics without the tricks, movements and dances assimilated from old Sixties soul revues, bits of stage business with the drummer and the black tenorist, a gift for mimicry, and this big, dramatic whisper that Springsteen employed as one weapon in his vocal armoury – a whisper roughed out hoarse and attractive, played off against an acoustic piano and a violin at certain sections in his performance.

More than ever, too, it was apparent that his musical roots were embedded in the thundering symphonies of Spectorland, secured especially in the styles of Spector's girlie groups: in the Crystals and Ronnie and the Ronettes, several of the girls themselves from New Jersey, of course. One of his proudest possessions, it later emerged, was a signed colour photograph of Ronnie Spector.

Springsteen's heart, evidently, was back there in the Fifties and early Sixties. His poetic intellect had absorbed the songwriting advances of the Sixties and Seventies – those knotty problems of metre and internal rhyme – but he intuitively anticipated in his new audiences the response for that uncluttered, emotional freshness embodied in a song like "And He Kissed Me."

The number, in fact with which he closed his Avery Hall show that night was the old, joyful rabble-rouser, Gary Bonds "Quarter To Three."

In those few months since the Bottom Line performances his album sales have started to pick up in America, especially those of his second record, which has gone past the 80,000 mark. Still, that isn't too great; by big league standards it's even a failure.

So the people who know about these things are forever badgering him to bring in a big-time producer instead of Mike Appel, someone like Richard Perry, maybe, or Bob Johnson, or . . . or Spector.

Springsteen says no, summoning a rueful smile for his elders and betters. He and Appel managed it okay together, as far as he's concerned. All his records had been commercial, he thought, and no sounds had gone down he disagreed with.

Though there's a smell of burning somewhere, he remains very loyal to Appel, while Appel announces, in very precise tones, that his artist's "presence on stage dwarfs any musical attempt on vinyl. Any album is a disaster in comparison."

His record company, meanwhile, bites its nails and waits for the release of the third album in the early part of next year.

Other artists, maybe, will break his songs first. David Bowie has recorded "Growing Up" and "It's Hard To Be A Saint In The City," the Hollies have done "4th Of July Asbury Park," and Allan Clark "If I Were The Priest."

But Springsteen doesn't want to be just a fat cat on some publisher's shelf. He's looking for the main action.

OF THESE musical politics, however, the good people of Austin, Texas, know nothing, though the name of Bruce Springsteen is well-remembered from a gig last year at the Armadillo World Headquarters, a big, 2,000-capacity club that likes to think of itself as a Fillmore in a city with pretensions to the cultural cosiness of old-time San Francisco.

Austin, situated on the Colorado river in the Texan interior, if that's the phrase, plays home to Doug Sahm and the 40,000-student University of Texas, and once, indeed, to Charles Whitman, who from the top of a tower near the main drag rifled 18 people to death.

Kinky Friedman, another Texan, and a Jew to boot, wrote a catchy ballad about it; that's one way to achieve immortality.

During the day a travelling band in this city might occupy itself looking through a number of thrift shops for old 45s and 78s on Dial, Duke/Peacock, Josie and other, more arcane labels.

But at night after a cloud-burst the visitor is greeted only with streets dripping empty and miserable, surfaces black and shiny, with the neon strips of hamburger joints little more than cold comfort.

We find Springsteen late at night in the Fun Arcade on Main Street, which is where one would have expected him arriving in a strange town.

He's literally running from game to game – from the pool tables, to the pin-football – at which the Tex-Mex kids are so adept – to Pong (the official name for "television tennis"), and on to Air Hockey, a two-player game that involves slamming a puck between goalmouths across an air-cushioned tabletop.

He's a small guy, about five foot seven, with a deceptively rumpled, sleepy face – deceptive because he's winning at all these games.

Tufts of curly hair grow out from under a grey cloth 'po' boy cap, his skin is sallow, and the beard is scraggy.

But with his rubbed jeans, beat-up leather jacket, and this hat tipped raffishly over one eye, he becomes at second glance something quite charismatic . . . a pool hall hustler, a Fifties runaway, floating cool with his hard-earned savvy, the kind of character that Kerouac would immediately have recognised and set down.

A peculiarly anachronistic air clings to Springsteen. After observing him a few moments shooting pool and rattling up big scores with much intensity, I start to think he should've been a Beat poet himself, hopping on boxcars around America, sharing a bottle of wine with ol' Ti Jean and the hobos out in the yards and then writing down his fleeting sensations, each rush of thought, on scraps of paper he stuffed about his clothes.

That was another age, when electric guitars weren't so common, but Springsteen still gives off this heady whiff of pristine romance, of nostalgia for a wide-open America that this rock generation has never known, some outlaw quality of adventuring that cuts right across all this business of middle-class white boys leaving school to sing black men's music.

And again, the well-thumbed line comes straight to mind, that nobody ever taught him how to live out on the street. Because he already knew, knew instinctively.

ON THE Thursday morning, when the New York Times calls the Sheraton Inn in Austin, Springsteen turns to the man from CBS and asks if he's really got to do the interview.

"It's only ten minutes out of your life."

"But why."

"It can help you. They want to do a big story."

Springsteen brightens at a sudden thought. "You got the wheels right? Okay, lets go out and play. Lets go get some hamburgers" – his favourite food, since fancy cuisine makes him uncomfortable.

He treats the CBS man to a hoarse, compulsive chuckle. His voice has a husk on it like a kernel.

"You really should talk to him. It is the New York Times."

There's a pause before he grumbles assent. "Aw, okay."

Springsteen avoids interviews if he can, apparently not out of bolshevism or with any attempt to envelop himself in mystique, but because he finds it hard to adjust to the brittle game of question and answer, of careful probing, smart deceptions and double-guessings that are supposed to elicit some approximation of the truth.

He is too real to put his faith in the glamour of headlines, too mindful of his privacy to undervalue his personal feelings at the sight of a notebook or tape recorder.

This attitude is really a corollory of his dislike of rock stardom, which he professes to find as meaningless as most rock stars are unappealing to him.

They're jokes, hoaxes, gyps he's fond of saying, because every other person can be one if he's willing to surrender himself to a public relations man.

"They're just people who wanna crawl back in the womb," he will say, "people who have built their own reality and are afraid of reality itself." Being a rock star was letting yourself be controlled, and that way you cheated yourself.

So no, he doesn't ever want to be a big, hyped-up rock star, playing at Madison Square Garden, where the kids will need binoculars to see him. "I hope somebody shoots me offstage," he says, "if they ever see me there, because then I'll deserve it."

The band, guys who've been out on the road for some years several of them spent with Springsteen, are less sure of what's involved. The organist, for one, Danny Federici, a taciturn, sandy-haired man who also played with Bruce in a group called Steel Mill back in the old Jersey days.

"I don't know what to think of the whole thing," he says. "I don't even know what to think of the way the audiences respond. I know Bruce is good, I know that, but I don't really understand what it is, or how they let it all out the way some of the people do for our concerts."

Still, it's essentially Springsteen's responsibility. He supervises the music as totally as he orchestrates the audience's emotions, and the E Street Band is a group in which personal expression has to be sublimated in the collective effort in which there's a group sound and infrequent soloing, since one of Springsteen's musical ideals is the sound-mesh that Dylan achieved on his electric albums.

Only Danny, briefly, gets a large slice of the spotlight, just as it was Al Kooper alone who was allowed to rise out of the mix on "Highway 61."

Springsteen has picked them all carefully. The bassist, Garry W. Tallent, has been with him since '71 when Bruce led another band of Jersey renown, Dr. Zoom and the Sonic Boom.

The pianist, Roy Bitton, arrived in September after long-time keyboards-man Davey Sancious became too idiosyncratic with his prepared piano pieces and iconoclastic Debussy style, while the present drummer, Max Weinberg was auditioned around the same time.

He's a number one pupil of Pretty Purdie, and, among other former occupations, an ex-Broadway pit player (The Magic Show and Godspell), showbiz experience that Springsteen particularly utilises in his rapid number of time switches and off-the-cuff routines.

But his main man is Clarence Clemons, a big, imposing black tenorist, who was a football player with the Cleveland Browns until he got a leg injury, and who once held down a spot as one of James Brown's Famous Flames.

Clarence also sings harmonies, and he's a kind of foil for Springsteen, this huge dude, standing front left setting off the diminutive singer – Clarence in his white suit, black shirt and hat, with the shades, counterpointing this skinny, hungry-looking kid who looks as if he's been leaning on fire hydrants all his life.

The band is as tight as the fingers on a hand, all living within ten miles of each other in New Jersey, near the beach and not far from Asbury Park, just so's rehearsals will be easier to arrange.

ON THURSDAY at the Armadillo there are no visiting dignitaries, but the audience is greater than the previous evening's, a crowd of tall Texan gals and young longhairs in dirty-cream cowboy hats cocked back on their heads, in their hands huge pitchers of pale beer which they slop in the glasses of whoever is standing near.

It's a crowd that wants to boogie and crack those empty cans of Lone Star beer under their scuffed boot-heels in this large barn of a joint, warm but still redolent of the rainy night outside.

So they're unprepared and somewhat off-balance when Springsteen walks out in his battered duds with little, scholarly Roy, the pianist, and Suki, who just happens to be the wife of his sound engineer, Louis Lehav, and spent time in the Israeli Youth Ork – this slight, tiny blonde, a heart-stealer in rolled-up denims and boots, a thumb-nail sketch of charming, fragile femininity, who crooks a violin in her shoulder.

And Bruce, in his muscle tee-shirt with his hair haloed by the lighting, a tender John Garfield characterisation with one hand fingering the veins in his arm, eyes hooded in shades, Bruce starts in on his uptown drama of Spanish Johnny, sad-eyed Romeo figure, looking for a sweet word from his girl, all the sounds of the city in the song, with the violin like a breath of night wind across the West River.

And the cowpokes, even if they're all maths students most likely at the university, cease their crunching and slurping. "And from out of the shadows came a young girl's voice, that said: 'Johnny don't cry' . . ."

Springsteen whispering over the mike in a long moment of total magnetic concentration, until on the last piano note, a single, delicate droplet, the crowd bellows out its huge roar of rough approval.

And from that instant Springsteen has them, Austin and Texas by the horns, all out to ride the emotions off 'em.

He always performs this single song, "Incident On 57th Street," as his opening number, and then brings on the rest of his band: Clemons, clutching his gleaming horn; Gary Tallent, vaguely Leon Russell with his flowing brown hair and beard; Max's face virtually obscured by the hovering cymbals, and Danny on last, the sandy moustache with its hint of truculence, sitting right across the stage from Roy Bitton.

They ease out with the familiar Crystals oldie, altered naturally to "And She Kissed Me," and then Bruce's own "Spirit In The Night," Clemons and Tallent on the harmonies, a rasping big band sound, Weinberg driving and hopping them along, Bruce skinny-legging it around the stage, and the audience fully twitching now, caught in the spill of the event.

The music is truly overwhelming a wild, heady mixture of lyrical mosaics refracted through a warm glow of nostalgia, memories of nights spent listening to the radio under the bed covers, when music was undiluted and young, the same almost forgotten stab of joy, but undeniably Seventies R & B, the music brought clean and wailing into the present times and suggesting at every other turn the influence of jazz and Latin sounds.

The measure of its exciting effect is its refusal to be pinned down, but for me at least it touches some particularly sensitive chord, submerged deep in the rubble of the subconscious, that's exhilarating but also disturbing, because it's rarely exposed so completely.

I listen to Springsteen like I used to listen to Dylan, John Lennon and Chuck Berry – as though a life depended on it and no more can be said than that.

Just one impressive factor about Bruce Springsteen is his encyclopaedic knowledge of rock 'n' roll and the intuitive use to which he puts it.

Eddie Cochran brushes shoulders with the Crickets and Bo Diddley, Phil Spector appears all over the place, and in the live version of "Rosalita" he throws in a Four Tops riff.

On "Sandy" he even uses Federici on accordion, possibly inspired by the Beach Boys' "God Only Knows."

But the noise and smells of street-life crowd in on him. I shut my eyes and I can see those dirty New York yellow cabs, nosing in wolfpacks down the hot asphalt on Eighth Avenue, the charred stink of bagels in the air. Manhattan or the tackytowns of New Jersey, he hasn't wandered far from either.

"It's hard to be a saint in the city," he sings with an edge of pride, a sentiment chock-full of New York attitudinising.

Tough cops, bar fights, jukeboxes pimps, alleyways, Harleys, greasers, filthy denims, circuses, boardwalks, Spanish razorboys, trains and tenements – this is his literary stomping ground.

SPRINGSTEEN, born in Freehold, New Jersey, lives these days in an outlying district of Asbury called West End. Asbury Park is a seaside town in Eastern New Jersey, with a population about 50 per cent black, and crammed in the summer with tourists who haven't got the money to go to Atlantic City up the coast.

It was the usual story. His mother had bought him a guitar when he was 9, but he hadn't taken it seriously until he was 13 around the tail-end of that golden age of rock 'n' roll, and just before the Beatles arrived to whip up every white kid's latent fantasy of success in the adult world.

Elvis, the Chiffons, Sam Cooke, the Shirelles, Chuck Berry, the Isley Brothers – every night he went home and put those babies on the record player, seeking out that release promised in the black grooves.

Rock 'n' roll, he swore, was what kept him from going nuts but it was the genuine, horny old stuff he dug. The Beatles were pop, and the Rolling Stones he stopped buying after "December's Children." Something to do with the fancy production.

He was in and out of various bands, even making nightly trips to the Cafe Wha! in Greenwich Village, but his first important group was Child.

Danny Federici was another member, Bruce was 18, and the band went off to San Francisco and cut a four-hour tape for Bill Graham's Fillmore records – so good, according to Federici, that Graham offered their manager 2,000 dollars to sign which wasn't considered enough.

They came back and changed their name to Steel Mill, playing heavy rock, and picked up a reputation in the Jersey towns, where they could play to two and three thousand people a time for 500 dollars and 50 per cent of the gate, even without a record company.

He wrote a lot more in those days. Every weekend the band had a new repertoire. And he was into the image, sexy with his shoulder-length hair and his guitar slung low, low down.

Until one night it wasn't enough any longer. They were a big local act, and yet one evening Bruce walks out onstage and he doesn't feel it any more, it's almost as if he were parodying himself, and there and then he decides to bust it up.

It was hard on Federici. His wife had just left him and here was Bruce saying it was all over. He still has this mental picture of himself stuck in his hallway with his suitcase, trying to figure where to go next. The next two years he never played with anyone unless they paid him upfront, he felt so hurt.

As for Springsteen, he set up another band, Dr. Zoom and the Sonic Boom, which included Garry Tallent and practically everyone else he knew who could play an instrument.

He was still searching for the right vehicle, and then hitched his name to a ten-piece band, loaded with horns and R & B riffs, that eventually whittled itself down to seven, and then to five.

They had been friendly for a time with Looking Glass, seen how they hit the jack-pot with "Brandy," a Number One American single, and wondered why they weren't hitting it, with Bruce writing these great, colourful songs – and wondered especially why Tinker, Springsteen's manager from way back, hadn't ever clinched that record deal.

A vote was taken, and one morning Springsteen went sorrowfully back to the surfboard factory where he and Tinker lived, and delivered the black spot. The guy was fixing his truck, underneath it. He didn't say a word.

It was through him that Springsteen met Mike Appel.

BY THE time we've all boarded the group bus that Friday morning, ready to leave a very rained-out Austin, a rather unnerving change has swept through the whole party.

Five or six of us are wearing hats like Springsteen's, bought in town from the Texas Hatter and pulled down low over one ear in the true style of the Depression era, so that we resemble young Okies, or the Little Rascals, depending on your imagination.

Springsteen looks amused at his groupies, but he never says a word. From this point, leather jackets, jeans and caps, beat up and lived in, become something of a uniform.

The bus pulls out at midday on its 200-mile trek to Corpus Christi, a town on the Gulf of Mexico which combines, one is led to understand, the palm-treed pleasures of a resort with the financial income of oil refineries.

Just above Springsteen's bunk, where he's curled up in a blanket, a single red rose hangs from the roof, a tribute cast by an admirer at the Tower Theatre in Philadelphia. But Bruce is suspended in his own uneasy limbo, drained of sleep by the previous two days' performances.

He dreams he's being driven across a rough landscape and up a huge mountain, slowly and terrifyingly, because the incline is vertical. And then it stops, and he's poised, safety resting on a clenched breath, his body almost upside down, jagged edges below . . .

When he awakens, sweaty and anxious, to cars speeding by on the highway, he fishes around for an explanation of the dream. "And the mountain was named Success, right?" grins one of the party.

He explains that during a performance he has to fulfil two needs, the physical and the emotional, and that sometimes you do one, sometimes the other, but usually you fall short on both.

Inside himself he envisions these little gates, and throughout the performance he goes through each one until BOOM! – the big release! But always there's another one there, always just one, and the intensity of the feeling burns in his stomach, needing to be released, because performing is the only thing he ever does in his life and he has to go all the way with it.

His philosophy is, you have to drain yourself, your band and your audience, and in its place the performer leaves something else, an indefinable something. But for all parties it's the sense of release that's important. Music is simply the modus operandi.

"Because," he will elaborate, "a movie, music, a book – whatever – everybody uses these things to satisfy a need. Creating is a release in itself. Everything's a release.

"That's what it's about in this society – you gotta get released," laughing at his own intensity.

"That's what everybody wants, that's why the audience come, man. They don't come to say, 'hey, you're great!' or to be jived with rock stars and stuff – they mightn't even know why they come – but they come to get release to be set free.

"They think they're gonna get something they need, and it's gotta be more than just jump up and down and 'boogie, boogie!'.

"What happens is that people cheat themselves and they don't know it. I would never cheat myself. If you don't cheat yourself you don't cheat anybody. You can never play too much, for example, there are never too many encores.

"If you can't let me do an encore let me smash a chair or somethin'. I don't know if there's ever enough of a release. Maybe it comes when you die, the Ultimate Release . . ."

IN Corpus Christi that night, where he's topping the bill over old Sir Douglas Quintet organist, Augie Meyer, the local cat from San Antonio, he does four encores, even though there are only 300 people in the 1,700-seater Ritz Theatre.

There's been no airplay on him, no announcements, no advertising. As a word of mouth he's a whisper down here in darkest Texas . . . but the audience is ecstatic, going totally bananas in this bare, white-bricked theatre that was built back in the 1920s as a vaudeville hall.

And Springsteen gushes, coming off really high, saying, "no, man, it doesn't matter how many are there. Sometimes it's even better when there's not a lot there. You get off on yourself and the band."

He knows that next time he played here it would be full; but it's unlikely there will be a next time.

For this is an altogether grey, creepy town. Several years ago a hurricane blew in from the Gulf and took Corpus away with it, and though the physical scars have been patched up, in spirit it's only one graduation from a ghost town.

So much for sun-kissed beaches. The resort has shut down for winter, the air is clammy with cold.

So no-one was unhappy to leave that alien town for Houston, a wide, expanding sprawl of a city, not unlike Los Angeles in its centre-less architectural concept. Sitting, later, in his Houston hotel room, Springsteen can look back on his Corpus performance and say, "I had a good time, but right now it seems like a kind of a void. It didn't seem complete enough."

If only he could have done a final encore, he broods, the show at the Houston Music Hall might have come close to the perfect emotional dissolve that he's seeking.

But the management's fear of the unions prevented them performing and he wanders off dejectedly as the audience swarms out, upset that he's not physically spent, that there's energy left with no place to go . . .

SO, LATE this Saturday evening, in Houston's downtown Holiday Inn, Bruce Springsteen is slowly shaking off his post-performance blues and equalising his emotions.

He's saying that when he gets back to New Jersey he has to make a lot of changes in the band, to get more depth. He feels he's just on the perimeter of what he should be doing.

But perhaps inside he's remembering that night years ago when he walked out on-stage and suddenly found he was only parodying himself, that it had become a bore. He's only too aware now of how he needs that shiny hit record to sustain his momentum, that elusive combustible which will break open another door for him, just as he once stepped through a door that took him into rock 'n' roll and off the streets.

And yet change is all around him. He spends long weeks on the road now. He will see less and less of Asbury Park which, though no millionaires' row, has been a big source of inspiration for his music. He's rarely written on the road before, but he will have to adjust. His consciousness is developing. He has to work it all out.

He's a guy who might have gone bad, or just become a bum, but found this little seed within himself and learned what makes it grow, till he's filled up inside with lots of different goodies.

Everybody has it but most people just never figure it out. Springsteen says his father was one of those. "And there are guys still out there, guys my age, guys a lot older."

So with this perspective he sees his function, his role, if he has any at all, as one of trying to show people some quality, some emotion, that is real, and the way he tells it is less pompous than it sounds.

He says, "You've got to be able to see yourself for what you are, and not until then can you improve on what you are and be what you want to be. But people throw it away for a hoax, the Big American Hoax. For me I can't deal with life in reference to governments and politics, I have to deal with it on a personal level.

"If you look at Bob Dylan, that's what he was doin'. 'Blowin' In The Wind' was all right, but I don't like it half as much as 'I Want You,' 'Like A Rolling Stone,' or anything on 'Blonde On Blonde.'

" 'I want you' – that's it, that's the ultimate statement you can make to anybody. What else can you say? And that's the greatest lyric in the song, those three words, in the whole damn song!

"I put that on, man, and I get blown away, I get blown down the street, 'cause there's no hoax there, it was real, real as hell."

In his own songs Springsteen tries for that same honesty, searching however wildly, for some clear picture of himself. "I don't know what I'm writing from," he says, "but the main thing I've always been worried about was me.

"I had to write about me all the time, every song, 'cause in a way you're trying to find out what that 'me' is. That's why I choose where I grew up, and where I live, and I take situations I'm in, and people I know, and take 'em to the limits."

But in pursuing this self-discovery, away from the stage he's grown self-contained, untouched by people in the final analysis. Although easy and friendly, not a bit aloof, he's still a lone star, moving on his own, independent trajectory.

He's into none of the musician's usual trips – doping up, drinking and heavy womanising. The girls he meets on the road he never turns into groupies, to be discussed with appropriate lip-smacking noises in the bus next day. Dope was not even important to him as a teenager.

"People do it because their friends do it," he explains carefully, "and at the time I didn't have any friends in Asbury . . . I had a guy I'd see once in a while and a girl, but outside of that there was nobody, I wasn't in that circle.

"Consequently, I was oblivious to a lotta social pressures and stuff within the scene, 'cause I was on the outside, on the outside looking in . . . until I started to play, and then people come closer to you. You don't go to them, they come to you."

He pauses, his hands rumpling through his hair. "But by then it was too late. I was totally involved in what I was doin', and I had no need for anything else, or for anybody. I was there, and that was it, for me."

He gets up and turns the television off and then goes back to the bed, where he sits cross-legged.

"Y'know, you have to be self-contained. That way you don't get pushed around. It depends on what you need. I eat loneliness, man. I feed off it. I live on a lotta different levels, y'know, because I've learned to cope with people, which is – be cool all the time. I can do that, because . . . I've got too much going on inside to be upset over things that are trivial to me.

"So I've learned to really flow with it on the surface. I can roll with the punches. It's a way of getting along."

Still he's in the ring now, moving up the rankings, with other managers fastening their beady eyes upon him. Suddenly it's become a big deal, and he needs all the help he can get. He and Appel battle it out together, managing on a shoestring, until The Breakthrough arrives.

One day he wants to have that big pile of money, wants to hold a million dollars in his hand, just to see what it's like.

And come that day, he's promised himself he'll ride in a limousine and go to some spiffy high society do where they'll have to announce him.

Then – thinking dutifully – there's his mother who's worked every day since she was 17, and she's old now. He'd like her to stop – his old man, too. Oh – there's all kinds of dreams wrapped up in that million bucks. But mostly he knows what he wants, and it's to do with an attitude.

"I wanna be able to spit on the floor when I like," he says with passion. "I just wanna be in control. I don't wanna be controlled through the air, man. I wanna spit in the air . . ."

IN THE early hours of Sunday morning we confront ourselves at a celebration party held in Roberto's home, a large, wooden-frame building set back from the road amidst tall grass. The rain has stopped momentarily, but the vegetation on the drive swishes heavily.

Inside it's a great melee, with people crushed drunkenly together. Ice rattles in a big tub holding cans of beer. Over in one corner several people play gin-rummy on a big, battered old table. There are cigarettes stubbed out in the potato salad. The party is on its last legs . . .

It's well after 3 a.m. when Roberto, mad Chicano that he is, portentously raises his hand and calls, in thunderous fashion, for silence. As the hubbub cuts out, he draws Bruce to him and makes a little speech about how honoured he is to have such a rising star in his home, he, Roberto.

And while Springsteen looks sheepish, the guests raise their cans of beer to him for a brief deep moment. Then someone coughs, and the party limps to its close.

Later, in the car back to the hotel, Springsteen says, "Do you know what he gave me?" And he pulls out of his pocket Roberto's absurd Lone Ranger mask. We all have a good laugh at that, and then we head for the nearest hamburger joint, because Bruce is feeling very hungry by now.

Michael Watts

5

Exiles on main street

THE ROLLING STONES
December 23 1974

For ten years now it has been an incredible fact, the partnership between this replete feline with his bumpy, giblet lips as Tom Wolfe described him, and the lean and hollowed axe-man, features like a funky waste-land, image that of hoodlum bike-boy from "Scorpio Rising."

A decade is a long time in the brittle world of rock and roll, whatever it might have been to Rodgers and Hart or Kern and Hammerstein. Fissures appear in the superstructure, psychological scars open and bleed again, there are pressures, both vague and tangible.

And all the time there's this accretion of myth, building, billowing out, obscuring until finally the whole edifice collapses and crushes the individual under its weight.

They say that's what happened to Brian. As a rhythm and blues band was swallowed up by pop mania, he couldn't adjust to the whole myth which developed, to the fact that the singer was now getting all the attention – and he, Brian, had started the whole show, had been the leader, the one who collected the two pounds ten or whatever after those early gigs! The innate paranoias mushroomed. It was insidious at first, and then crushing.

But for Mick and Keith it may have been a good thing. After that the air was cleared. The balance neatly tipped between them. No hang-ups.

They grew into their roles, and though the mythology of hothouse exotica increased even – the whole fin de siecle, prince of darkness, decadence syndrome – they became secure in handling, even manipulating it. It's like the guitarist in the studio.

What's played in the room doesn't necessarily come out on the final tape, nor is that always desired. Distortion!

The dichotomy between reality and public fantasy is often baffling. Truman Capote, who toured America this year with the Stones, could find no illuminating spark. In the end he gave up his attempt to write a story and simply dismissed them as "unisexual zombies."

Chuck Berry, says Jagger, is a great example of a confusing myth: "He can destroy what you want, what you thought of him, but on the other hand, the next time you meet him he can make up for it."

Unisex. Zombies. Satanists. Kenneth Anger calls Keith Richard his "right hand man."

In fact they are so different, even from each other, Mick and Keith.

The one is nearly as much a socialite and movie star celebrity as he is a rock singer. Photographed entering Max's Kansas City and leaving it. In Andy Warhol's Interview magazine. On the fashion pages. Top of the ten best-dressed men league. The group's press agent, most willing to talk to reporters. The original rock androgynous.

And the other, pure hundred per cent musician. Apostle of raunch. Equally as fascinating, perhaps more so, in his gaunt and wasted pose. He still best represents the politics of delinquency and the spurious glamour of the drug culture.

The establishment's whipping boy, yet he continues to ride it out, with just a contemptuous glance over his shoulder.

Mick is fidgety, a coil of strung-out energy, his body always posturing, his hands beating at something. . . the flat of his thighs, a table-top, picking things up compulsively.

Keith is slow motion, almost abstract. Even gentle. A cloak of world-weariness on his shoulders. The answers seem to come from far away, as if the questions have long been considered and debated within.

Close-to he's less raunch. When he shakes hands, his is soft and boneless.

IT IS five days to Keith's 29th birthday and he is sitting at a table more than three thousand miles away from London. Jagger appears off and on.

We are speaking of England. Keith talks about its tremendous capacity for absorbing attitudes, "like a big piece of wet cotton wool."

"It doesn't matter what it is he's saying, it will just absorb it until it's part of the establishment. That's England's big trick. After all, didn't they do it to the Beatles? Slap a medal on them. They could never pin an MBE to the Stones, but still, all those things they put them through. . .

"You only have to listen to BBC. Once every day to be completely in touch with what is going on in England."

It's not the most prolific place in the world, he admits, but he dislikes not to be able to live there, for tax reasons.

There are far worse places, like Switzerland, where he's been living for most of the past four months since the American tour ended. There they've sacrificed everything creative for their feeling of security – financial, physical and everything else.

He's seen the kids in Switzerland: "They come up to me in the street and say, 'hey, you're a Rolling Stone! I'm in a band. How do we get to be really big and earn lots of money? What do you have to do to make a good group?'

"And I say, 'well, look, why don't you try starving?' They can't even comprehend that, man, they're so rich. I mean, have you ever heard of a good Swiss musician, a good Swiss painter or writer?

"England gets fooled by the newspapers and TV that if it doesn't have the best standard of living in the world at least it's got the second best. England doesn't even know, man! They're being fooled all along the line!

"People in Switzerland, France and Germany live twice as good as anybody in England. They're twice as bourgeois, twice as rich."

He sighs. He's still searching for THE place, but he can only find the answer by moving around. He prefers now not to live anywhere, but just to travel between places he knows and a few he doesn't.

This Christmas he's rented a house with Jagger in Jamaica. He'll move in Anita and the kid. He hesitates.

"It's a drag not to be able to go and see me mum," he says obliquely. "Just because of some stupid tax."

And then there was France, of course. What had made him unhappy about France? And he replies, well, really, it was a question of what made them unhappy about him.

Before he'd even known what drugs were everybody had believed they were out of their heads. They had come up to them in Richmond and Ealing with that sidelong look that people had in those days, when it was very taboo and mysterioso exotic, and they'd whisper, "what are you on?" And he'd reply, well, actually, he'd just had a brown and mild.

KEITH doesn't think musicians are necessarily attracted to a drug lifestyle. They just come into contact with it more than most people because. . . look, a cat plays a club, and that's where the local pusher hangs out to supply the kids; the guy naturally gets into contact with the musicians playing there.

That's the only connection he can think of in the first place. There may be a whole culture on the West Coast devoted to drugs but it hasn't sustained anything musically. He doesn't think drugs have added anything to music, let's put it that way.

"They might have flashed the inspiration for a couple of good songs, but I don't think there's anything fantastic been written under the influence of drugs that couldn't have been written without. But you find out what it's like because it's there."

It's like the desire to climb Everest, to attempt it because it challenges the experimental instincts.

But dangerous, too. The newspaper headlines stand out vividly. "Hendrix, Morrison, Joplin – victims of the drug culture."

Because they died, because they died, he repeats. Before they weren't seen as that. With Hendrix, people either just dug him or they thought he was some evil, nasty, drug-taking black man, which was the other half of his image to moms and dads across the land. But once you were dead, you were the "victim of the drug culture."

He casts an ironic eye. They may all have died because they had "J" and "I" in their name, who knows? Brian Jones, Jim Morrison, Janis Joplin, Jimi Hendrix. . . Mick Jagger!

"Somebody tried to lay a hex on us last year because of that. There was some incredible scheme worked out by somebody in America about letters "I" and "J." Apparently, Mick was the next.

"And the cat has got some incredible story about a painting by Franz Hals who was a Dutch warlock who painted a picture in the 16th, 17th, century, of a guy playing the lute, called "The Minstrel" or something like that – the cat looks just like Mick!

"So the guy worked on these two coincidences to the point where everyone was walking around. . ." He does an eyeball-rolling impression of an acid freak.

"It was really amazing. I mean, his date came and went and nothing happened, but I got a copy of the painting, just to see. It's incredibly like Mick, an incredible likeness. It looks just like Jagger. Same haircut, same mouth."

But Jagger looks like several people.

"Exactly, exactly. If you put a frame round the face and paint it black it'd look like Hendrix, too. A wig it'd be Janis Joplin." Faint smile. "A pair of spots and it'd look like Carly Simon."

HE STARES into a vodka Collins that's been laid before him. His current favourite drink. Tequila Sunrise was the American tour.

The death of rock stars. It's got a romantic tinge to it, but actually it's very sordid.

"It's always sad when somebody really good and obviously still into it suddenly just. . . (He snaps his fingers abruptly) just like that. I mean, some people do die young and that's all there is to it.

"Some people have said it all by the time they're 22 or 25, but I don't get that feeling with Hendrix or Janis Joplin. I don't think they were finished, or that it was their time to go."

The sense of death and decadence, Edgar Allan Poe. There are always people drawn to the Stones because they think they see an aura of decadence.

It's never just the Palm Court Orchestra in town to play for the night. You can't divorce the music entirely from the scene that it's all built on. It's all part of "the Stones are the Stones, warts and all."

The daily media's horror of rock groups seems to begin and end with them. They don't get excited about anybody else's excesses as much.

A shrug of resignation.

"I know," he says, "I know. I guess you can only have one bad boy at a time, really, and we're it.

"There's not really much you can do about it. They can print what they like about us because people believe it, anyway.

"It amuses me personally, but on another level it's kind of frightening – the generalisations they can make without anybody apparently having to take any responsibility for it."

Did he feel this incredible pressure from the establishment weighing upon him?

"God, no! If I felt it, man, I'd just give up and go away! I'm not unconscious of it but. . . I don't feel there's any kind of weight. It seems that the press turn you into what they want you to be, and as far as the people are concerned that's what you are."

Someone else at the table, from another paper, says "we'll say you're nice."

"We don't give a –" comes the short reply.

IT'S JAGGER, leaning into the conversation. He's been making long hops between this table and the telephone.

Bianca, in London, stricken with flu. There's this solid impression that Mick is . . . keeping an eye on the talk, on Keith. The PR man. There's something protective there.

Anyway, the Stones versus the establishment, and Mick is saying it's all political, and that on his side he likes to live outside legality, to do what he likes, and on their side there's this. . . well, not exactly a conspiracy, but it does become that.

"Once you plant some idea in people's minds there doesn't have to be. The conspiratorial element is there. Once you've got the idea underlying they can re-use it, and that is a conspiracy.

"For us it's a big drag. No one quite throws their hands up in horror at us anymore, but we do object to the politics of it. We feel that our right to be able to play where we want to and when we want to is being interfered with.

"No one else gets the hassles we get and we don't do anything no one else doesn't do."

Poor Mick. But the times do change. Take the American tour. It was their most successful yet, musically and financially. And there was no trouble, no cop crushed, no deaths.

America had changed since the last time in '69. The atmosphere less intense, the audiences more into just having a good evening.

In '69 they were coming to watch. . . messiahs. This time it was no longer ominous. The campuses were quiet.

There's a different generation in there who obviously don't give a cuss for getting beaten on the head, teargassed and maced, which the previous generation seemed to have a capacity for taking.

Has anything really happened? Or have we gone the full 360 degrees, back to the beginning.

There's always a surge forward and then a slump, says Keith, until it seems nothing has happened at all, but in actual fact lessons have been learned.

"America has changed, believe me, quite considerably in the last ten years, but it doesn't appear to if you just look at the country.

"Take the FBI. It still pokes its nose, but not only does it now have another chief, it's lost the guy who started the whole shebang, who was the FBI.

"Ten years ago America was just a big put-on. It was exactly what every

English person thought it to be, except much more so, with dating rings, holding hands, hamburgers and teenage heaven – it was all there! In '63, '64. Ugh! Would you kiss her on your first date? That was the burning question, then.

". . . Only if she's got bad breath," mutters Jagger. And now? The crafty look at the pusher. "Oh, it's 'want some acid, man, want some acid?' You know."

The drug culture, with its fantastic grip on the American young.

"Sociologists ask why.

"Is it because America has refused to face up to the problem, like England has, which is just to give people who want smack smack. 'Give it to' em and then it's cool.

"In England there hasn't been that enormous increase in junkies, and also they don't go around thieving, stealing and mugging to get bread for their next fix, which is what happens in America.

"For a nation that can put a man on the moon it isn't that much of a problem to find a cure for heroin addiction, not if they really wanted to.

"You know, during the war the number of junkies in America dropped to almost zero because they just policed the f — ports properly.

"In wartime everything just snaps into action, right? You can't get anything into that country unless they want it in.

"Which means they can do it if they want to, if they really wanted to stop it. But you can make more money out of heroin than of anything else."

DRUGS, money, politics – revolution! There's lots of causes but no revolution, Jagger is saying.

"There are charities, there's people in jail who need money, there's people who don't have anything to eat that need money, there's all these people – but there isn't a revolutionary movement."

Fifteen hundred miles away in New York's East Village "The Trials Of Oz" is just opening to celebrities from the theatre and movie world: the media. Music by Mick Jagger.

Mick and Keith, the most famous and enduring partnership of them all! Capote's unisexual zombies! Five days away from Keith's birthday. For Mick's 29th. Ahmet Ertegun threw a huge party in New York with Zsa Zsa Gabor and all those socialites.

"It's probably because the newspapers ain't as interested in me as in Jagger." A faint, wry smile. "All you 'ear about me is when the warrants are out.

"Another Vodka Collins, please."

Michael Watts

6

'Don't deal with dark things'

BOB MARLEY

June 12 1976

Don't want success. Success mean nuttin'. Plenty people been successful, but dey still living dead – Bob Marley.

It's no ordinary rehearsal room, the doorless out-house in the garden of Bob Marley's house in Hope Road, Kingston, just a few minutes along from the Prime Minister's residence.

The Wailers practise here, in a room about twice the size of the average British lounge. What makes it extraordinary in atmosphere is the unmistakable feeling that when the musicians are in here, playing and smoking and planning a concert or an album, it's as if nothing had ever happened and they were still jamming purely for fun, as they did ten years ago. With few cares or considerations beyond the next tune, the new single, and not the faintest prospect of world tours and hit albums. A drum kit lies idle, an empty guitar case here, a chair or two . . . but what's this? A running order is scribbled and stuck to the wall, reading as follows:

Revolution/Natty Dread/So Jah Seh/No Woman/I Shot The Sheriff/Talking

Blues/Road Block/Bellyfull/Jah Live/Trenchtown Rock/Nice Time/Concrete Jungle/Kinky Reggae/Midnight Ravers/No More Trouble/Bend Down Low/Get Up Stand Up/Rat Race/Bumin' And Lootin'/Stir It Up/Duppy Conqueror/Slave Driver/Rock My Boat/One Love/Thank You Lord.

On another wall, an article of faith: a portrait with the words: "His Imperial Majesty, Emperor Haile Selassie, King of Kings, Lord of Lords."

Incongruously, a sticker is pinned beneath it: "Album Of The Year – Natty Dread."

Bob Marley lives here, works here, plays here and if there's one thing absolutely endearing about the whole Jamaican-Rastafarian/Reggae story as it reaches its British peak with Bob Marley's tour next week, it's this: what you see, and what they say, is all there is.

There's no hiding behind poses, and the uncluttered sound of their music runs synonymously with their personalities. The rehearsal room is the opposite of pretentious.

Marley is hard to reach. Even his friends say that strangers, particularly white ones, should not go to his house unless accompanied by a face which Marley recognises.

It's virtually impossible to make an appointment to see him, because he appears not to recognise schedules, even for himself. But eventually on that hot evening, he appeared from the table tennis room in his house and walked me outside, saying he would think better with some air.

His house is large and old and rambling, and bears the vibrations of a commune. People drift in and out, by car and on foot, and he waved to them all, while remaining seated on the steps.

The house is a positive statement by Marley. Opposite, there are some terrible new apartments which look like prison cells, and Bob continually laughs at the fact that they have bars up, protecting them from burglars. "No way to live, no way to live!" he keeps saying. "Must run home like mind. Keep open."

Thus, Marley's home, Island House, in Hope Road, Kingston, is open to all-comers. Especially Rastafarians.

As the Marley/Wailers success gathers momentum, so their allegiance to Rastafarian principles becomes more concentrated. Every other sentence of Marley's speech is punctuated by a reference to Jah (God) and as he drew harder on his cigar-sized spliff (joint), repeating: "Righteousness must cover the earth like the water cover the sea," I had visions of a sermon rather than a conversation, and certainly fading hopes of a lucid conversation.

And yet it's too easy to dismiss the obsession with Rasta as excluding their attachment to reality. It's impossible to catch, first time round, every word and nuance of what Marley is saying, but his drift is quite simple to understand, and while he keeps returning to his declarations that commercial gain is not his aim, he is acutely aware of all that's happening around him. His mind moves very quickly indeed, and his powers of observation are uncanny.

I asked him first about his evident need to smoke ganja (herb), of which he partakes a pound a week, and why the smoking of it was so dovetailed into his Rasta beliefs.

"Herb is the healing of a nation," he said quietly. "When you smoke, you don't frighten so easy. Herb bring all brethren together, all thinking alike and that's why they lock you up when you smoke herb, because it makes people think same way, but if people don't smoke herb they think different from each other, can be told what to do and get . . . confused.

"In Babylon we give thanks for herb, and if we didn't have herb to educate us, we be educated by fools who tell us to live like funny, like in Babylon. Herb is the healing of a nation, Bible say that. Herb come out of the ground!"

Did this contempt, then, for materialism and Babylon (Western culture) and even for organised society represent Black Power, and did Bob feel his music was preaching TO white ears, or to blacks about whites?

"My music fight against the system. My music defend righteousness. If you're white and you're wrong, then you're wrong, if you're black and you're wrong, you're wrong. People are PEOPLE. Black, blue, pink, green, – God make no rules about colour, only society make rules where my people suffer and that why we must have redemption and redemption is now.

"Against white people? Couldn't say that. I fight against the system that teach you to live and die."

So his music existed for propaganda? He laughed at the seriousness of the word. "No. If God had-na given me a song to sing, I wouldn't have a song to sing. So it's not MY music, from my soul, doing these things, saying these words.

"I don't know about propaganda but in telling truth, and I don't deal with the wrong things of life, and I don't want to know them because as soon as you know them, you . . . know them, and because you're not perfect you might try to change.

"Don't like idea of propaganda, that's not how I-and-I see it. Don't deal with dark things."

And yet many of his songs, I said, were laced with stabs at various inequalities. "Bellyfull," for example, was surely a commentary on the starvation of some as compared with the abundant wealth of others?

Not exactly, Marley answered. It was more subtle than that – your belly's full, but we're hungry for your LOVE of your brethren. Food's in your stomach, but cannot you see there is more to living than filling it? Where's the love for your brother?

No, he averred, it wasn't entirely a materialistic commentary, more a sad declaration of the bankruptcy of believing that everything ended with self-gratification.

But he was positively not playing a role. Asked if he felt any responsibility as the most popular star reggae had produced, he said: "I don't think about it, you know. Too busy working.

"People come to me, say: 'Bob Marley, big international artist' and I laugh. I don't know what that mean. If it mean more people listen, enjoy music, then good. That's all."

Still, he had been watching the adoption of reggae by others, and he liked Johnny Nash's "Stir It Up," a world hit version of the Marley song, and he was interested in other incursions into the style, mentioning Paul Simon's "Mother And Child Reunion" ("nice.")

"See, dem American players come down here and play with Jamaican musicians who are very friendly. Make good records. It happens all the time."

So there was no determination to keep reggae as a wholly private scene, and Jamaica was happy for the world to go into Kingston and join in?

"Nah, world cannot take it," Bob replied immediately. "This is one of them things the world cannot take. It's like gold is gold and silver is silver, and what is . . . imitation can be seen t'be imitation.

"So the real thing, nobody can take away from here. You have to really come in to this thing at our time to have the feel, y'know. It's art, y'know, art. Not just a purposeful thing, but from knowing.

"That's why I-and-I know nobody can take it. They can go anywhere and play funky and soul, but reggae – too hard, reggae. Must have a bond with it. The real reggae must come from Jamaica, because other people could not play it all the while, anyway – it would go against their whole life. Reggae has t'be . . . inside you."

Marley was now trying to get himself to define reggae music as clearly as possible, and the nearest he could get was to say it was like jazz.

"Jazz – a complete music," he declared, still smoking. "Reggae complete too. Reggae is funky, but it's also different from funky, and sometimes I think funky soul music goes little too far in what it tries to do.

"Reggae music is simple, all the while. Different from soul as well. Cannot be taught, that's a fact."

It relied on a mental attitude, he explained. If he was depressed and was going into a studio, he could not make music properly. But then, it might easily have something to do with the people and their vibrations.

He felt – well, not uneasy in the company of non-Rastafarians, but not relaxed either. He wanted to stress, though, there was no antipathy towards white non-Rastas.

"Well, I say give a man a chance if he's not Rasta. The Bible full of stories of people not treated right for not believing. Problem is not with people who are not in touch with Rasta, but with people who are once Rasta and then have left it and have to go back to it. These can be difficult and . . . confused people."

Propaganda for Rastafarianism was something he admitted, if not for black repression.

Are you trying to make audiences outside Jamaica appreciate what Rastafarianism stands for?

"Yeh, mon. Rasta Man Vibration gonna cover the earth! Jah say: until the philosophy which places one race superior and one race inferior is finally and permanently discredited and abandoned, then we won't have no peace.

"Babylon believe in divide and rule, but Rasta one way only, the right way, and we can do it but it take longer. We have redemption now, nobody can stop it . . ."

Marley said he read a chapter of the Bible every day, and based his belief on that, including his diet. He is a vegetarian, although that is not a prerequisite of Rastafarianism.

He didn't drink, he said, because it was obvious that pumping chemicals into his body would make him ill. "A little wine, sometimes," he reflected.

"The reason people drink is because they want to feel how I feel when I smoke. Everybody need to get a little high sometimes, just that some people get high on the wrong thing. Herb does grow. How much do I smoke? Plenty."

Could someone be a Rasta and not smoke?

"Yeh . . . but if you believe in Rasta and fight against the herb, you are wrong. Herb needs to, be understood properly, but, in hands of Rasta, it is the healing of a nation."

Smoking is highly illegal in Jamaica, however, and Marley repeats his view that society is frightened of people thinking the same way.

"Vampires!" he roared. "Most people are negative out there, but Rasta people think positive. Most people in Babylon want power. Devil want power. God don't want power, but Devil need power, 'cos Devil insecure."

Insecurity never bothered him. Even when he travelled outside Jamaica, he remained confident, secure, positive.

The only country he would contemplate settling in, except Jamaica, was Africa – this was naturally bound up with his Rasta convictions – but even without the prospect of settling there, he planned a trip there soon.

Friends say they dread the day Marley goes there, because he's such a highly-charged, sensitive man that it is bound to change his entire attitude, one way or the other, towards his beliefs.

He said the system taught people that they must live and die, but he and his brethren did not agree. Furthermore, they were totally opposed to the worshipping of material goods to the point where people in "Babylon" (Bob's all-embracing word for the centre of the world's problems) died working for material objects which would do nothing to enrich their lives.

It wasn't that he personally renounced materially useful things: bicycles, cars, were OK in the Rasta creed, but they were merely a means to an end. "If somebody gave me a spaceship, I would give it back to him because I could not use it," Marley continued.

He pointed to that ugly block of new houses opposite, and laughed, sadly. "Those people over there are working to live in a situation not good, but the system educates them to think that is the end of their life," he said.

"People not taught to be at peace with themselves. Education all wrong. Put you in a bracket where you earn enough money to pay for THESE things!" (He pointed at the houses again).

"Well, you have to be a Rasta man to beat the system, and when they can get a Rasta man in jail, they do, and then they try to get you back there. Everyone wants the biggest this, the biggest car, refrigerator, crazy, mon – this is the system I keep talking about. . . ."

He started to sing "Rat Race."

What about the race for the title of the biggest reggae band in the world, then? Did he concede such a contest existed?

"Can't say that," he answered, convincingly. "I-and-I, and my brethren, only answer to myself and to Jah. If de Wailers are in some race, we must have been put there by somebody, but not us."

How about the future of the band, Bob? Does it plan to change, progress in any foreseeable way?

"When I feel that the job has been done that I-and-I have been sent to do, I-and-I pack it up," he stated firmly. When would that be?

"When I feel satisfied and when Jah tells me I am finished with this work. It might be at the end of the American visit, or the English visit – I will know that when as many people as possible have learned what we have to say." When the system is challenged?

"System bound to go," he answered.

THE personal manager of Bob Marley is Jamaican-born Don Taylor, who has worked with Tamla Motown in Detroit, and especially closely with Marvin Gaye, Little Anthony, Martha Reeves and Chuck Jackson.

He's managed Marley for a year, and says he was warned against taking on Bob by locals who described Marley as a "problem, difficult character."

"What you must remember," said Taylor one day as he contemplated the escalating Marley story yet again, "is that Bob's sharper than all of us.

"Right now, he's getting to the position he was in ten years ago, of not trusting people and that's a pity. Lots of people hang around the studios, for instance, saying they are broke and asking him for ten dollars just like they used to.

"He always used to give friends dollars if they needed it, but now the whole world seems to be joining in.

"Maybe it's because there's jealousy in this town because Bob's the one who made it, and people are out to take him for a ride. This is real bad, y'know – they should realise that he's made it possible for everyone to make it.

"Instead, people are talking behind his back and speaking all this crap about selling out. Listen, the same guys who knew Marley when he was in Trenchtown are talking behind his back now, and it's sickening. . . ."

Bob Marley, he declared, knew all about the rats and the roaches of Trenchtown living. "He also knows all those old slogans about no money, no jobs, no future. Well, Marley's GIVING them a future."

FLYING out of Kingston next day aboard Air Jamaica, I asked the hostess her views on reggae, Rastafarianism, and Bob Marley. She was about 25, a black Jamaican.

"Rastafarianism? Oh, it's quite popular but only among the very young here. I don't think reggae will ever catch on much. It's really dance music for the young. What would you like to drink?"

Ray Coleman

7

What's going on

MARVIN GAYE

October 9 1976

MARVIN PENZE GAYE. Born April 2, 1939, in Washington D.C., the son of a minister. First sang in father's church aged three. Played guitar, piano, drums in school orchestra and organ in church. In 1957, two ex-Rainbows plus Marvin and Reese Palmer formed the Marquees. They recorded "Wyatt Earp" under auspices of Bo Diddley for Okeh and backed the bluesman on Checker label's "I'm Sorry." In 1958 Harvey Fuqua's Moonglows group split. The leader went to Washington to form a new line-up. He chose the Marquees, adding Chuck Barsdale. They made two singles for Chess in '59, Gaye sang lead on one.

Fuqua married Gwen Gordy, who ran Chess's Detroit-based subsidiary, Anna. Gaye moved to Detroit with Fuqua, married Anna Gordy and all joined forces at brother Berry Gordy Jr's emerging Tamla Motown's set-up. Initially, Gaye was session drummer; worked the road with Smokey Robinson & the Miracles; sang back-up.

His first single, "Let Your Conscience Be Your Guide," issued in the States in May, 1961. A flop. Two others followed. In July 1962 his fourth single, "Stubborn Kind Of Fellow," broke into the American R & B Top Ten and the pop Top 50, since when, without exception, 47 subsequent singles (solo and duo) charted.

In Britain he didn't make the charts until 1967 with "It Takes Two," a duo with Kim Weston. In 1969 "I Heard It Through The Grapevine," produced by Norman Whitfield, became his first solo hit in Britain and remains one of Tamla Motown's biggest-selling records ever.

Gaye's handsome visage and adaptable voice led him to be paired with outstanding Motown female vocalists. First was Mary Wells ("Once Upon A Time," "What's The Matter With You Baby?") in 1964, then Kim Weston (notably "It Takes Two") in 1966 and Tammi Terrell from 1967 until her death in March 1970.

After Tammi's death, Marvin withdrew into a shell, became introspective, reclusive, obviously affected by events. He metamorphosed into committed writer/performer/producer with 1971's "What's Going On," an album of sweeping social comment ranging across topics of moment like poverty, pollution, ecology, drug addiction and Vietnam veterans.

Having established his credentials afresh with powerfully observed lyrics of "What's Happening Brother," "Save The Children," "Inner City Blues (Make Me Wanna Holler)," "Mercy Mercy Me (The Ecology)," Gaye turned his attention to less cerebral matters with 1973's "Let's Get It On," an album of immense sensuality, one of the most direct celebrations of the sexes imaginable.

Sandwiched between those two releases came "Trouble Man," Marvin's first film soundtrack. The movie was fairly execrable; Gaye's music was its only saving grace and, according to interviews with Marvin, it's one of the works he's most satisfied with.

The upsurge in creativity gave Marvin the confidence to perform live again and, tentatively at first, he stretched those feathery vocal wings once more to fly. In July 1973 he said to an American magazine: "I don't have any fears now of failing as a performer because I feel, quite frankly, that I can stand on my record at this point. . . . There's one little fear I have – I love to be liked and it bugs me that somebody might not like me."

That, he admitted, sounded like, and was, egotism. Allied to the fact that he merely had no burning desire or fiscal need to perform, his withdrawal seemed logical if hard on his many fans.

When he finally sang before a live audience again even his slightest fears were utterly quashed as the squealing response of his fans heard on "Marvin Gaye Live!" testifies. Recorded at the Oakland Coliseum in '74 in front of 14,000 audibly ecstatic admirers, the album had one new song ("Jan"), two songs from "What's Going On" and "Let's Get It On" and the title track from "Trouble Man," plus an oldies medley. After the six-year performing hiatus had been broken, Marvin worked the road more regularly.

He revived the male/female duo facet of his work by teaming up with Motown's first lady, Diana Ross, for one album in 1973 and, just last March, he presented his latest solo album, "I Want You."

When he flew into Britain last week to start his tour at the Royal Albert Hall with two sold-out shows, he was still unsure as to what his reception would be – despite the constant reassurances of promoter Jeffrey Kruger that his coming was awaited with impatience, anxiety and great excitement.

By Monday evening, at 11.30pm, as the second RAH house emptied he could be in no doubt that his long, long overdue stage appearance in Britain had been a total success.

BY 7.15 p.m. on a darkening Tuesday night, the night after his debut British concerts, Marvin Gaye had tippled a third of the way through his fourth bottle of red wine. He was in a loquacious mood.

He's a tall man, about six feet, and has filled out since his slim early Sixties publicity shots caught him looking like a razor. But there's still not much spare flesh on him. He still looks the athlete.

He wears a royal blue bathrobe with a livid red trim. It's one of those bathrobes fastened at the side by three thin cords so that the material drapes loosely like a curtain showing a generous expanse of bare skin. The gap in Marvin's bathrobe was big enough to drive a truck through.

He is seated at a round table by the 14th floor hotel window looking out over Knightsbridge, a view which occasionally holds his attention. Spread out in front of him on the table are photographs of his family over which he pores, shuffling them around as though they were tarot cards. He sips the wine frequently and tosses peanuts one by one into his mouth.

Twice he breaks the mood of the interview to stare directly into a photographer's camera with an unnerving intensity – his animated face suddenly becoming utterly sober and expressionless. It's as though he is trying to petrify the camera's shutter.

The talk is sprawling and philosophical. Marvin Gaye's history is well known enough; it's his motivation which holds the darkest secrets and is most pertinent to his writing though, of course, his career has not been without drama.

Indeed, it has been noted that there's a strong correlation between his career and that of Daniel Stone, a fictitious character in Elaine Jesmer's book Number One With A Bullet, the publication of which Motown unsuccessfully tried to prevent.

Stone is portrayed as a handsome singer who joins a young label, marries into the family which runs it, becomes a star, has drug problems, battles with his label and shrinks from the spotlight into seclusion.

True, the book is fairly cheap sensationalism a la Jacqueline Susann and Harold Robbins, but the picture of Stone looks, you'll agree, not unlike a shadowy outline of Gaye.

We begin, rather naturally, with discussion of the previous night's shows. Marvin has enjoyed the first the most. "The band were conscious of the show and the surroundings and the sound. The second show got very loose and kind of loud and everything and I found myself shouting, which I didn't want to do. Outside of that, I liked it."

Obviously his standards are mighty high, for to me he'd sung with a fine control and vivacity quite unrivalled.

"The sound effects are terrific at the Royal Albert Hall and I found myself really experimenting with it, even doing little numbers with my voice so I can like hear it come back at me in certain ways, but eventually the music got too loud and I couldn't do that. It just soaked up my voice."

Surely, most singers found their echo distracting? "You do so many theatres and you're involved in so much sound that you know instinctively when the effects are good. The best person to judge the effects is an artist."

Still, it's not as controllable an environment as a recording studio. "There it becomes very technical. The same problems exist but they're only very technical and hidden.

"It takes a very technical mind because arithmetic is involved and physically it's not one of involvement, it becomes numbers and figures and wires, whereas with the theatre you do have some control because it's largely physical."

Despite being a self-producer of considerable excellence, Marvin insists that he has little technical expertise "and I don't want to know. I can run a studio I could record myself if I had to, simply because I've watched people twist knobs for so many years and plug in jacks and that sort of thing, until I've learned, not because I wanted to, but because I've seen it so much.

"The same way I learned piano over the years by watching good musicians' hands."

Marvin says he's been asked many times why he has suddenly chosen to visit Britain after so long – and each time he gives a different answer. "I wonder what the real answer is?" He smiles to himself. "The more wine I drink, the uh . . ." He breaks into a laugh.

The day before he'd said he had no desire to come to Britain because he felt his records didn't sell here. "Ah yes, back to that . . . If my royalty payments don't reflect that I'm popular in England then it's difficult to get up for it."

Could it be that his record sales here are poorer, proportionately, than in the States simply because he hasn't toured Britain before?"

"Could be that. Could be that. But the whole thing is if that is the bottom line and you're that kind of artist then that would come to mind. But I'm not monetarily structured. I'm out to gain the world, of course, but not in a monetary way.

"Monetarily speaking, I make a good enough living selling records in the States. I'm not a greedy man so I wouldn't say 'Oh boy now I've got to conquer England recordwise'.

"Although I have looked at the charts, and all my life I've always wanted to have a Number One record in England.

"I understand that in the earlier years when I was recording in the Sixties my records did quite well on the English charts, but the Seventies . . . of course I can understand that for one thing I didn't put anything out (grins), on the other hand I'm sorta underground all over."

It's as though he's elusive? "I don't like to feel that way. I think I am because I need a lot of time to myself because I do a lot of thinking. I haven't put a lot of the thoughts into action. But I shall in due time.

"I'm only me. I'm not trying to be anybody else or anything else. Because I'm the way I am. I'm not particularly the way artists should be. I don't fall into the category or mould of most artists. Artists like myself just prefer to be however we are, and if we're honest with ourselves and the people around us that's okay.

"I don't think, if I were another kind of artist, that I'd've got the reception I got last night. I think I was received that way because, basically, people believe I'm honest and they believe something about me.

"Marvin Gaye is something a little different and that little difference is that I'm concerned and I'm not concerned about money and things like that.

"I make a lot of money and I'm probably a very rich man but I don't necessarily need it. I can do a concert in America and make as much as 100,000 dollars for one show, which ain't bad (laughs).

"The thing is I got some letter about eight years ago from a bunch of English people and I was so shocked, there were so many of them.

"These kids were in school and all of the letters, there were about a thousand of them, and they were all in this book and the book was about this thick (indicates the depth of two telephone directories) and I was thumbing through it, they were saying how much they loved me and my records and I never got that out of my mind."

He's sure the memory of that book and the fans' devotion helped put him on the Concorde the Sunday he flew to Britain, convinced that though his albums broke no records here, he was nevertheless wanted. Badly. "I feel if I'm wanted, I have to go."

There was an air of reluctance. He doesn't like being on the road, he says.

"The road is dangerous for one thing. The other thing is I don't like to be away from my family.

"And number three, I feel many times that after working one show after another," he sighs, tapping two fingers in an arc around the table's edge, "for a series of days or months or weeks, that an element of hypocrisy creeps into performance which I hate with a passion because I become tired and I want to quit but I can't because I got nine more days.

"So I'm not performing truly, honestly. I'm performing tired and I don't really want to do it and regardless of what people say it becomes very tiring."

Nowadays, Marvin lives as far from cities as he can. "People live together because people need people. They tend to place their security in people.

"The only opportunity there is in the country is the opportunity to find oneself and to obey Mother Nature and Her laws, which is the greatest opportunity in the world. In the city you have to obey man and his laws."

Yet Gaye's music remains basically urban in its mood and subject matter, accepting the presence in his catalogue of a few ecology songs.

He'd said earlier that he'd had many thoughts which he wanted to put into action. Could he talk about them?

"When did I say that?" Five minutes ago. "Well, I never. Well . . . feeling I know my mission in life and my purpose, which is something that most people don't really know and what I feel that most people should try and understand, I'm going to put those thoughts to music, because that is the best way I can help anybody.

"It's what I do best. I do everything good," he grins, "but I do music best."

Were the years he spent as a recluse the most productive in terms of soul-searching and idea-provoking?

"No. Strangely enough, I get most of my direction when I'm on the road and I'm close to people and when I can see situations.

"I look at people in the eyes and see their problems, their fears, their miseries. I can read them a lot of times and I get my energy when I read them.

"When I'm away, I'm away for knowledge only. And wisdom. My feeling, what makes me want to write and what motivates me, is my contact with people when I'm on the road.

"I don't need to be on the road a hundred days a year to get that because the problems are everywhere I go.

"There's no place without problems, there are fewer problems in the country because there is greater understanding, greater tolerance. They don't tend to be affected by the modern things other people are affected by."

The city, he summates, encourages people to make small things over-important. Country folk have a better sense of proportion, of the balance of life and of values.

"Such as clothes. City folk tend to make them a mountain . . . it can be most influential in your life, how you approach your dress. Your dress can change you, you adapt to what you wear, you become what you put on.

"If you put on a slick pin-stripe suit, very sharp and exquisite and Wall Street-looking and brainy, you try to emulate it."

Conversation meanders back to the previous night's show and the crowd's ecstatic response. He'd been told it would be that way, he says "but I was surprised at the extent of their exuberance."

It's rare, too, to see a cool London audience clamber on stage, give the artist a hug or a kiss which seems a mixture of gratitude and respect and, having paid homage, leave the stage free to the artist. There was something almost religious about it – at least at the second show.

The first had been a much more physical sort of celebration with Gaye venturing along the aisles, shaking hands like an electioneering politician and ultimately having great difficulty getting back to the stage.

"I know that English audiences are reserved for the most part, they show their appreciation after you're through with the performance, after each number.

"They really don't do that sort of thing young ladies and teenyboppers . . . even old ladies! I was surprised in that. It bolstered my ego fifteen, twenty, thirty notches.

"And let's face it we all need a little ego bolstering. It helped me a lot and so, you know, I put out. I really put out."

He hadn't gone among the audiences in the States since he was doing his night club act in the Sixties, he says: "That will give you an idea what that sort of electricity will do to an artist."

Basically, he says, there are two types of artist. The mechanical who "learn an act and who'll do tremendous things whereby they know they'll receive a certain reaction from the audience every time. If they don't feel good one night they'll get the same reactions as if they feel great. They maintain an average.

"I'm not that type. I'm the type that can be lousy. I can do the same act but I can be lousy. So if the audience is lousy," he laughs, "or they're too reserved or if I get any feelings up there, I'll be lousy too. I can't do it. I just cannot do it.

"And I'll be glad when I'm off, the audience'll be glad when I'm off and everybody'll be happy. We come out even."

The chuckle with which he started has become a throaty laugh. "And I go out another night and the people go Wham! and I go 'Here I AM and I can do it, man, waddya want? I'LL do a double flip, anything'. And I would too, I'd try anything. And when they give it to me, I give it back. If they don't give it to me it's hard for me to give it out."

Texture, as much as anything else, is crucial to Gaye's music. When an artist like Marvin works as a sort of sound painter he must have a fairly flexible framework as far as band arrangements go, yet, too, there must be a certain amount of formality.

"I've had trouble finding the right combination of musicians because I'm a very, uh, hey, my musicians won't read this, but I'm a very . . ." He pauses, sighs.

"I have a respect for music that very few musicians have and it's difficult to find musicians generally who have the same kind of respect for music. And if I ever find those musicians we will play music that the world will never forget as long as there's a world.

"And I won't do my music until I find them and if I never find them my son will do it for me. I know that.

"I have only scraped the beginning. I have a lot of music in me. I have written a lot of music that's unpublished that I think is great. But I cannot afford to do it.

"The record companies and the industry as it is now are so ridiculous until . . . I would just rather save it. It'll be something for my son, here, Frank." he says, twirling one of the snapshots on the table.

That music includes a two-movement symphony. "It's not that great but who knows. Might be. I don't think it's that good," he laughs.

Marvin's gospel-based singing and mostly his earnest, ethereal conversation gives one the impression of him as a deep, spiritually motivated man with concurrently a highly developed appreciation of the more luxuriant earthly delights.

Spirit, he softly explains, is a strange, uncomfortable and unfair word because it brings fear. And he knows fear.

"What I would say is that I am a very aware person and I have certain qualities that I think excel the average human, only because I think the other person will not commit himself to getting into areas that are unknown in one's present environment.

"These are areas that are taboo. There are sorcerers. There are bad sorcerers and good sorcerers. But sorcery is where it's at.

"I think there are men and there are MEN. There are men who're born and are strong enough to be sorcerers. Those who are strong enough to become sorcerers can certainly imply themselves to become warriors. Impeccable Warriors. Impeccable Sorcerers.

"Nobody is strong enough to teach them. The word is taboo. The practice is taboo. It's a very strong practice and a very viable practice.

"Sorcery is beautiful. I say again there are good sorcerers and there are bad sorcerers. All men don't handle the power with respect."

Meaning using the power for evil, which most do? "No. You have to have an understanding of sorcery before you can even use the word evil. Another word that's not understood.

"There are people on this earth who are strong in righteousness and strong in Godliness and strong in awareness and strong in humanitarianism and strong in all the things that would be placed on the side of a line called The Good".

Balancing, he says, is the side of men strong in lying and deceit and brute force, who turn situations to their own ends.

"This side" he says, indicating good, "ultimately wins out, maybe. I haven't decided yet. You see there has to be a balance. It all sort of balances out.

"If you're impeccable enough he (indicating the bad side) can't hurt you, if you're impeccable enough in your belief". In tone and intent he sounded like a quiet, serious preacher.

He would love to become an Impeccable Warrior. "One who has little need for the earthly things such as the wines and the women and the clothes and the diamonds and the nice place to live.

"I'd love to develop a distaste for those things and become only interested in knowledge and power. Knowledge and power this earth will give you if you're willing to put in the time and the effort and it takes years, of course.

"I would love to quit show business and go after that knowledge. Have the power that the truly gifted sorcerer has. The power's here. It's in the rocks, it's in the air, it's in the trees, it's in the animals.

"There are men who can take those forces and elements and cause tremendous things to happen to the body to transform themselves, to do many, many marvellous things. We don't like to think that's true but I tell you it's true.

"I would like to become a man of power and knowledge. I would like to use it in a good fashion. To better the world's conditions.

"To have people understand that if they don't achieve the powers they can at least get on the trail and try, because what is life except to know oneself and so to become a superior being so that your genes are transferred to your children, and they get a better start than we ever had and they become more and more powerful and strong.

"You impart to them how to live, how to be, how to acquire power, acquire wisdom, how to acquire knowledge. They transfer it to their children and then, all of a sudden, you have a master society that can communicate without telephones, that can do unbelievable athletic feats. It's beautiful. That's the way life was at one time. We are uncivilised in a sense.

"This society will definitely come to an end and it may not be so far away. But that is how it's always been and that is how it has to be".

Man, he says, has always reached a point of knowledge and then destroyed himself. He wants to reach that point and catapult society into the area of "Superknowledge." Mother Nature, he says, is the key.

"There are those of us, the artists who write songs about things, you know 'the good things in life are free' and Stevie (Wonder) did a song about 'Sunshine Of My Life'. And 'shine on shine on harvest moon'.

"Those songs aren't written for nothing. They don't know, those writers, half the time but they're just forced to bring Mother Nature into the picture.

"People have to really start digging on Mother Nature and their environment and what's around them and start protecting it.

"You just have to quit trying to have a Cadillac and a Rolls and I know people say 'Nah Marvin Gaye, you're a rich guy' and all that stuff but this business makes you that. If you become popular that comes with it.

"I have everything I want but I don't really want anything. Most of the things I have are to try to make other people happy really. And to try to keep the Government from taking it all!

"There are a lot of things I desire. I desire peace and happiness and love and understanding. That sounds so ridiculous to a lot of people. 'Who is this guy wanting all that? Another Trouble Maker'."

Essentially Gaye is saying that "people who chose to be Righteous and Good" should have a strong and powerful ally because their beliefs and positions make them vulnerable. He would like to teach the righteous to find their protector.

And the weapon is his music? "Sure. Sure. They don't use it".

Does he find communicating through music difficult? Is the process of composition arduous?

"It's difficult, sometimes. Everything's difficult sometimes. But for the most part I find it fairly easy. The most difficult thing to do is to find the proper subject matter and then to condense it properly so that everybody can understand it and there are no ethnic differences when I'm finished with it."

Would not something as totally committed, politically and socially, as "What's Going On" refer specifically or, even, predominantly to blacks?

"Perhaps. The only, uh, ethnicity . . . I know that's not a word . . . about it is the fact that its author is black. But I don't think the social content or the musical content is ethnic at all. I think it can apply to anybody, the entire album. Any race. Any creed. Any body.

"And that's the way I want it. I wanted to say a statement that anybody could identify with and check out if they wanted to get a little spiritual voltage or shock, rejuvenate themselves."

After "What's Going On" Gay's commentary on life through his records changed tack from the political and social to the sexual, which dominated both "Let's Get It On" and "I Want You".

"The only thing I can say about that is that I'm my own artist and I'll certainly do whatever I like. And the next album might be the same," he laughs. "And I'm sorry. I'm not going to be dictated to by fans, certainly. I'm dictated enough to by my record company to last me a million years.

"I will sing about fairly much what I like to sing about and they don't have to purchase it. I'd probably be upset that they felt that way but I'd probably adjust and I'd probably, at that point, do something to make them happy if it came to that, but for the most part I'd like to keep my individuality and my freedom to write and sing about what I choose to sing about."

He says that fans ought to know that when he made a record it wasn't for personal reasons and that "I'm really trying to make them happy."

"What I was really trying to do with the last album was to say that there's a lot of closet freakery going on around the world and I was trying to, by musically coming out and saying things on an album, say that if this is what you intend to do there's no sense in having a deviation attached to it and if you're going to make love and going to do these things, which in some societies are considered deviations then let's make it an honest situation.

"If love is the bottom line, if you do love somebody, then you certainly have the right to do what you please if it makes you happy. That's what I was trying to say. I'm not sure it came across that way."

He reiterates that he felt it necessary that he is distanced from his "fans" in order to be an "observer". "And try to find something out of the observation to write about in order to help them or make them feel more at ease, which I actually don't feel I did with the last album.

"One reason", he continues, "was that I didn't produce it myself. Had I produced that album they would've had the effect I wanted. Totally. But what I did was I took someone else's ideas (Leon Ware's) and thought and I put on it what I thought would work since the music lent itself to something soft and bedroomish and sexual.

"Which wasn't the intent. Had I done it my way it would've been as good as 'Let's Get It On'. I'm sure, had I produced it from its insurgence.

"I'm just a servant, you know, at the bottom line. No matter how I feel or who I am, I'm still their (the fans) servant".

Geoff Brown

"

8

Rotten!

THE SEX PISTOLS

June 4 1977

JOHN ROTTEN stands with his arms casually outstretched in a sardonic parody of the crucifixion, a look of languid hatred flickering for a moment across his pallid features before giving away to an expression of petulant contempt.

A policeman searches Rotten's pockets and frisks his scrawny frame with dedicated efficiency.

He finds nothing.

John lowers his arms and curls his lips around a can of lager, taking a defiant swig as the police constable who has stopped him in the fierce sunlight along Westbourne Grove in Notting Hill diverts his attention toward Sid Vicious.

Sid smiles malevolently as he turns out his pockets and P.C. B510 takes out his notebook to scribble down a few pertinent details.

Imagine the conversation:

"Name?"

"Sid Vicious."

"V-I-C-I-O-U-S?"

" 'Spose so."

"Address?"

"Here and there."

"Date of birth?"

"How should I know?"

Rotten looks on in disgust: he and Sid had been walking along the street after a photo session for the Melody Maker when the Old Bill appeared suddenly and turned them over.

"We look different, see, and it frightens them," he says in that sarcastic intonation he so effectively employs. "I can understand it, though. This is called living in England in 1977. If they ask for violence, then we'll give them violence. What else can they expect if they treat people like this?"

A guy from Pistols manager Malcolm McLaren's office has the temerity to ask the officer why, precisely, he stopped John and Sid.

"Turn out your pockets," the officer replies to our disbelief.

"Arrest him, officer," Sid thoughtfully advises our friend P.C. B510. "He's a Nazi . . ."

"And you're a big mouth," responds B510. "And if you don't move along I'll book you."

"IT HAPPENS all the time," says John Rotten as he, Sid, Paul Cook and Steve Jones collapse into the interview room at Virgin Records' offices just off the Portobello Road. "All the time. Everywhere I go. Wherever I go. Every time I walk down a street. If it ain't a copper, it's some big, fat ignorant turd. It happened yesterday. In Highgate. I was just walking along . . ."

"On your way to the f— pub," interrupts Sid.

"Nah, acourse not," John replies wearily. "They've banned me from all the pubs up there. I can't even get a drink in Highgate anymore."

THIS bright Tuesday afternoon is the first time that all four members of the Sex Pistols have visited the offices of their new record company, with whom they signed only three weeks ago (for £45,000, according to McLaren; "for an unspecified amount of money," according to Virgin; "for no advance at all," according to Rotten).

Now, for all its enterprise, Virgin has never had to deal with a pack of maverick delinquents like the Sex Pistols in its entire history.

And here they are with a group whose capacity for outrage has antagonised over the last year the entire nation and provoked their enforced departure from two major record companies. No, Virgin has always been more closely associated with the Woolly Hat Brigade (Gong, and various compatible hippy combos) and rather serious European ensembles rather than the rock and roll defiance expressed by the Pistols.

The shock waves of the signing seem to be reverberating still through the company; and you should have seen the concerned and apprehensive expressions decorating the bemused faces at Vernon's Yard last week when the Pistols staggered, like the Wild Bunch swaggering defiantly into Ague Verda for their final stand in Peckinpah's movie (I rather fancifully thought), down the cobblestone alley and into the reception area at Virgin.

"Where's old Branson-pickle, who's that c—, and where can I get something to f— eat?" demanded Sid Vicious as he dropped in a looselimbed pile of rags and leather onto a couch.

"More to the point," countered John Rotten, "where can I get a bleedin' drink?"

Steve Jones, looking burly and aggressive, and Paul Cook (as ever quite amiable), wandered about clocking the premises, amused at the confusion they were causing. We were joined by the staff of the Virgin press office and drinks and sandwiches were promised to appease John and Sid, who complained constantly of being a dying man.

"I'm so f— ill I'm going to puke," he observed colourfully.

"You've just got a big spot on the end of your nose," he was rebuffed by Jones.

"I know, it's because of all that f— pressure I'm under. I'm too f— sensitive to have to put up with all this," Sid commented weakly.

"Where's that booze?" asked John irritably.

"Give us some free albums," Sid, reviving suddenly, demanded of Virgin PR, Al Clark. The request was politely declined. "If you don't give us them we'll steal them," Sid warned.

It was immediately clear that his recent illness had not blunted young Sid's rapier-like wit.

"Stand a bit closer," he subsequently ordered a photographer. "I can't gob that far in my present state."

I FIRST saw the Sex Pistols in April, 1975, at the Nashville in London when they supported Joe Strummer's 101'ers.

John Rotten stumbled to the front of the stage, held together with safety pins and wild conceit, his blond hair spiky and greasy, his dark eyes alive with venom. "I bet," he screamed at the bewildered audience, few of whom were at all familiar with the group or its nascent attitude, "that YOU don't hate US as much as WE hate YOU!"

He was quite mistaken; the audience responded to Rotten's jeering abuse with extrovert disdain and made clear their instinctive dislike for the Pistols' leering aggression and crude music.

I went away that evening and wrote a review of the band that concluded with the profound hope that no more would be heard of them. Some hope.

By the end of the year they had become the most notorious group in the country; controversy, disaster and constant publicity elevated them from obscurity to international disrepute in a blur of months of persistent outrage.

Their history – as short as it is – reads like a series of reports from a battlefront, so full of incident has it so far been. They precipitated a whole new wave of bands cast in a similarly aggressive stance: the Clash, the Damned, the Buzzcocks, Generation X, Chelsea, the Slits . . . all of them owe a debt to the Sex Pistols.

The media, faced with the explosive anger and rebellion expressed by these bands, reeled in confusion. The music press was split in arguments over the respective merits of these young groups; their admirers congratulated them for the energy and passion of their music and applauded the violence with which they had disturbed the complacency that had recently settled on the rock establishment.

Their critics conversely condemned them for their inarticulate anarchy, their apparent nihilism and their musical incompetence. Those of us in this latter category floundered in our attempts to place these groups in any correct perspective and may even have felt slightly threatened by the collective aggression and determined disregard for convention displayed so arrogantly by these new wave renegades with their punk toughness and volatile outbursts.

We may even have wished, despite our increasing fascination with the movement, that they'd all just shut up and make some music or disappear up the slipstream of their own invective . . .

"YOU were probably right when you wrote that rave review," John Rotten comments sarcastically as he tugs on another lager. "We were probably really bad then. Don't f – apologise. The point is that we were just starting. We just went out and we DID IT. We formed when music was becoming too serious.

"Rock and roll is supposed to be FUN. You remember fun, dontcha? You're supposed to enjoy it. It's not supposed to be about critics, or about spending 100 f— years learning a million chords on the guitar. It's the spirit. It's what you say that's important."

There is something to be said, I ventured, for a certain musical eloquence; you can't survive indefinitely on undiluted energy and passion.

"Yeah," Rotten replies, his voice undulating in that particular sarcastic rhythm of his, "I understand that, and we are concerned about the quality of what we play . . . but, like, when you criticised us we were just starting. We just went out and we done it in front of the public. We didn't stay in a rehearsal studio until we were so perfect we were boring.

"The whole idea was to get out and have some fun and we hoped that someone out there would see us and have fun, too. We just wanted to get out and play and we hoped that some people would see us and go away and form their own bands. We wanted to make a new scene."

"We f— did," comments Steve Jones, and then adds with a curious sense of disenchantment, "and for a while it was good . . ."

ROTTEN sits clutching the inevitable can of lager, his legs stretched out before him. He looks, momentarily, abstracted and tired. He runs his fingers nervously through his bright red hair; his mood has changed now from the aggressive punk stance he had earlier assumed and relentlessly sarcastic, he's more open and polite.

His attitude seems constantly to shift from one of defensive condescension to passionate concern. His conversation may be scattered profusely with scatological expletives, but he remains abrasively articulate.

Steve Jones sits opposite him; more immediately extrovert in his opinions than Rotten, his characteristic bellicosity is mitigated only by his gruff humour. His contributions to the conversation are more pointed and emphatic. Paul Cook, the quietest of the quartet, sits beside him listening more than he speaks.

Sid Vicious is slumped beside John; he's so dreadfully pale and wasted that he makes Keith Richard look like Steve Reeves. He lapses often into a comatose silence that is broken only by frequent statements to the effect that there are certain individuals to whom he would like to deliver "a good kicking". He's a sweet lad, our Sid.

Rotten suddenly jerks forward, staring intensely.

"The Pistols are the best," he says simply. "The only honest band that's hit this planet in about two thousand million years. We've been treated like some kind of fashion parade of a bunch of no-talents. People have said those things for their own reasons.

"And it's very hard to stop that, because when you do an interview with someone they only print what they want to print. You can't control it. So you just give up; you just say, 'Shut your face and f— off!' 'Cos it's not worth the hassle of talking to them."

"Nobody," adds Paul Cook "writes the truth. Especially about us."

"That's right," Rotten continues. "And the worse load of f— b— is from people like Caroline Coon. Always going on about the sociological implications of the Sex Pistols. Makes me cringe. Absolutely DIRE stuff.

"She hates me . . . I mean, I really thought that people would recognise that what appears about us in the newspapers is b—. But they don't. That's what shocks me about the general attitude of the public. They're excessively stupid. Their whole lives are centred around what the Daily Mirror or the Sun says.

"There was all that crap after the Bill Grundy thing. I just couldn't understand how they could take it all so seriously. I thought it was a great laugh. People are so very gullible. It doesn't matter what anybody thinks about us. It doesn't matter what you think about us. You could go away and slag us off. I don't care. I don't expect anything from anyone."

"Because of what they've read in the national press," Steve Jones observes, "people think all we do is go around giving people good kickings, fighting, drinking, f— things up, spitting, swearing . . ."

He actually sounds disturbed that this should be the case.

"But we won't change," emphasises Rotten, his eyes glaring. "We'll always tell people to f— off if they try to tell us what to do. That's why we have trouble with record companies. This deal's fine. We don't want to f— this one up . . .

"We set our OWN direction. We don't follow anyone. And there's no one who can follow us. The rest of those f— bands like the Clash, the Damned and the Stranglers and all the rest, are just doing what every other band before them has done, it's the same big, fat, hippy trip. Those bands are no different. They make me cringe."

The way John delivers that final word makes my flesh creep.

"I think it's absolutely vile," Rotten speeds on, "when I go to see a band that's obviously trying to imitate us. I think it's absolutely disgusting. That shows a complete lack of intelligence. It shows they have no reason for being on stage.

"You have to do your own thing. You have to be yourself; otherwise you can't offer anything. And if you can't offer anything, you're in the wrong place and you should f— off. You have to be honest. You have to believe in yourself, whatever anyone says or whatever happens. You can't give in.

"That's another reason people hate us: we don't conform to their stupid standards. Like at press conferences, you know, they try to get us to be nice and polite to all the 'right' people. That's dreadful.

"If someone says to me, 'Watch that person, they're in a position to really slag you off,' then I just go up and say, 'You c—. I hate you.' I don't need all that."

"People have described us as a kamikaze band," offers Steve Jones. "But we just play music, we don't crash f— planes. It's just that we don't back down. We just do it.

"The other bands don't have the nerve to follow us. They were all right in the beginning, but now they've signed their contracts they're f— up. I feel sorry for them. And now they say that we've f— the scene up. They've forgotten that WE started it. We opened ALL the doors."

"The doors and the windows," says Sid, coming back to life for a moment.

I'd heard the Pistols described as martyrs recently for the reason that they'd sacrificed themselves in the initial assault on the establishment that led eventually to the present commercial success of those bands – like the Clash and the Damned – whom they originally supported.

"That's right," says Rotten. "We helped all them bands in the beginning. We helped them start off. The Anarchy tour, right . . . WE paid for all that. We gave them hotels, money – the works.

"Well," and here he gives one of his nervously evil little laughs, "I ain't seen any of it come back. We've lost a lot of money. Thousands. And the tax is doing us for 80 per cent of everything we ever got. Which is ridiculous. You saw us squabbling over a quid. It ain't funny. The shortage of money is pathetic.

"But we don't need any sympathy and we ain't martyrs. Martyrs are failures. We ain't failures, 'cos we never give up. They're not going to get rid of us. We'll only finish it the day it gets boring."

"I DON'T even know the name of the Prime Minister," asserts Steve Jones, "so I don't really see how anyone could describe us as a political band."

"We don't support no one," emphasises John Rotten. "Politics is b—."

We've been discussing the political overtones of the Sex Pistols, as exemplified most significantly by their singles, "Anarchy In The UK" and "God Save The Queen"; as far as I'm concerned the infectious irreverence and spirited venom of these two songs is considerably more appealing than the wearing political stance adopted by, let's say, the Clash.

Rotten agrees and articulates my own feelings when he stresses that music and politics enjoy an uneasy, frequently loathsome, relationship if the political views expressed are incoherent and immature. He's clearly of the opinion that the Clash are incoherent and immature.

"Music," he says, "should be FUN. It's meant to be a relief from working 9 to 5 in a factory. It shouldn't be about some c— on a stage yapping about how terrible it is to be on the dole."

"And they've just made a mint. I don't think Clash even know what they're talking about."

"Right," agrees Paul Cook. "People talk about us being Malcolm's puppets. That's ridiculous. The Clash are the puppets."

"Malcolm's a good manager," insists Rotten, "but he wouldn't dream of telling us what to do."

"He wouldn't dare," Jones grins. "We'd turn Sid on him to give him a good kicking."

"F— right," quips Sid, without opening his eyes.

"Strummer's no politician. Never was. Never will be," asserts Jones. "I mean that single that he had out with the 101'ers on Chiswick ('Keys To Your Heart'), it was a little love song. Now he's shouting about 'Hate and War'. He don't know what he's on about."

"The Clash ain't got no guts anyway," Sid thoughtfully opines. "They sound as weak as the Damned. Pathetic, the lot of them. That Damned record sounds like an early Searchers album. All tinny. And that Clash album sounds like a folk album. They're going to end up singing ballads, the Clash."

Rotten mentions the new Chelsea single, "Right To Work", and breaks out in a malicious grin: "That's Gene October. Him screaming about wanting the right to work is hysterical. He's got a job. He's in a f— group. Ridiculous."

"We take our songs seriously," Rotten comments, "but we don't take ourselves seriously. We believe totally in the songs, though. That's why we play them, and that's why we're prepared to put up with so much aggravation to get them out.

"Yeah, I know I said music should be fun. I ain't contradicting myself. I know we sing about unemployment and all that. You should write about what's happening, but there has to be fun, too.

"Of course, there's no fun in being bored or on the dole. But music should offer a relief from all that. It shouldn't be depressing. If a song's about boredom, it should be about ways to overcome that boredom. It has to be true, but there should be humour. Optimism. And that's not political.

" 'Anarchy In The UK' was about MUSICAL anarchy . . . I don't think you can be a political rock and roll band. It's a loser stance."

It seems an opportune moment to bring up the issue of the Pistols and the National Front, with whom they were associated in a cheap, sensationalist piece in the London Evening News (there have been suggestions elsewhere, too). Rotten, I know, was disgusted and hurt by the piece. It still shows.

"We got f— all to do with the National Front," says Steve Jones first.

"That was someone trying to discredit us and make out that we were for them. It was someone putting the boot in. Just a cheap bit of publicity. My God, that thing in the Evening News made me sick. They said that the National Front used to turn up at our gigs and that's b—. I wouldn't play for the National Front."

He looks at me icily and with a chilling venom proclaims, "I hate them. I despise them. I'm Irish, right, and if they took over I'd be on the next boat back. I believe you should be allowed to live where you want, when you want and how you want.

"If the National Front need a rock group to support they should go after the Clash. They want a Clash movement. Military thing. Like, you know, one of the songs on that album has some stupid lyric about conscription being what we need . . . that's Strummer on that album. I heard that and I creased up. That's disgusting."

"If you want to join the army, sure – go ahead. But you shouldn't be forced into it. No one should have the right to do that to anyone. That's wrong. Evil."

"We should call the next single, 'We Hate The National Front'," Sid volunteers helpfully.

"If a load of c— like the National Front get into power," says John with cold conviction, "I'm afraid I won't stay around. What's the use in staying to fight? How can you fight an army? . . . I dunno, though. They might give me a good reason to die. Just get a machine gun and kill as many as possible. Nah, I don't think that would be a romantic end. I don't find anything romantic about dying."

"Neither do I," Sid says after some consideration of the matter. "And I find the idea of being shot to pieces by a million bullets from the National Front really unromantic. We're all going to die from alcohol poisoning anyway . . .

"I like getting drunk," he then adds on a more cheerful note. "I like getting out of my brain. It's good fun. Ordinary life is so dull that I get out of it as much as possible."

THE NIGHT before the Sex Pistols were unceremoniously thrown out of the window by the panic-stricken fuhrers at A&M, says John Rotten, they were told by a paternal Derek Green that they were very fortunate young men; if they had tried to release a record as provocative as "God Save The Queen" in, say, an Eastern European country they would be savagely repressed and would in all probability spend the rest of their days in slave labour in Siberia or somewhere as equally unpleasant.

Be glad and thankful, they were told, that they lived in a free country where freedom of expression was a cherished virtue.

The next day the Pistols were again without a record company.

"We just laughed and said, 'B— to you' and had a big p— up," says Steve Jones when asked for his reaction to that fiasco.

Rotten, however, is less flippant: "Someone at the top put the boot in. We don't know who, but someone doesn't want us to make it. Someone wants us silenced. Someone wants to prevent us from working again. It seems that some of the local councils are lifting their bans, but we still can't get a gig.

"We can't book a hall because we can't get an insurance company behind us. And there's no hall that'll book us without an insurance company, because they think we're mad and that we'll just go in there and smash the place up and walk out the back door, waving a big fat cheque in the breeze. It's bloody ridiculous.

"I mean we were SO disappointed that we didn't get that record out. The record was ready to be released, right? It was going to come out then. We wanted it out then. I think it's a good record. It was disgusting that it wasn't allowed to get out. They signed us up without really knowing what the hell we were about. It was stupid. Pathetic.

"I don't trust anybody any more. I've been let down too often for that. I just keep away from as many people in this business as possible. This deal with Virgin ain't like the record deals we had with the other companies. These people here are working for us and we like it. With the others we ended up trying to use them as much as they were using us. That wasn't easy, but we had to do it all the same. They don't tell us what to do here. NO ONE tells US what to do."

He's convinced that there exists some kind of conspiracy that's attempting to subvert the potential success of the Sex Pistols. He mentions the attempt to associate them with the NF and the media campaign that continually stresses their obnoxious behaviour.

"I hate that attitude that people have. They think that if you ain't been to university you must be an ignorant lout who doesn't know his own mind and can't form an opinion about anything.

"Some of the most intelligent people I know have come straight out of the gutter. I mean, that goes straight down to boot boys who get fun kicking people. They still have their brains together. They know what they like and dislike. The trouble is, the media poisons them. That's the worst part about it."

He despises, too, the continual attempts to associate the Pistols with every outbreak of violence at new wave gigs and elsewhere. He's particularly angry about the band being blamed for the violence at the 100 Club Punk Festival late last year when a girl's eye was gouged out.

"That was despicable. We were blamed for something that happened when we were 200 miles away. That was caused by a fight between the Vibrators and the Damned. But what can we do? We were blamed for it and everybody believed it was our fault. But this is a fact: wherever we play, when we hit the stage people don't smash each other up. They watch US. They can't take their eyes off us.

"Look, we've got a very varied audience. We've played places where we've had teddy boys dancing at the back. Up north we've had bike mobs to see us. There's been no wars. That's the way it should be; a lot of people having fun together. F— the rest if they won't allow it to happen – THAT'S when you get trouble, when you try to stop it."

I wonder whether he was personally frightened by the violence that sometimes attends new wave gigs.

"Wouldn't you be?" he asks simply.

"Most of it is ridiculously posed," he continues. "You get people in the audience saying, 'Come down here, we'll take you on.' And you look at them and you want to cringe and die, because it is not necessary. They should be having fun. And it's not funny or glamorous being smashed to a pulp. It's ugly and nasty. I've been beaten up frequently, old bean. And it ain't funny . . .

"You know, sometimes you go out for a quiet drink somewhere and there's a mob in the place and they take a dislike to you because they've seen your face in the papers. And there's nothing you can do. And then it's for real. And it ain't glamorous when it happens."

"You know we get people coming up to us and wanting to take us on 'cos they've heard all about the Sex Pistols," contributes Steve Jones. "Now we ain't going to start on them, but whatever happens we'll get the blame. That's the way it goes.

"Like that Speakeasy thing was just squabble and it was all blown up and we got the blame. It was a load of b— I mean, if a big guy comes up and starts on me I run . . . and if he's a little guy I give him a good kicking."

Rotten laughs at the idea that the Pistols, like the members of the rock elite, surround themselves with bodyguards.

"F— that. I hate those c—," he says vehemently. "They're full of lies. Always contradicting themselves.

"Like I was reading a thing about Pete Townshend talking about punk. And I thought, 'WHO ARE YOU? How dare YOU presume to have the right to tell us what it's all about?' He half admits that he doesn't understand what's happening on the streets. I don't think he ever knew."

"It's that other c— I hate," interjected Jones. "Roger Daltrey."

"I'd like to give him a good kicking," soliloquised Sid Vicious.

"I don't give a f— for any of them," John continued. "I mean, I never even liked the Stones. Jagger was always too distant. No way could you ever imagine talking to Michael Jagger (he delivers the name with a venomous sneer) like you could talk to someone on the street. And you should be able to. I don't see why he has to have f— bodyguards carting him about all over the place."

"He came down to Sex (McLaren's shop in the King's Road) one afternoon," reflected Sid. "Stood outside for three hours 'cos he was terrified to come inside. And then just as he was about to come in, John slammed the door in his face. He's a f— comedian."

"Ian Hunter's a c— too," observed Steve Jones. "All that talk about coming off the street."

"I know that we frighten these people," Rotten insists. "You read the music papers and they all mention us. This I find very funny. People like Ian Anderson always have to slag us off to promote themselves. I find it trivial and silly and childish. Steve Harley's the same.

"You might expect it of US, 'cos that's what we're supposed to be like. But they're SUPPOSED to be ever so intelligent. If they WERE intelligent they wouldn't have to say things like that . . . and it's like they have to be seen at the same places that we go to.

"Like Robert Plant came down the Roxy, surrounded by millions of body-guards. One of them came up to me and said, 'Robert Plant wants to talk to you. Now, you aren't going to start anything, are you?' And all these heavies are around me waiting for me to have a go at him. And he's twice my f— size. What am I going to do?

"I just looked at him and he's like a real ignorant old northerner, and I felt really sorry for him. The geezer looked so shy. Now how can you respect somebody like that?"

I WONDERED finally whether Rotten could envisage the 'Pistols one day becoming part of the rock establishment they now so openly despise.

"NEVER," John replied without hesitation, and I found myself believing him. "We're still the only band that doesn't hold press conferences every two weeks and pay for some far out binge for the social elite and grovel around or fly every other reporter in the music press over to New York on a private plane. F— that.

"But we're going to be around. We've got a record out now and we're going to finish the album and we'll find somewhere to play. They won't stop us.

"They can shut us out, but they'll never shut us up."

Allan Jones

9

'Don't make me cry— there's only one Lou Reed'

May 13 1978

CARMINE **flipped a quarter into the juke-box and swayed un-steadily beneath the dull neon glow of the Miller High Life sign. He looked as ripped as hell; eyeballs spinning deep inside bruised** sockets, like the principal dancers in a kinetic ballet, nerve ends jangling like hysterical air-raid sirens. You could catch his panic like a hot, impatient breath on the back of your neck. He was shaking so furiously that he might have been grooving to some demon beat pounding a dangerous rhythm in his brain, like wardrums on the horizon.

His nervous shuffle brought him to the bar; he smacked at its scarred, polished surface with the flat of his hand, forcing through his cracked teeth a colourful obscenity. He hung back a beer with a hungry gulp and listened with vague attention to the cowboy lament (some romantic pap by Michael Murphey) on the Wurlitzer. He swore at the barman, who ignored him and continued to pick meanly at the coins left as tips along the counter. Carmine bit his lip and scrambled frantically up the bar towards us, cursing his own bad luck and demanding conversation.

"Some real bad s— gone down tonight," he complained fiercely, his voice a blurred speedfreak whine. "Real bad, you know. Like . . . uh, those b—, man, they really screwed me, you know . . . Like, we wuz in the car, man . . . I had an ounce of grass man . . . real quality grass . . . an', uh, you know, I was, like, rolling some J's for the gig, man . . . I had like five, six on the back seat, rolled, man . . .

"And, uh, these guys I wuz with, man . . . these assholes . . . like, they couldn't wait, man. I had, like, one more to roll . . . it was in my hand, man . . . and these idiots get outta the goddam car . . . and I'm goin', like, 'Ferchrissakes, get back in the car, we'll get busted, man!'

"But these assholes, they wouldn't lissen . . . assholes . . . an' the cops are, like, cruisin' down the block, man . . . and they see these three guys standin' outside this car, and the doors is, like, open . . . so, what are they gonna think? It's like, New Jersey on a Saturday night, man. They think these guys is rippin' off the goddam car!

"An' I'm sitting there in the back, man, with, like, five loose J's an'a ounce of grass. Christ, the assholes . . . I'm gonna wring their f— necks, man . . . an' the cops, man, they stop and they come over to us . . . and they start shinin' these lights through the windows, man, and it's like Christmas with all these lights, you know, an' I'm sittin' there like a turkey, man. Jesus. Those assholes."

Carmine hurled back another bullet of beer with angry zeal.

"So . . . they took the grass, man . . . an OUNCE of really incredible grass . . . the mothers. They wuz gonna pull me down to the station house, but I wasn't into that . . . I showed 'em my discharge papers, man . . . Like, I was in the Marines man. I got papers, an'a citation. The MARINES, man. Crazy mothers. I was in Nam, man.

"So . . . they just took all my grass. An' I just, like, wanted ONE J, man . . . Cuz, like, after the gig, man, I wuz just gonna go home, take my German Shepherd an' go sit on the cliffs an' look at the sea an' blow this, man . . . that's so cool, man . . . But, I still got these . . ."

He fumbled in his overall pockets and emerged with a phial full of rather dubious looking pills. "Black Beauties, man. I'm gonna hit these, man, an' then I'm gonna go lookin' for those guys I wuz with . . . an' believe me, man . . . I'm gonna be in the mood to KILL."

I wanted no part of any impending massacre; let's not form a bloody posse, I thought squeamishly (I panic quickly, especially when confronted by a potential homicidal maniac in an anonymous bar in New Jersey – "they're all animals in Jersey," I remember Jim telling me). I told Carmine that I sympathised with his predicament, and that I was sure it would all work out for the best in the end.

Then we split as if our tails were on fire and God was serving free beer in the bar of the Capitol Theatre, just across the road in downtown Passaic.

"See you again, man," said Carmine, wrestling with my thumb.

YES, we're in Passaic, New Jersey. To see Lou Reed, of course; Arista, Louis' record company, having coughed up enough crackers to wing across the Atlantic a quartet of European correspondents (two from Blighty, one from France and another from Germany).

Louis, you see, after more than five years spent suffering the indifference and hostility of Yankee critics, has come close to blowing them away with his most recent tortured opus, "Street Hassle". The carefully orchestrated jeers of the yahoos has now surrendered to a chorus of applause; "Street Hassle" has been cheered onto the racks and Louis is in the unusual position of having his new album being declared a masterpiece, a brilliant vindication of those wilderness years on the vicious borderline of defeat and squalid neglect.

And his present ocean-to-ocean American tour is, similarly, driving the hacks to their typewriters, filing superlatives to the probable confusion and surprise of their editors who'd had Lou typed as a terminal loser, long bereft of his original talent and now merely wasting everybody's time waiting for obscurity's undertakers to take him on that final, cruel drive into history's footnotes.

Blah, to them: Louis is back on the case with a venomous urgency.

And we're here to wave the flag for the resurrection.

THE Europeans made their initial connection with Louis in Philadelphia. A three-hour drive out of New York City, with Elvis Costello's "Pump It Up" screaming across the airwaves, the Jack Daniels and Blue Nun bottles rolling empty on the Cadillac floor before we were off the New Jersey turnpike, and the moon coming down like a day-glo yo-yo, wearing the clouds like shades ... and, eventually we're burning rubber a half block down from the Tower Theatre ...

Louis is sprawled out in this grubby armpit of a dressing room, backstage at the Tower, still flashed on the energy he'd been pumping out minutes earlier as his set had climaxed with a two-pronged encore of "Sweet Jane" and "Rock 'n' Roll", seminal monsters that will forever hang about his neck.

I had last seen him a year ago, after a night of hysterical chaos in Gottenburg in Sweden (I really must tell you about that sometime – you'll love the bit where we sank all the remote control boats in the seafood restaurant), flat out drunk on the wall-to-wall of his hotel room.

We'd destroyed a case of brandy and – a last ditch effort, this – quarrelled over a bottle of Schnapps. The latter did it for us both. I had to be carried to bed as dawn laughed through the windows; Lou was unconscious when I left him. There were no coherent alibis.

I stroll into the dressing room. He greets me politely.

"Jesus God!" he smirks. "It's the faggot dwarf. You grew. What happened? We thought you were dead. You look well. What happened . . . you get religion? Your head's still too big for your body.

"You still drink? Have a beer. Jesus. Last time we saw you, man, you looked worse than anybody I've ever seen, except myself. You still working for Melody Maker, trying to influence the diseased minds of the cretins?

"Say hi to the band, faggot . . . isn't this a great band? Weren't we great tonight? Weren't we the best rock 'n' roll band you saw in your life?

"God above, we aren't a rock 'n' roll band. We're a f— orchestra! And did you ever hear anyone play guitar like I did tonight? Wasn't I just great? No. Save your superlatives for the article . . .

"Oh, man, I got this guitar now (it's the Roland Guitar, freaks!) . . . man, with THIS, I sound like the Dante of the rock 'n' roll guitar. THIS is the sound I've been after for years.

"I was playing like this all the time . . . you know that . . . I just had to wait for all those stupid, pallid imitators to die off. I was just waiting for the cretins to get the tickets, so's I could take over man . . . this is where it really starts to hurt."

I was relieved that Louis had lost none of his overwhelming modesty in the year since we'd last met.

"Oh . . . oh, I still KNOW I'm the BEST, man. Who else is there? Kansas? Mel Torme? Come ON. I'm Dante with a beat, man. When I get onstage with this f— monster (the Roland Guitar Synthesizer, fans) I'm like . . . like, Bach, Bartok and Little Richard. I'm so hot at the moment, I burn myself every time I touch a guitar. . . .

"What did you think of 'Street Hassle' tonight? Great, uh? That gets spooky, man . . . like, I thought tonight they'd have to carry me off screaming . . . that's ME on the line out there. Like Dante, man. It gets really close in there . . . but, f— it. . . ."

"If they put ME in purgatory, man, I'd be the landlord . . . hey, why didn't you come see us the last time we were in Europe?"

You didn't play England, I explain (Lou did a Continental trek late last summer after his last London concerts in May).

"That's an excuse, NOT an answer. We'll let it pass. You're right. We played places like Germany. Hell. You gotta be careful there, man. The hotels are like concentration camps. All Dobermans and suspect showers . . . 'You wanna shower?' 'Uh . . . no thanks, man . . . uh, yeah . . . okay . . . but easy on the Zyklon B . . .' Who needs it?"

A friend worked on that tour; he told me several horror stories about Lou holding to ransom Continental promoters.

Like, at one place he's said to have stalked off stage in the middle of his set and threatened the promoter with a switchblade, and demanded more money for the gig. He got it, too. . . .

"You're well informed for an idiot," he replies cheerfully when I confront him with this piece of scurrillous gossip. "But it wasn't a blade . . . it was a can opener . . . I didn't have my blade with me.

"It was upstairs in the dressing room . . . what was I gonna DO? Say, 'Look, I'm threatening you, but I don't have my blade . . . could you just stay there a minute looking scared while I go get my knife?' I just used whatever came to hand.

"If I hadn't found the can opener, I'd have used the leg of a chair, I was so angry . . . Like, I don't stand for being pissed around, man. On this tour we had a sound guy who had no brains. Right? So I came out one night and said, 'Hey . . . let's talk. There was no talking. So he kicked his monitors off stage and I sacked the mentally retarted cripple . . . I don't f— about."

Louis is still bitching about this incident two days later when we meet him in New York; we'd been talking about his audience, his attitude to them, whether he thought of his performances as entertainment and how he felt about them constantly barracking him from the stalls.

"F— it," he says succinctly. "I'm not one of those people who NEEDS applause. I know what those people in the audience are like. I can do without it. I only need my own applause.

"But, listen . . . I don't insult my audience. I respond to them in their own way. And they know what I'm saying. They're just not used to anybody onstage taking them seriously enough to have a dialogue with them. . . . I'm that serious. All my songs are that serious. This is MY life on the LINE.

" 'Street Hassle' is THAT serious. It's ME on the Line. And I'm talking to them one to one. And it gets very intense out there. I realise that . . . like, 'Street Hassle', I realise I did myself a hell of a good speech in that. And it's scary 'cos it looks like I'm making myself too vulnerable, at least from the audience point of view.

"It's scary when an artist does that, 'cos it would be so easy to get him, that is, me. Anybody who's like a Bob Hope or a Don Rickles – it isn't gonna be so easy to get HIM.

"But here's a guy who's gonna be a songwriter and perform songs like THAT . . . and you can heckle him or throw beer cans at him. . . . He IS vulnerable. And, . . . like, what reason can a guy have for doing that? It would be easier not to do it. Obviously. So I must be serious about my audience and what I'm doing to bring attention to it. . . .

"But I don't want to leave them with a part of me, or change the way they think. . . . Oh, no . . . On the other hand; I'm not beyond entertainment. It's just that I'm a very rare and exquisite kind of entertainment . . . if you want to call it entertainment.

"On an entertainment level, I think I function pretty well. If you're looking for that, I'm pretty good.

"I wouldn't recommend me as entertainment, though. If I was going out, I'm not the person I'd go see . . . then again, if I wanted to take a chance – I might.

"No. I don't get upset when they yell at me. Why should I? They're at a rock 'n' roll show. Not in a museum. Like I told that mixer who was f— me around, I said, 'This ain't a seminary in here, man, crank it up . . . they don't get little booklets with the lyrics. Turn the thing up!' And he said. 'But they can't hear every golden word!'

"And I said, 'They're not supposed to . . . if they wanna hear the words they can go home and listen to the records.' "

MEANWHILE: backstage here at the Tower Theatre, Philadelphia, Louis wants to know what's happening in England. Someone spouts some facts 'n' info about Rotten's latest plans . . . "Johnny Rotten," sez Louis benevolently, "should stick a safety pin in the end of his p – and shove it through his nose. . . ."

Mention is made of the current rumours of a joint enterprise involving ex-Pistols Steve Jones and Paul Cook and former NY Dolls Heartbreakers' guitarist, Johnny Thunders.

"Johnny Thunders," laughs Louis. "Don't make me cry . . . there's only one Lou Reed."

He starts talking about his band again; yes, they were great, we agree.

"I'm gonna call them New York," he tells us, "what do you think?" We-eee-ell, I hesitate, I think it sounds a little precious.

"Oh . . . oh!" squeals Louis. "The dwarf thinks it's precious . . . okay, faggot, we'll call the band MUTTON, how does that feel?"

Uncomfortable, I think; I switch the subject . . . He and Bowie are currently carving across the States on tours. When was the last time you saw David Bowie, Lou?

"Well . . ." he stalls, and then in a flash, "I looked in the mirror this morning and he looked fine . . . ah! But why are we talking about 'me' when we could be talking about ME."

Good point; let's get back to the gig.

IAN DURY and the Blockheads are chasing the applause to the end of their set at the Tower Theatre, Philadelphia, when The Europeans arrive.

("Ian's great," Lou will say later. "But his act needs subtitles. Can you understand him? First time I heard him I thought he was Rumanian. Call that English? It sounds like a tongue disease. I know, by the way, why he calls the band the Blockheads . . . I spoke to one of them for the first time, yesterday.")

Ian, backstage, is talking to an American girl. She wants to know who he likes, who his influences might be.

"Ever 'eard of Syd Barrett?" he ventures. She smiles vaguely. "Worrabhat Cyd Charise, then?"

LOUIS stalks out on to the stage of the Tower in Philadelphia like a man looking for revenge. He's whipped off his shades before he hits the mike; and he stands there for a second zeroing in on the audience, prepared to decimate every last excuse for these last years of flabby alibis, confused embarrassment and idiot posing.

He's looking for revenge; both upon himself and the more fickle amongst us in tonight's audience, for these last squandered years.

"KER-BLOODY-THWAAA CKKK!" he hits the mike. A straight arm chop from the waist. I didn't even see it coming and the band are lobbing hand-grenades in the specific direction of "Gimmie Some Good Times", which also opens the "Street Hassle" album. . . .

"Gimmiegimmie some goooooodtimes, gimmie gimmie gimmie some PAIN," yowls Lou, "dontcha know things always looook ugly – to me they always look the SAME . . ." And the band takes care of the rest.

From the last time he appeared in London, he's retained on keyboards the dazzling Michael Fonfara, on saxophones Marty Fogel, and on drums, the assbashing Michael Suchorsky, who has all the violent kick and simultaneous sensitivity of former Roxy Music drummer Paul Thompson.

Stuart Heinrich is on guitar (such blissfully evil sounds he concocts!). "This is a guitarist," Lou will say in New Jersey, "that can make Hunter and Wagner eat s—!"

Ellard "Moose" Bowles, a monstrous black bass player, lays the boisterous foundations for the evening's success alongside Suchorsky. Two foxy dames, Angela Howard and Christine Wiltshire, are at hand to provide back-up and harmony vocals.

"Satellite Of Love" follows; a radical exercise in reorganisation, it lacks entirely the slight charm of the original on "Transformer", as Louis peels away its initial insignificance to reveal a dark perspective on hatred and betrayal.

It leaves me suddenly breathless as he goes into the originally burlesque routine of "I've been told that you've been bold with Harry, Mark and John . . ." which he here reels off with real hurt, confronting a lover with her betrayal.

And, God, this is beginning to hurt; he's pulling no more punches, he's getting right down there in the grime and deceit of it all and he's still snarling and biting.

When he did this in Passaic, New Jersey, accentuating every muscle of every syllable, almost bleeding with venom, I began to wish I was taking my chances with Carmine on the prowl for his buddies; especially when Lou straps on his perspex guitar and winds up for a solo that sounds as if he's stringing together every moment of pain he's felt during the last whenever.

His guitar growls and bites and staggers back on itself; and it's over, this solo, before you've really locked onto it. He doesn't play it for inspection or applause. He hits you with it, like a challenge.

I could've done with maybe a walk around the parking lot to clear my head, but Louis, smashing out a riff so obsessive that it clearly needs psychoanalysis, urges the band into "Leave Me Alone"; a frightening/frightened plea, whose power I barely recognised on "Street Hassle".

This version unwinds with a power so annihilating it would demand an apology from disaster; Louis rants with shivering rage as the band chant the title line behind his aggressive, taunting lead.

Heinrich knocks out phrases that send shivers through the theatre and Fogel's saxophone screams like it's having its toenails pulled out.

My God, I thought, they're going to have to arrest these people before they do us some serious damage!

Then Lou calms it down with that touching epistle about racial harmony, "I Wanna Be Black", the sheer bad taste of which elevates it to levels few others would ever have considered.

I was choking with laughter, but a few of those weirdo college students there in the audience clearly thought this was taking it all a little too far.

"Walk On The Wild Side" – inevitably part of the repertoire – fills the next space. A version full of conceit – Reed stops in the middle of the first verse, lights a Marlboro, takes one drag and throws it at someone in the front row of the stalls. "Hey, BITCH, let's take a walkonth'wild siiiide," he drawls, hitting the mike with another of those righthand smacks that bolts you upright.

This, however, has so far been a preliminary skirmish; the real warfare is just now cruising around the corner and into view.

It starts with Lou standing in a blue spotlight crooning to himself, distracted, almost; concentrating upon nothing but his memories and his anger and pain . . . "Let's hear it for the Excellents," he mumbles. "They did it first . . . I stole it from them and it's called 'Coney Island Baby'."

There's a waver of applause, but no one seems to know what the hell he's talking about (it transpires that a group called the Excellents recorded in about 1965 a song that inspired his own painful saga – oh: you knew; well it was news to me, too). The music begins to drift past us, followed by Lou's monologue.

"When I was a young man in high school, I wanted to play football for the coach . . . and all those older guys, they said he was mean and cruel, but you know, I wanted to play football for the coach.

"They said I was a little lightweight to play lineback, but I gotta play football for the coach . . . You know something, man, you gotta stand up straight, or else you're gonna fall . . . and then you're gonna DIE. . . ."

Heinrich's guitar creeps in here, carrying its own pack of Kleenex to wipe away the tears.

"You know," Lou continues, laying it all on the line, "when you're all alone and lonely in your midnight hour and you find your soul's been up for sale, and you begin to think about all the things you've done and you begin to hate just about EVERYTHING . . . and all your two-bit friends.

"You got any two-bit friends?" he asks Philadelphia, "or are they all dollar 50 friends like mine, who sold you for a SUBWAY RIDE? And then started talking behind your back saying, 'Hey, Lou Reed – there ain't no way you're ever gonna be no human being. . . .' "

The blue spot hits him again and he begins to scratch at the melody, playing a fractured guitar phrase . . . "I'm sending this out one more time to Lou and . . . uh . . . Rachel. I'm just a f— up Coney Island Baby . . ."

He stands away from the microphone, his voice dying away as the singers repeat and phrase behind him in a vocal dive that carries with it an extraordinary anguish. And then I realise that Lou is really bringing it all back home this time with a kamikaze vengeance. This is musical autobiography with the chapter headings written in painful self-examination.

"This song's called 'Dirt'," he announces; and we spend the next ten minutes eating it. The band lurch into the kind of superheavy riff that even

Zeppelin would've left in the closet. It doesn't hit you so much as smother you. This is for real, pop-pickers; none of that fashionable, stylised menace passing for venom.

Then he performs "Street Hassle", and if God had any tears left to cry the audience would drown.

"Street Hassle" isn't just another song about degenerate street rats; it's a tragedy about lust, betrayal, disappointment, death and despair on a universal scale that is challenged by few contemporary examples of rock songwriting.

It derives its enormous strength and impact from those specific qualities Lou Reed was thought to have long since lost.

His immaculate sense of observation and ear for dialogue serves him brilliantly, especially in the second of the three fragments where he recounts the conversation of two of the protagonists in the drama, one of whose old lady has OD'd to the minor discomfort of the other who decides that the best solution would be to drag her body down onto the street, wait for a car to slam over it and claim her death "as just another hit and run".

And nowhere has his powerful poetic gift been better displayed than in the final passage, where he sings with authentic passion, "Love has gone away/Took the rings off my fingers/And now there's nothing left to say. . . ."

This final elegy is performed with an understated elegance that culminates in a display of dreadful and overwhelming poignancy and desperate longing for all that has been lost and can never be replaced. The final echo of the hypnotic central theme that holds together the three segments (carried by Fonfara's discreet use of the synthesizer), whispers into the wings, followed by Reed and the band.

And it's all over, but for the encores, "Sweet Jane" and "Rock 'n' Roll" (in New Jersey he will perform a 15-minute arrangement of "Sister Ray", but only after making his audience wait for over ten minutes while he recovered from the emotional outpouring of "Street Hassle").

Yes. The wasted years have almost entirely been vindicated; but he won't let us forget how much they cost him. . . .

SUNDAY morning in New York City. The police sirens are screaming like renegade banshees through Central Park. The Europeans are waiting for Lou Reed in the bar of the Essex House hotel. He shows up an hour late and demands an Irish coffee from the barman. "I'll just send for an Irishman to make it," he wisecracks.

Louis is not amused. "Hey," he snaps. "If I'd wanted a comedian, I'd have called room service. Just fix the drink. Make it a double."

"What you want? TWO Irish coffees?"

"No. I want a doubleshot. And don't miss the glass. I don't want to have to lick the bar again." The drink is served. The cream is whipped into a sickly curl. Lou looks as it with distaste.

The incident annoys him. He decides to return to his room. We follow at a safe distance (no use upsetting him at this stage).

LOU REED'S room looks like a warehouse after a four-day aerial bombardment. Amplifiers, guitars, synthesizers, video games, stacks of disco cassettes, trailing miles of wires and cables cover the carpets and every other available surface. Clothes and boots are strewn everywhere. Trays of drinks, bottletops, glasses crack underfoot. Now, I could hardly be described as Miss Tidy 1978; but this is ridiculous.

Lou is sitting amid this rubble, revealing no visible concern for the outrageous clutter. I fling half-a-ton of debris from the bed and collapse upon it. Lou is fiddling about with the Roland Guitar Synthesizer.

"Isn't this the greatest? I'd tell you about it, but you just wouldn't understand. Anyway, it doesn't come with an information booklet and I haven't figured it out yet myself . . . (he starts whacking out some Hendrix-derived riff).

"Hear that? I used to take acid too, you know. This is marvellous. Delusions of grandeur. That's always been my style, anyway.

"This is the greatest guitar ever built by human people. It makes every other guitar look tragic. This thing is the invention of the age. I haven't been this excited since the first record I made . . . you gotta realise, the Virgin Thrill has long gone." He points to the video patterns of the television screen. "Isn't that impressive? No? Then f— you.

"This is the sound I heard in my head at the time of 'Sister Ray.' I've done nothing but track this one sound down. It's been frustrating, 'cos I always approached the guitar as if it was an orchestra – am I not the king of flash? That's what distortion was all about.

"But I didn't know what I was doing then. I just had, like a Vox Super Beetle . . . but, oh look, man. Who can remember back then? Who can remember what we were doing . . ."

His attention is caught once more by the video patterns. "See that? That's what we're gonna be using as a backdrop. Can you imagine it? That as a backdrop, with six little figures at the bottom. Six little dots, man."

Hey, Lou – you don't really see yourself as a dot, do you?

"Why not, I'd rather look at that than me. What kinda question is that? That's such a loaded question."

I just thought you'd want the audience to know that they were watching Lou Reed, not just a dot.

"But how could they doubt it for a minute?" he responds with a marvellous gesture. "So who else would do that? We've already established what I LOOK like. Now we can go past it. All this time, it's just been like saying 'hello.' Now that's settled. So just look at this."

LISTEN, a word of advice. You don't interview Lou Reed, you sit there and he talks to you and you're damn lucky if you can squeeze a word in sideways.

"My life can't be caught up in other people's conversation," he says at one point. "I don't talk to that many people. I do most of the talking because I deserve to. If somebody's faster and smarter than me I'd shut up and listen. It doesn't happen too often, though."

So we sit here, this French journalist and me, and we listen to Lou and we agree with him when he tells us how great he is; and it becomes increasingly clear that he's in quite a dislocated mood.

His conversation follows no convenient logic; so we just dig and try to ride out the cresting waves of high speed raps and try to make sense of his more, uh, abstract flights.

I try to force him to focus on these last confused years, and to explain his survival when almost everyone had given him up for lost.

"I'm, uh, very legitimate on a number of levels," he begins, piecing together a coherent statement. "And that's the only reason I think I'm still here . . . Like, people think on many levels that I'm a vicious and conniving this and that, who doesn't do the right thing, who's self-destructive, who can't be trusted.

"The thing is, it was always like, LOU REED . . . he was always doing it. I'm the only honest commodity around. I always was. I mean, even if I was an asshole, I was an asshole on my own terms. It's not like I'm dumb and I didn't know.

"Even when I was an asshole, I was a literate lunatic. Even my bull was head and shoulders above everyone else's. It's always been honest and personal, you know . . . When you buy a Lou Reed record you gotta expect LOU REED. 'Metal Machine' took care of that . . ."

When, in your career do you think you were the biggest asshole, I ask.

"Hey . . . you're really pushing it aren't you . . . I don't think I WAS an asshole."

I was using your own words.

"Yeah . . . yeah, I know," he says wearily. "But I think an asshole is somebody who wastes time. It's not a question of good or bad. It's just that during this

"

period I hadn't reached a conclusion about things. I didn't CARE. I was having a little dialogue with myself, about life, the world, my vocation, what I wanted to do.

"No. I wasn't looking for an identity. I had an identity. I was a lot of people, I'm a pretty expansive creature. I can be one thing and then another. No one of them is any more me than the other. But they're all parts. I mean, it's not that hard . . . In novels no one would think twice about it. It's just that rock'n'roll has been treated as such a mutant, idiot child medium . . .

"But that," he says, winging off at a tangent, "made it easier for anyone with even half a mind to walk in and just dominate that end of it. The trick was not to become intellectual flash . . . On the other hand, I didn't HAVE to worry about that because I didn't CARE . . .

"I always assumed that I was great. I never doubted it. People's opinion of me don't matter. I know my opinion is the one that's right. I took me a long time to learn that.

"The only mistake I ever made over the years was listening to other people. 'Hey, Lou,' I finally said, 'can't you understand that you're right, that you've always been right? Why do you insist on bringing in all these other people?'

"Now I don't. But, it's frightening if you're always right and you're never having to work for it."

Why are you so convinced, Lou, that you're always so right?

"Because I can do it right in front of you like THAT (he snaps his fingers for emphasis and almost falls off his chair). It's not very hard for me. Apparently, it is for other people.

"But now I MADE my decision, and I'm looking out at the world and, like, it's 'Jesus Christ, Lou – you really are a very rare commodity!'

"I've only known a few people I thought were that good. Delmore Schwarz. Warhol . . . I mean, I get tons of publicity. I don't go looking for it. I always assumed that I'd get it. And I DO.

"There are some people who get press agents . . . but they wouldn't be able to stay in the same room as me. It'd be hopeless. The thing is – I'm convinced I'm right.

"And I am, for me . . . I ended up in rock'n'roll, 'cos there was a working machine that was just sitting there that needed overhauling and somebody to pay attention to it. And I realised that I could do that very well, 'cos I was doing it anyway. And since I was doing it I thought I might as well do it in the open market place.

"And if you look back at the Velvet Underground, in retrospect it's remarkable. If you look at other areas, there's nothing. The Velvet Underground is legitimate. It can hold its own. I mean, I didn't write Death Of A Salesman. But then, I didn't find that an interesting play, anyway.

"Even now I don't think there's anyone in rock'n'roll who's writing lyrics that mean anything, other than ME. You can listen to me and actually hear a voice. These other people are MORONS. They really are."

Oh come on, Lou, I exclaim, exasperated. What about Bowie? Dylan? Neil Young? These people aren't exactly compiling shopping lists.

"Oh . . . uh . . . yeah. I was wondering about that the other day. I was thinking 'Who the f— is there around, who was, like, with me, from the year one who's still viable?' David hasn't been around as long as I have.

"And David is gaining and losing ground at the same time. He's managed to scuttle as much of one part of his audience as possible, and tried to go for another and they aren't there yet. I think he lacks people around him who might challenge him. He's in danger of becoming a guru . . ."

But, counters my charming French companion, you – Lou – have been a guru to a lot of people.

"And you might've been a German Shepherd to a lot of people," Lou responds lightheartedly. "That has nothing to do with me. I know that that exists, and I make room for that.

"Like, I went through that very early. Like people said, 'I took heroin because of you.' I don't wanna KNOW . . . It's so AWFUL to have that kind of power over these poor sick savages. Please, leave me out of it.

"At least I like to think I told them about it gently – ah! I don't get involved in that kind of tedious dialogue. I don't bother even thinking about it. It's bulls— thinking. It has nothing to do with me. I just always have that power over people. It's up to me whether I want to live with it . . ."

I still want an answer to his outrageous dismissal of his contemporaries. And I'm in the mood to pester him until I get it.

"Right . . . right . . . David's right there. But he's getting more and more isolated. I listened to that last album, man. It's scary. I don't relate to it. It's interesting and I admire it; the technique, the craft, the use of language and the acting involved in it. But it's not something I identify with.

"Dylan? Dylan's not around anymore. Of course, he was NEVER around for me. But he did have a nice flair for words that didn't mean anything. And he knew it. They were just marijuana throwaways. But they loved him for it. But he became dull. Then, he was dull anyway.

"He did write some nice stuff, though, that I don't think maybe he appreciates . . . But he's never made a rock'n'roll record. Of course he hasn't. Can you imagine what it was like where he was . . . on the other hand, isn't it a shame that he's such a loser. Sure I think he's a loser. He's not strong. I know I'M strong.

"If I couldn't handle this thing, I'd remove myself. I'm a sensible guy."

NEW YORK has its own resident symphony orchestra; the sirens of the police cars that chase each other through the city. Right now the solo violinist is screeching past the open window of Lou Reed's hotel room on Central Park South.

"You know,' he says, "it's, like, war right from the top. The minute you wake up in THEIR world and you tune into the fact that you gotta get out, it's war. And they'll do anything to stop you.

"I usually have a commonsense view of it all, but I know that right down on the bottom line, it's absolute warfare from the very first. No question about it.

"I claim that THEY are poisoning us from the start, and that we don't stand a chance. I really believe there's a war, and that we're on one side and they're on the other. And I think that rock'n'roll is terribly, terribly political and subversive and that they're absolutely right to be afraid of it.

"And right across the board there are a lot of albums with words like mine. I'm just more of a threat because of what I represent. I am an enticement to THEIR children. I'm still banned on the radio, not because of what I look like, but because I represent certain ideas.

"I mean, I don't have long hair, I don't wear earrings or glitter. Maybe they just don't like Jewish faggots. How seriously can you take it? So they don't play me on the radio? What's the radio? Who's the radio run by? Who's it played for?

"They should take me very seriously . . . they do. They wanna keep me locked away. I'm dangerous."

"They're afraid of that. And they really should be because a lot of us really aren't kidding, and we just keep going. And they can't stop us, man."

I SPOKE to Lou after the Philadelphia concert and caught in the euphoria of that success he proceeded to trash all the albums that had preceded "Street Hassle"; I remind him of this statement. He'd like to clarify it.

" 'Street Hassle' is the best album I've done. 'Coney Island Baby' was good, but I was, like, under siege 'Berlin' was 'Berlin'. 'Rock'n'Roll Heart' is good – compared to the rest of the s— that's around. As opposed to 'Street Hassle,' they're babies. 'Coney Island Baby' is a very shaky album, in a lot of respects; because it's a very bare Lou Reed you've got there. It may not sound vulnerable to whoever's listening to it. But you were getting a photo after the fact."

But do you think you've achieved as much as you should or could have over the last four or five years?

"That's another unanswerable question," he says flatly. "I achieved as much as I could have, by definition. There's a school of thought that says it's incredible that I'm still here at all, right here with this one.

"The ending's the only thing that counts in my life. I've lived through people saying, 'Oh, Lou. That's the best thing you ever did . . . Like beat 'Heroin' . . . beat 'Sister Ray' . . .' Well, people are beginning to realise that that's exactly what I'm doing.

"I've just been out of work for a long time, you know. I didn't care about all those albums. They were the best I could've done at the time. No one asked me to do my best. I was told not to, man.

"I thought that I was lucky to be making records at all after 'Metal Machine'. Like I know a lot of people who aren't even allowed to make a noise in the house. I just thought I was lucky.

"But really I want to be able to listen to my own records, and at one point it was not exciting, because I was the only one there and no one was interested in what I wanted to hear and or say . . . But I didn't take any easy options. It was a situation of no choice.

"I don't look back, though. I think people who look back are making a mistake. They're wasting time. I coped with whatever I was coping with. And I assume I did the best I could, because I always do, you know. No doubt about it. If somebody doesn't like it or think that I could've done better – fine. That's just the way I did it.

"I know when I'm good and when I'm bad. And I'm NEVER bad, some-times I just don't bother. And for a long time I didn't bother . . . But like Andy says, 'If you complete one thing, even if you don't know what you're talking about, you're miles ahead of everyone else'. So shut up and DO IT.

"If you have an idea, start it and finish it. And I started it when I put 'Heroin' out. I started it with the Velvet Underground. That's when it started. Then I left it for two years.

"But I decided that I hadn't finished what I started. But I had to really think about coming back and finishing it, about involving myself with all these people in this business.

"Because you're talking about people who're not creative people. Because there are very few creative people – and most of them are lunatics.

"If you wanna make adult rock records you gotta take care of all these people along the way. And it's not child's play. You're talking about managers, accountants. You're talking about the lowest level of human beings.

"You're talking about lighting people tacking on an extra 200 dollars a night AFTER kickbacks. You're talking about road managers selling cut cocaine to musicians. You're talking about people who're putting down on a corporation payroll 50 people who don't even exist.

"You're talking about people who won't file your taxes, an officer of the corporation who doesn't pay your holding tax, so you find yourself owing to the government and in contempt of court, and heading for jail, money that's going out for drugs is going down on YOUR tab.

"You're talking about a situation where the artist wonders where all his money went, and he's in litigation with his record company and his manager and he doesn't have any money to defend himself, so no lawyer will even touch him.

"But the people who stole the money can defend themselves with the money they stole, which is his. But no one will touch him, because in a pop medium your lifespan as a moneymaker is two to three years at the most. And there's no known case of a manager losing to an artist, and the record companies know that so they'll back the manager.

"And maybe they're right to do that, because the act maybe is not that bright and/or f— up and doesn't even have the strength or stamina to get out of the situation, anyway. 'Cos when you decide to get hot'n'heavy with these people it's no use saying, 'Oh, man – I just play guitar.'

"Musician protect thyself 'cos the heavens are coming down. That's when it comes down to, 'Do I even want to make a record?' Given the way the people are generally, given the trouble you have to go through just to get the lyrics on there – like I was told THREE times to ditch 'Street Hassle' . . . I never thought that these people knew what they were talking about, but inevitably they made me feel very insecure.

"My only problem, then was that at that point, I assumed that was it. There was nobody I met who I wasn't disappointed with or found out was a sleaze . . . But I'd decided to come back and finish it.

"What else was I gonna do? Walk away and leave it? But I don't want all those people who've put their faith in me thinking that I turned out to be a total sham, like everyone else they ever believed in.

"I want to keep the illusion."

"I AM of a mood these days," says Lou Reed, "that tells me that I'm a right wing fascist liberal. I cover all bases. I cover it all from all points of view, and you know there's something to be said for them all, given the lay of the land.

"I don't think of people as sheep. I think of them as dogs. There's not much you can do for them except treat them as people. Most of them aren't civilised. They live in their houses and they read their newspapers and they agree with what's in there.

"Why shouldn't they? They don't travel a whole lot. Nobody ever told them anything. They've got no psychological difficulties with their religions or their schools.

"It's amazing that people aren't at war 24 hours a day. I'm surprised more people aren't shooting each other in the street . . . I just don't know how it all got set up this way.

"I can go to Japan and they got highways that look like the ones in Nebraska. Jesus. It's like a primitive attempt at logic. Like 'We all go this way on the highway and we'll be there in an hour.' Wow. They're really trying, aren't they? It's pretty sophisticated, uh? They all move at roughly the same pace. Except the blacks in Africa and I guess they're pretty f— anyway."

We have been talking now for close on two hours. Even Lou's sounding tired of his own voice. He started chain-smoking, about 90 minutes ago. He'd start one and leave it burning in the ashtray. Then he'd light another one. To save embarrassment, I started smoking his. Then he started smoking mine and pretty soon it was like musical chairs with nicotine. We've ended up juggling a pack and half between us. . . .

"What it's all about," he's saying, "is doing it on your own terms. Reasonably. Without getting killed by somebody or shot on the street. But you still gotta satisfy your own standards. It would be easy to satisfy THEIR standards.

"It would be difficult for me now, 'cos I've started manipulating people again. 'Street Hassle' proved that people listened if I shouted loud enough. I can't manage to get through on THEIR standards anymore. But I admire people who can.

"It's a talent to be consistently mediocre. But it's usually real pap. Like, Jacqueline Susann-type pap. But that is a talent. But it's not Dostoevsky . . . but, like, how many Dostoevskys are there?"

God, Lou, you don't want to be the Dostoevsky of rock'n'roll, do you?

"No . . . I don't wanna be Dostoevsky . . . I don't wanna be Jacqueline Susann, either. I don't see why I can't be both. And STILL be brilliant. Because I'M the ONLY ONE. There's nobody even coming up behind me. I'm still there, man.

"And even when they tried to stop me making records they couldn't stop me. Lou Reed was always there. They couldn't change me. Like, 'Sally Can't Dance' . . . with all that junk in there, it's still Lou Reed. I sound terrible, but I was singing about the worst s— in the world.

"They said, 'Oh – Lou's parodying himself.' But I was doing better than that. I was right down there. That WASN'T a parody. That was what was

111

happening. All my records are for real, man. I don't know HOW to kid around. They're all REAL close to home.

" 'Berlin' was REAL close to home. People would say, 'Lou – is that autobiographical?' And, I'd say, 'Mmmmmmm – not bad.' Jesus. Autobiographical? If only they KNEW!

"Like, during the recording session my old lady – who was an asshole, but I needed to have a female asshole around to bolster me up; I needed a sycophant who I could bounce around and she fit the bill . . . but she called it love, ha! – anyway, my old lady, during a recording session, she tried to commit suicide in the bathtub in the hotel . . . Cut her wrists . . . She lived . . .

"But we had to leave a roadie with her from then on. It's funny, another girlfriend of mine told her. 'Look – if you're doing it for real, slice THIS way – and not THAT way, darling.' Anyway, she lived, so it's a bulls— scam . . . ON THE OTHER HAND . . . one rock star's wife DID commit suicide during an album recording. So these things DO happen.

"But why, my dear, should it frighten me . . .? What do you want me to do? Hide in the closet? There are car accidents outside. Muggings. TYPHOID. There's cancer. We're all gonna die and have heart attacks. So, what would you like me to do? Feel sad? Get upset? Get religion? Act better?

"I'd just like to have some FUN. As long as I'm going through with this thing, I would like to have fun. You know it's garbage from top to bottom – so why not?

"I'm gonna have fun . . . It's the only thing you can do . . . And you gotta hold out until they end it or they kill you . . . or you get away with it."

Allan Jones

”

10

Portrait of the artist as a working man

ERIC CLAPTON
December 9 1978

ERIC CLAPTON, whose remarks in support of Enoch Powell two years ago gave the initial impetus to the formation of Rock Against Racism, this week spoke to the MM about his political beliefs – and repeated his praise for the controversial MP's stance on immigration.

Echoing his famous impromptu speech at a Birmingham concert in the summer of 1976, Clapton said: "I think Enoch is a prophet. He's not a racist – I don't think he cares about colour of any kind."

Clapton continued: "I think his whole idea is for us to stop being unfair to immigrants, because it's getting out of hand. The Government is being incredibly unfair to people abroad to lure them to the promised land where there is actually no work.

"The racist business starts when white guys see immigrants getting jobs and they're not.

"That whole thing about me talking about Enoch was that it occurred to me that he was the only bloke who was telling the truth, for the good of the country."

Asked how he responded to the heavy criticism of his original statement, Clapton replied: "I don't mind. I believe Enoch is a very religious man. And you can't be religious and racist at the same time. The two things are incompatible."

RAR commented: "Before Eric Clapton opens his mouth he should not only understand the facts, but also the political climate in which he makes his statements – and, as a popular musician, he should exercise that responsibility.

"He obviously doesn't know what he is talking about. Powell has never said anything with the welfare of the ethnic minorities in mind – the result of his 'Rivers of Blood' speech and subsequent racist outbursts in fact made racism respectable and racist violence the norm. The only difference between Powell and the Nazis is that Powell would ask the blacks to go back and the National Front would tell them."

IT HAS often been said that one of Eric Clapton's major problems over the years has been to find his own identity, one in which he can be comfortable and assured. He has been through the most historically important groups of our time, undergone the pressures of an extraordinary fame, been himself up to all the excesses of the rock 'n' roll lifestyle, been close to death, known misery and oblivion, and come out of it with his talent and sanity intact.

Eric has appeared in many guises: the eager, flippant art school kid of the Yardbirds, the macho blues man with John Mayall, even a psychedelic hippie with Cream in the era of pink boots and frizzy hair. With his old pal Jeffrey (George Harrison to you), he became drawn for a while to matters spiritual.

But now he has settled down to the role of a kind of musical labourer as he seeks security and stability in the English working class ethics and manners. His speech has that inbred authority of a saloon-bar host who divides the world into two groups of people – beer drinkers, and non-beer drinkers.

He may not be 100 per cent the real Eric Clapton, but it's a good solid base to work from, and it makes life less complicated – although, even here, I suspect that taking a stand on one lifestyle is not always easy.

While Eric enjoys talking about football to strangers in the bar, the commitment to being English and working class requires entrenched, conservative attitudes.

A few years ago, at Birmingham during a gig, Eric made a few remarks that seemed to support Enoch Powell's view on repatriation. As a direct result of this, Rock Against Racism was born. The left rose to fight what they feared might be popular support for the right.

But Eric is non-political and can hardly be called a racist. He has long idolised black music and musicians. Nevertheless he seems to feel that unchecked immigration is still an issue, and it was one of the matters we touched on during a long conversation at Southampton's Polygon Hotel on Saturday afternoon. At first it seemed that Eric might well be lured off to a football match; but to start at the beginning . . .

THE day dawned wet and miserable at Waterloo Station. Adrian Boot, hero of the Grateful Dead's Egyptian campaign, appeared clutching his trunk load of cameras and reported that Jona Lewie of Stiff Tour fame was in the coffee shop.

Jona, a smartly dressed gent, clutching a piano accordion, was intrigued to hear of the expedition to see Clapton. He was on his way to a spot of promotion himself, down in Portsmouth, and remembered that the last time he saw Clapton was when Jona was in Brett Marvin and the Thunderbolts. "We did a tour with Derek & The Dominoes back in 1970. I remember Eric as a very thin man. He's bloomed out a bit since then."

Andy Murray, one of Stiff's hierarchy, recalled that he had seen Eric play a secret holiday camp gig at Hayling Island. "He played 'Layla' for all these mums, dads and kids, and nobody seemed to recognise it, but when he played 'I Shot The Sheriff' they knew it was a hit. He was going to play at another Butlin's but they had 7,000 applications for tickets. They panicked and cancelled the show."

Another show that had to be cancelled more recently was the ill-fated Cream reunion, when Ginger Baker wanted to bring Eric and Jack Bruce together again at his polo club. Unfortunately word was leaked to the national press and the polo fraternity also panicked, expecting an invasion of fans.

Andy laid Jona's album on me, apologised for blagging at 9.30 a.m. on Waterloo Station, and we went our separate ways.

AT Southampton, an hour away, football fans were already streaming into town for the afternoon's match. But at the Polygon Hotel, most of the Clapton camp were still sound asleep after a night of merriment following their gig at the Gaumont.

115

Roger Forrester, Eric's manager, was awake, however, bleary-eyed and clad in a dressing gown, but keen that the long-delayed interview would take place.

"You know what I had to do to get Eric to agree to an interview?" he demanded, ordering coffee from room service. "I had to go on stage last night and announce the group. I was terrified. But once Eric gets an idea into his head he keeps on and on about it. So as I had to go on stage, he's GOT to do the interview."

Not for another couple of hours was it deemed sensible to start knocking on Eric's door. He had not been to bed until 5 a.m., having been out dancing at the local discotheque. Rumour was that the local girls had not been impressed by Eric's John Travolta-style routine, and refused to join him on the floor, so in the end he had put a bandana round his head and danced alone.

It seemed odd that after years of avoiding publicity and trying to shake off his fame Eric was now approaching that state known to many a rock star in their 30s, when the younger generation fails to recognise them.

It seemed the height of irony when two girls sitting in the hotel bar (where we eventually found Eric, surrounded by football fans) revealed they had not the faintest idea who he was. Their favourite band was Showaddywaddy. They'd never heard of Cream or Bob Dylan, for that matter.

ERIC has cut back on drinking considerably, but he felt that a glass or two of brandy might help ease us into the interview and was most affable and amenable. There was a moment when I tried to draw him away from the subject of football, and back to more pressing matters like Rock Against Racism, when he chided: "Never mind what we were talking about. Now be courteous!"

What Eric had been saying about immigration was really just saloon-bar talk, and stemmed from a remark shouted at him the night before.

"Someone shouted out 'Enoch Powell' last night. And I had to spend half-an-hour after the gig explaining to Carl Radle that he wasn't the George Wallace of England. But I think Enoch is a prophet, see? His diplomacy is wrong, and he's got no idea how to present things. His ideas are right. You go to Heathrow any day, mate, and you'll see thousands of Indian people sitting there waiting to know whether or not they can come into the country. And you go to Jamaica and there's adverts on TV saying 'Come to lovely England,' and pictures of double-decker buses."

But didn't Eric think that Enoch was a racist?

"No, he's not," said Eric firmly. "I don't think he cares about colour of any kind. I think his whole idea is for us to stop being unfair to immigrants because it's getting out of order. A husband comes over, lives off the dole to try and save enough to bring his wife and six kids over. It's splitting up families, and I think the Government is being incredibly unfair to people abroad to lure them to the promised land where there is actually no work.

"The racist business starts when white guys see immigrants getting jobs and they're not. Enoch said six years ago, stop it, give 'em a grand, and tell 'em to go home.

"That whole thing about me talking about Enoch was that it occurred to me that he was the only bloke who was telling the truth, for the good of the country. I mean there's all sorts of things going on, smuggling routes. . . . you can get as many people in this country as you like. And it's their families that suffer because they're left behind. I saw an Indian woman being grilled at Heathrow and it was the most anguishing scene you've ever seen in your life."

"The woman has completely broken down, because she can hardly speak English, and she's come here expecting to be greeted by her husband and go to a new house. Next minute, she's back on the 'plane."

Eric got a lot of stick for his previous outburst.

"Yeah, I did. But I don't mind. So did Enoch. They shoved him into Ireland. But he can do as much good there as he can anywhere. I believe he is a very religious man. And you can't be religious and racist at the same time. The two things are incompatible."

But people might think that you are being racist yourself?

"Yeah, yeah. That was the original mistake."

MEANWHILE the dialogue between Eric and his new-found mates, the football fans, went something like this:

> 1st Football fan: "Wodger work – five nights a week?"
>
> Eric: "Nah, I couldn't 'andle that. I'm getting old, mate.
>
> 1st Football fan: "You must be, because when I was a kid you were still going." (Shouts of laughter from all the company.)
>
> Eric: "THANK you."
>
> 2nd Football fan: "Oh yeah, was it with Cream or summink?"
>
> Eric: "All right, none of that . . ."
>
> 1st Football fan: "'Ee was going afore that . . ."

Eric hastily changes the subject and looks across at the two rather beautiful girls sitting across the lounge. He leans towards me in conspiratorial fashion. "'Ere, go across and ask 'em how old they are." What – those chicks? "Yeah, the grumble. Well, it's company isn't it."

At this point Roger Forrester appears in his manager's cap to borrow a couple of quid.

"Here you are, son, now go and enjoy yourself," says Eric enjoying the situation, and producing a tenner.

"Oh Eric, I don't want all that, do I? That's very nice of you . . ."

The fans chuckle in good humour, throw back their beers, and – having failed to seduce Eric to the match – set off to watch Southampton beat Birmingham.

The two girls come over to join us for drinks, with bright, nervous smiles. They sense that somehow Eric is the centre of attraction, but reveal a charming ignorance.

"What do you work at?" asks one.

"Musician," he responds, as if he were saying "bricklayer" or "industrial cleaning contractor."

"What sort?"

"A rock 'n' roll musician."

The girls persist with their probing questions. What was he doing here in Southampton, they'd like to know.

"I've come to do a gig here, haven't I," says Eric. "We played the Gaumont. Last night." He begins to sound testy. We wonder who has been doing the promotion.

"Roger!" says Eric. "He stands outside and offers people money to go in. I've been geeing Roger up, because he showed me last week's Melody Maker, and I wanted to know how much he paid to get us on the front page. How much was it, Chris?" Eric seems quite convinced that jiggery-pokery had been afoot.

"I mean, you don't like me," he added.

I hastened to point out that quite a lot of water had rolled under the bridge. Past knocks had stemmed from duff gigs, but the band up in Glasgow the week before had been great.

"It was good fun, wasn't it?" said Eric quietly. "Last night was a gas! Not many. Dear o Lor'. It steamed along. The band is incredibly tight."

Was he happy working as a four-piece?

"It was the original deal. But it took us four years to get around to it. The original plan was that Carl would bring Dick Sims and Jamie Oldaker to Miami. Only they arrived late – being Tulsa people – and George Terry was already around, so he joined. It was a stitch-up if you ask me! No he hasn't quit. I just called him up and said that we were going out as a quartet. I was scared shitless of the idea, but it ended up him telling me not to worry. His attitude was fantastic.

"The first gig was a walkover, probably as good as any of the others. In fact it's easier with a four-piece. 'Cos when we had the girls and George, I was always looking from one side of the stage to the other to check out what was going on, and like two of the girls would be redundant a lot of the time, just sitting in chairs. That saps your energy and I don't think it was good for anybody. Wasn't good for them – or me.

"Trouble is – I can't fire people. Yvonne left because she wanted to pursue a solo career, and that was like saying 'Can I go?'

"The Dominoes was a four-piece band and I enjoyed that. It's the whole thing about having a Booker T-type feel. One guitar, keyboards, drums and bass. I have to work more, it's true, and that's what I really enjoy doing. Everybody has to work. We started out this tour trying too hard. Over-compensating. Now it's a lot more simplified. Booker T was your complete unit. You could add horns to it, and singers as you wanted."

So Eric would stay with this band for a while?

"I think so. We've already done nine months' work . . ."

And how was he shaping up, physically?

"I'm tired, man, really tired.

"WE went to a disco last night, and there were some really ugly birds there. There were about 20 bouncers to every fella. I spent most of my time chatting up the bouncers – so I wouldn't get hit! And there's no place to go to in London any more. The only club I go to is Rags. But that's a man's club. You never see women in there ever. They've got a pool table, backgammon and cards. You go in there and drink until everyone's fed up with it, or you play pool and that's it. There's no chance of pulling anything! London's no place to go. I never go there unless I can help it. Only on business.

"I was going to have a dance competition last night. I was all wound up and going to give it plenty, but no chance. None of the girls wanted to dance. I've always been a dancer. I've been a dancer all me life. Do you remember the Scene Club? You could just dance on your own there. And there was some place in Archer Street, the only one in England they called a discotheque."

Eric was with the right label (RSO) for discos. How did he feel about the fantastic success of his old manager from the days of Cream, Robert Stigwood?

"I saw him recently and he doesn't know what's going on. He's transcended it completely. He's got more money than he knows what to do with. Billionaire – I should think. And yet he's exactly the same. He's still the same great bloke. He's a GREAT bloke. All he cares about is maintaining friendships, money can

119

get in the way of that, rapidly. In business all he has to say is yey or nay.

"Sometimes he comes up with some great ideas, other times he just gives his consent. Sgt. Pepper was one idea that died, though. It really died. He offered me a part in it. I was supposed to play a weather vane or something. Billy Preston ended up doing it."

Eric, who recently re-signed to the Stigwood organisation, stipulated in his contract that he would NOT be offered any film scripts. Apparently his experience in Tommy was enough, although he is keen to complete his own film documentary of the Clapton band on the road.

HE had seemingly fought shy of the media in recent years, rarely giving interviews, and those around him often complained vociferously of the treatment meted out to him in reviews and articles.

Australia was one place the Clapton camp vowed they would not return to again because of hounding by national newspaper reporters, who camped outside the door and ran stories about him and Patti Boyd. One paper had run a picture captioned "Ex-drug addict." But Eric seemed genuinely surprised at the heat this aroused in his friends and compatriots. For example, he wondered if I had been winding up Jamie Oldaker, who sprang to Eric's defence in last week's episode of the Clapton Saga.

"It sounded like he'd lost his temper. Did you wind him up or something? I didn't realise he cared so much. It's amazing, ennit?"

Had it been an accurate portrayal of how Eric felt about the press?

"Hmmm . . ." he thought for a moment. "No . . . the press is fine. But I don't think the press ever gets anything right. Reporting-wise, I mean. I don't think anyone has ever pulled that off. I don't think it can be done. Do you?"

My response was to refer to the hypothetical accident and the four hypothetical witnesses who all give different accounts. I referred back to the early days of Eric's comeback, when one got the impression that he didn't want to project himself too much, and his playing seemed listless.

"Yeah, well everyone likes to be lazy sometimes . . ."

The girls momentarily distracted Eric. Why was he talking to me all the time?

"Because I'm doing a bleeding interview," explained E.C.

ONE of Eric's happier memories of the past year was working with Bob Dylan on his historic European tour, and Eric's album title, "Backless," was a kind of in-joke about working for Bob Dylan's back, as the master had a habit of turning round and giving a fairly serious stare if the band were not entirely pulling their weight, a technique he may have borrowed from Benny Goodman, the jazz clarinettist also noted for "the ray."

"It was an inspiration working for Bob. Sometimes he'd turn round and it would be like 'Okay, you're not listening' and he knew all the time if you were paying attention or not. He knew what everyone was doing behind him.

"The best gig we did was in Nuremburg. It was the place where Adolf used to hold the rallies. The place where he used to come out and stand on his podium was directly opposite us. It was a black doorway. And he'd come out to an incredible atmosphere. The atmosphere was there, again but this time it was for a Jewish songwriter. And Bob didn't even know."

Eric had known and worked with Dylan over a number of years. What was he like as a . . .

Eric interrupted me, his attention again engaged by the girls.

"She doesn't even know who Bob Dylan is, do you realise that? I do get on with Bob very well, though. I love him, he's a fantastic guy. And I still love The Band. My soul brother is Richard Manuel, who plays the piano.

"The first time I worked with Bob was when I was with John Mayall. He came to London, and liked John who had made a record called 'Life Is Like A Slow Train Crawling Up A Hill,' and Bob was very freaked out by this. After calling up the Zoo and asking if he could have a giraffe delivered to his room, he called up John and we did a session at Chappell's in Bond Street. Tom Wilson was the producer and there was a huge entourage.

"Thousands of people were telling me, 'Don't play country style, play city, go electric, don't play acoustic.' It was all this. And Bob gets on the piano and starts playing. The next thing you know, there's nothing happening.

"And I said, 'what's happening, where's he gone?' And he'd gone to Madrid.

"This was back in '65. It's never been a serious friendship. We just jive. It's like working with Muddy, you know. We don't talk seriously. That's forbidden. It's an unwritten law. You don't say anything like 'I've always liked your music.'

"I can't watch Muddy. It drains me completely. When he does that song 'I'm A Man,' I have to scream. I didn't want Muddy on tour to begin with."

This seemed an astonishing statement, but he explained: "I thought it would be beyond my capabilities to follow Muddy. I just couldn't handle the idea of following Muddy on stage. Originally we tried to get the Paul Butterfield Band, because Paul and I are very much the same kind of characters. There's no big deal there, and he's a harp player. But at the last minute Paul couldn't get his band together."

I thought Eric was playing more powerful guitar.

"Well I've GOT to. Coming on after Muddy Waters, you've gotta do something, and it's gotta be right. Nah, I don't practice, I get it from the band. That's where it comes from. They're the source.

"If I'm on my own in a room, who have I got to play for? I'll write a song maybe, if it's there to write. I like to play for other people. It's always for someone else. You don't do anything for your own pleasure, do you? There is a point where you've got something almost right, and you don't want to present it to anybody unless it's absolutely right. But no. I'm not a perfectionist. Unskilled labour. Hard work. That's all it is."

DID Eric feel a sense of disorientation after his illness and cure from addiction?

"I was worried. I just didn't know where I was going. I didn't know whether I should carry on, or whether I should pack it in altogether.

"And then a song came along. It was 'Dear Lord, Give Me Strength.' It just kept coming through, like a dream. It kept coming back to me. I thought if I didn't do something, then I would be letting people down. That gave me the strength to carry on being a musician."

But there were practical considerations, too.

"I couldn't knock it on the head, anyway. Businesswise I was in breach of contract, because I hadn't done anything for three years. My contract said I had to make at least two albums a year and go on the road. So I HAD to and I knew that. It was in the back of my mind as well. It was really a matter of loyalty and word of honour. Robert Stigwood would never have come down on me, but I had given my word, whether it was written on paper or a handshake. That was a strong factor in pulling me through too. Now I'm enjoying playing and there's nothing in the way."

What did he think of the audiences, and the kids who came to see him today?

"I don't take any notice. Do you know what I look at? The exit signs. I can just about see the kids coming in and going out. At one gig the kids started shouting at me, 'Duane Allman'."

Eric began shouting at the top of his voice, causing the hotel fittings and fixtures to reverberate.

"Duane Allman!" he bellowed. "Jack Bruce!" Eric shook his head.

"They actually stand up and shout. It's a roar. They don't even seem to realise that Duane has been dead for about four years. So I just showed them the back of my guitar and walked off, after doing my alloted time, of course."

Does Eric feel that the past hangs over him like a cloud?

"It doesn't hang over me, I can handle it, but I feel for the band. Christ almighty, this is the LONGEST I've ever been with a band. And if they can't show some kind of appreciation for them . . .

"I mean, Jack has got his own life to lead, and so have I, and there are three other people playing on stage with me that are going to get hurt by all this. That incenses me, it really does." He paused to reflect.

"But then you don't always KNOW. How can you tell what's going through that guy's mind, when he shouts for Duane Allman? He might be meaning well. He might be saying 'Great, do you remember Duane Allman?' But I mean the Cream, with Jack and Ginger, was ten years ago. And I've been back on the road, now, longer than I was off it. For four-and-a-half years."

ERIC insisted his 81-year-old grandmother knew more about the rock business than most kids. "She can tell me exactly what position the record is in the chart. She's a great songwriter too and I'm going to do a couple of her songs. Rose, she's a born musician.

"Ahh, knock it on the 'ead, you're driving me round the bend."

I thought for a moment this was an abrupt termination of our interview, but realised that Eric was addressing his remarks to Adrian Boot, who was beavering away with his flashgun. But Eric relented and requested a picture of himself dancing.

"Did you know," he said, sounding like Michael Caine, "that John Travolta couldn't dance before he made that movie?"

I hazarded that he looked like one of Devo.

"The best dancer in the world is Bob Marley," said Clapton.

As far as Eric's current musical tastes go, his favourite is Elton John.

"I've been playing his album for the last three weeks. Every day. It's the greatest thing I've heard this year. It's gotta be the record of the year.

One of the girls decided to ask a question we had all overlooked.

"What do you do in the group?" she asked sweetly.

"I play guitar and sing," said Eric pleasantly.

"And the only person who asks me to do sessions these days," he said, returning to the official interview, "is George. And he's just finished a magnificent album but it won't be out until January because he's got held up over the cover. He probably can't make up his mind what to call it. He suggested that my next album should be called 'The Sound of One Man Clapton'. He's much happier and looser now. He's got a kid, as you know, and it's given him a new lease of life."

Has Eric thought of starting a family?

"I've tried, mate, I've tried. The first couple of kids I ever started to have were aborted because it was a bit dicey. But not having a family doesn't concern me really because I'm still a road musician and I can't see that going on forever. I'm a wanderer, a gypo. I get three days off, I go home and I have a row with everybody. I wander about and complain about things. Get back on the road, and I'm as happy as a sandboy."

That's good, I observed.

"It's NOT," corrected Eric. "No, it isn't, mate."

Well, it was good for Eric Clapton fans surely?

"Well I'm not one to put down roots, but Jamie has just got married again and he and his wife need to be close together, so he's got this incredible turmoil going on. He doesn't know whether to throw in the road and stick to a home life, or take her with him, and she doesn't like travelling. And I don't want that kind of problem.

"I've been on the road too long man, I can't give it up."

And how much further did he feel he could stay on the road?

"Until I drop, mate. 'Til I drop".

WHY had he always worked with American musicians, since the demise of Blind Faith back in '69?

"Well, they're the best. I think they play better than most British musicians. The only two I've ever met who can come anywhere near Jamie and Carl are Dave Markee and Henry Spinetti. I think they're fine. But they're session musicians, studio men. The Americans understand more about the music that has influenced me.

"It's like asking these girls about Howlin' Wolf. A blank, right? But the Americans, they know what I'm talking about, and with Carl it goes back to Louis Jordan. They know where it's all coming from."

Eric started off the whole British rock guitar hero thing. What does he think about his successors, and the development of the heavy rock guitar which could be traced from the Yardbirds, via Cream, Led Zeppelin, etc. to the present wave of heavy metal?

"I think it's great," said Eric unexpectedly (I thought he might disown the whole movement). "And the best person who is doing it is Brian May with Queen. I think that group is fantastic. And he is the only guitarist here who really knocks me out. Obviously there are lots more, but he's the one who comes straight to me head, because I love the way he plays."

But Eric's own guitar style over the years has remained free of flashy effects and all the inhuman sounds that technology can now unleash.

"I don't see how you can do all that and play at the same time. I mean, you've got to stop and think about what button you're going to press, and then you stop playing. That only applies to me. Probably there are other people who can do three things at once, what comes out of the guitar is the most important thing. I can still blow myself away. I can still do that, you know."

But for a long while Eric seemed to want to get away from the limelight, as a lead guitar player with a unique, universal appeal.

"Yeah, I was fed up with being dominated, all the time. It was just getting on my *nerves*. How can you live with that on your back? You can't. It's best just to be A Musician.

"Unskilled labour, that's what it's all about. And if you pull it out of the bag, all well and good. If you don't – it doesn't make any difference. If you are being WATCHED and EXAMINED, to see whether or not you can pull it off, and you blow it, Christ it comes down on you. It comes down hard, I tell you. People expect so much from you."

What does Eric think of his old mates, the guitar heroes of an earlier generation, now?

"Jeff Beck is my favourite. I think he's gotta be my favourite guitarist of all. He's mingling with the greats today, isn't he?

"And Peter Green, he came and stayed with me when he was having a really bad time, for about two weeks. And the first week, nothing. Not a chord. And every now and then he'd complain – Why are you doing this? Why are you listening to that? Why are you playing that way? And then one sunny day I caught him outside in the garden, dancing his head off, and laughing. It was so good to see him enjoying himself at last. And then we had a play, and he had it all there, it was exactly the same. I know where he's at.

"He's got it there, and he's just decided he's not going to use it, until he feels like it."

They were remarkable days in the Sixties that produced the likes of Clapton, Hendrix, Beck and Green.

What does he think of the British scene now? Is the talent still there?

"I don't think I'm the right person to ask. I'm looking at it from an older person's point of view. I'd be too critical."

Mention of Sid Vicious reminded Eric of an unpleasant but salutory experience from his younger days: "I once spent the night in jail in America. A County jail. I was busted for being in a place where smoke was being used. It was with Buffalo Springfield and they all got done. Neil Young had a fit, because he's had a history of epilepsy. He may be cured now.

"But in jail we had to take all our clothes off and line up for mug shots, and then they hosed us down and sprayed us with insecticide and took our clothes away. While they're doing all this, Neil just went 'wh-o-o-a!' and they took him out of the room, and it was the last I saw of him. I spent the night in a cell with three Black Panthers, and I had to convince them that I was a blues guitarist.

"When I look back, it was a good experience. I'll know never to get busted. No way. One night of that was hell. Because there was no word to the outside world. It's a good idea when they take young offenders to a prison and show them what it's like, because it's not like joining the army. And I had PINK boots on! And I had me frizzed-out hairstyle, and I was wearing all my psychedelic gear.

"They took all me bracelets and chains away from me and I got blue denims with LA County Jail written all over them. But they left me in the pink boots and threw me in the cell with three Black Panthers.

"It was like I was a punk, y'know? I just had to keep talking and tell them I was English and didn't really understand what was going on, but I played blues guitar and dug Willie Dixon and Muddy Waters, and Bo Diddley and Chuck Berry. It worked. It cooled them out – just about.

"I think they had been in for about three or four years. Eventually I applied for bail. There was one guy there who had been applying for bail every day for seven years, but nobody had put the money up for him."

WHAT is the driving force that keeps a musician like Eric on the road after a lifetime in bands, despite all the hassles?

A deathly silence greeted this, and he signalled with his eyes towards the girls sitting across the room.

"Robbie Robertson is asked by Ronnie Hawkins to join The Band in The Last Waltz, and Robbie asks: 'How much does it pay?' And Ronnie says: 'It don't pay nuthin' but you get more pussy than Frank Sinatra.'

And that's it, y'know. I play poker and I love winning money at poker, but I love women more."

Isn't money a motive?

"No, no. I've earned a lot of money, but I've lost a lot too. I've been frivolous, not generous. And Cream only broke even, you know. Most of the money we made from Cream went towards financing the Bee Gees."

"We joined up with Robert (Stigwood), went out on the road for six months at a time and made an incredible amount of money which went straight back into the company so that he could bring the Bee Gees back from Australia, and start them. But it balanced out. It was all in the company and it was like a family deal and it still is.

"The last year has been very tough because Robert hasn't been putting himself about much, he's got so many things in the pot. I've watched people losing their jobs without even knowing why, RSO people who have been in the family for as long as I've been with the label. They've been told to clear their desks and be out by Monday. And they don't know why.

"My contract was up, and I wondered, should I stay with this lot if they're going to get this cold? But I did re-sign because I don't think there is anybody else that I trust or love as much as Robert. When the contract came up, he said: 'You can write your own ticket.' So I signed.

"But there were clauses in the contract. One was that I didn't appear in any film unless it was under my own name. But I wouldn't mind making a guest spot in a film, as long as it was under my own name. Like those old jazz films which had Cab Calloway appearing as himself, not playing a role.

"Next year I'll probably make another album, go to America and tour for two or three months. That's the plan so far. And then I'll probably have a good time off, maybe six or seven months."

Would he start making model airplanes again?

"Ooch, no, not on your *Nellie*. That was only when I was really ill. That was the only thing that kept me alive. It was therapy. My eyes got so bad during that time, I ended up using magnifying glasses and old people's spectacles, just so I could paint the finest bits, like the eyes on a pilot."

WHAT'S his view of the "casualty" aspect of rock 'n' roll?

"A lot of people go down on the road, but you can't tell when it's going to happen. If a musician quits the road, it doesn't mean he ain't gonna get run over by a bus.

"Like when I had that accident right outside my house. I didn't know where I was for two weeks afterwards. I was in a Ferrari and had probably reached about 90 mph in a very short space of time, when a laundry van appeared. That was the last thing I can remember. All I know is I hit him and turned his van over. My skid marks were in a straight line and they found me with my head hanging through a side window. You only need to do that sort of thing once."

After his rehabilitation from drugs, he seemed to allow excessive drinking to replace one stairway to oblivion with another. Now he seems much more careful.

"I don't get legless much any more. When I'm at home and I've got nothing to do, then I'll have a drink. If I get one over the eight, I only have to look at Jamie, Dickie or Carl and I can see the disapproval straight away. They are depending on me to keep my end up. If I blow it, why should they bother?"

Now Eric has the responsibility of being a band leader.

"I'm not a very good one yet, but I'm learning every day. I never wanted to be a leader, and I still don't really enjoy it. As you were saying earlier, I always worshipped The Band. That was because there was no apparent bandleader. It turned out there was one – Robbie Robertson. But he was very much behind the scenes.

"Carl is mostly our leader. He's The Rock. He's The Elder. If ever I'm in doubt about anything, he'll put me straight. I'm not talking about the running order at gigs. I mean he can be a philosophical guide towards what is happening in your life. He's got all the answers you need. But he's not the closest to me. We're all pretty close. Some of us drift away for a day or two, then come back."

It was good to see E.C. back. Down in the lobby suitcases and bags began to pile up, and people began to ask each other who was in their room and who was ready to go.

Clapton was on the road once more, this time heading for Brighton, ready to play some guitar, sing a little and stomp with his friends. Let's hope we see him again soon.

"Well," said Eric, "you'll get a Christmas card from me this year. And I'll draw it myself."

Chris Welch

11

Say a prayer for the Pretenders

CHRISSIE HYNDE

February 17 1979

WE are dancing, Chrissie Hynde and I, to a **Sex Pistols** single, the exact title of which has been blurred by time and a good deal of alcohol. Heated discussions concerning the role of the rock journalist as public executioner have given way to abandoned physical exertion, although this is perhaps as much to maintain blood temperature on one of this winter's bitterest nights as to relieve the escalating excitability of the discussion I have been having with Chrissie Hynde and the rest of the Pretenders, and other occupants of a pleasantly decaying house near Tufnell Park.

Suddenly she grabs my arm and bellows above the Jones/Cook power riffs: "Look, you should give up all that journalism crap and get yourself a Fender, learn the piano or something. You can't write about rock 'n' roll if you can't play it."

As quite possibly the worst drummer ever to work the North-East club circuit, and a man who sings flatter than Lee Marvin, I'm forced to demur. But she has a point. In fact, it's currently apparent that several rock hacks have reached the same conclusion; even Uncle Mick Farren recently downed his felt-tip and struggled into his leather trews for a second tilt at stage credibility. And then, of course, there's Chrissie Hynde herself. But Chrissie's career as a rock scribe was fairly brief and totally accidental.

"I'd arrived in England naively thinking that I'd bump into Marc Bolan or Jeff Beck on every street corner. All I had was a coupla hundred dollars and three albums by Iggy and Lou Reed, and of course it was instant disillusion – I was living in these really cheap, scuzzy hotels, having to sell leather handbags in one of those sucker tourist markets on Oxford Street and modelling at St Martin's School of Art. And, like, no-one knew what the hell I was talking about when I mentioned the Stooges or Lou Reed.

"Anyway, I was pretty pissed off with England. Then I somehow got invited to this party, which seemed pretty boring, so I was coming on the loud-mouthed, vulgar American chick and talking about Iggy and how great he was, and this wiry, weird looking guy in the corner says, 'Oh year, I know Iggy, he's a friend of mine.' Which totally floored me.

"And that's how I met Nick Kent and I started running around with him, which was great, 'cause I was getting to see a lot of bands and one day I met one of the editors of his paper and I was badrapping some album or something, and he said, 'Well why don't you write a review for us, then?' Which shows where a big mouth can get you."

Some of Chrissie's pieces still stand up as good examples of shrewd rock observation. Her coverage of the prepubescent hordes awaiting David Cassidy's arrival at Heathrow is a minor classic, for example. But Chrissie's ambitions went further than a press card . . .

"I DIDN'T mind getting the review copies 'cause I didn't have a stereo, never have had since I've been in England, and so I didn't feel bad about selling the albums; I had to eat after all. Anyway, one day I was asked to write a retrospective of the Velvets, 'cause they couldn't come up with anything better, so I thought 'Well, screw that.' There was too much else going on."

Chrissie's life seems to be dogged by the GPO, for it's at this point that the first in a series of fateful phone calls comes through. Would she like to come to Paris and sing in a band? Well, hell – why not?

"See I've been playing guitar and stuff since I was 16, and my ultimate ambition has always been to play in a band. Not *front* a band as a solo singer," she emphasises, "but to work with a bunch of musicians."

These modest ambitions, incidently, were nurtured in last year's tinseltown, Akron, Ohio, where her brother Terry was a saxophonist. Afraid to expose her musical bent to the anticipated derision of her predominantly male peer group, she practised in clandestine solitude on a jumbo-sized ukelele, and later a proper guitar. She was in a band called Sat. Sun. Mat. with Mark Mothersbaugh, though.

BY that time she was already locked into the music of the major soul and R&B acts which from time to time passed through Ohio.

"One time I went to see Jackie Wilson, who was top of the bill over Aretha Franklin and B.B. King. Can you believe that? The place was full of spades, and by the time Jackie came on they were going bananas. And they had this stooge in the audience who was going down the front rows and picking out the prettiest girls and taking them up on to the stage where Jackie was lying down, man, lying down *singing*, and Jackie was giving each of them a big wet one and of course everyone was screaming their tits off. So then this guy comes up to me, and I'm mortified – but I get up and suddenly the screaming stops; the only white girl in the place being kissed by Jackie Wilson. Man, they were not ready for that!"

"I was pathetically shy then," she explains. But it didn't last long. She went to Kent State University, lived through the riots and the legalised homicide, "and ran around doing a lot of drugs and having a good time."

So Chrissie came to swinging England and thence to La Belle France, which is where we were a few stanzas back.

"PARIS was in the grip of the big punk thing at the time and this band, the Frenchies, were basically just another band. But it was okay . . . like I was starving again, but starving in France is pretty much the same as starving anywhere else."

One redeeming fact was that she met Chris Spedding via the Red Festival, a big left-wing gig held in the old Paris abattoir.

"I was getting very pissed off 'cause the promoters kept putting us further and further back in the running order until we were due to go on at 4 a.m. or something. And I can hardly speak French and there's no one speaking English, and I'm getting a bit out of it and more angry and rather depressed, so someone tells me that Chris Spedding is in town to record an album. I'm dying to see an English face, so the next day I find his hotel and there he is, sitting in the coffee shop. Sigh of relief. So life is made a little more bearable hanging out with him and his crowd while he's recording.

"So on the spur of the moment I upped and went to Cleveland, Ohio, where I got involved with this R&B group, Jack Rabbit. Naturally, I went like a shot.

"

Jack Rabbit were alright . . . I had to try and liven them up a bit with a few reggae tunes. But it wasn't the most inspiring period of my life, and when some of the band started having money problems, I split back to Paris."

Nothing happening there, so she decided to revert to the glamour of her Clapham digs. Once back, she reactivated her musical aspirations and began the long slog of trying to get a band together.

"It was so góddamn frustrating, cause a lot of my friends were forming bands, doing gigs and actually making records. It was the start of the punk thing; there were people who couldn't play half as well as I could – and I ain't great – who were becoming lead guitarists. I think I'd been around too long. I wasn't fresh enough for all that . . . I couldn't bitch enough about the music scene. I mean, after you've travelled around a bit and listened to Bobby Womack and stuff that's a lot more refined, you can't quite agree with kids who're saying that everything that went down before punk was a piece of shit.

"Basically, I had difficulty finding musicians who I felt I could work with. At one point, Malcolm McLaren wanted to have me dress up like a guy and get my hair cut short and put me in a band called the Loveboys with Richard Hell. Another of his scams was the Masters Of The Backside, which was basically me playing, not singing, with Dave Vanian and another really shy guy called Dave, doing the vocals. Chris Miller was discovered by McLaren because he was such an item, and then he said he had a mate from Croydon or somewhere who could play bass guitar, and along came Ray Burns with long hippie curls. That's where Rat Scabies and Captain Sensible started.

"It was a complete madhouse, of course, 'cos this shy Dave didn't want to do live gigs, and McLaren was too busy dealing with the Pistols, and the rest of the boys really wanted to gig. So they went off and formed the Damned and I was on my own again."

In '76 she liased briefly with Mick Jones, working out songs immediately prior to the formation of the Clash. Three months of fun and then another, less likely connection: a card on a music shop noticeboard led to Fred Mills (bass) and Dave Batchelor (drums), whom she christened the Berk Bros.

In the creative ambiance of Fred's parents' house in Croydon, they achieved the closest thing to reality, band-wise, that Chrissie had found in the UK – until the Croydon legend, Johnny Moped, came out of hiding.

After one gig with the man himself, onstage at the Roxy, "I knew I had no place standing next to such a charismatic figure, so I gracefully left . . . when he threw me out."

Then came another period in the doldrums, alleviated by some session work, doing back-up vocals with Chris Spedding, amongst others.

ANOTHER golden thread in the rich tapestry of CH's life was her unwitting and fleeting involvement with the Moors Murderers, a band that never was a band . . . something she must've been getting used to by now.

As far as she was concerned, it was just another opportunity for her to polish her licks, but a publicity hungry Welshman, Steve Strange, had other ideas. Not knowing the gruesome twosome from a hole in the ground, she agreed to help Strange out on a photo session.

"I just happened to be in that part of town the next day and although I wasn't really in the band, I knew he was anxious to make it. He asked me to put a black plastic bag over my head like the rest of the band, and I thought, "Well, if they're all doing it, why not? What I didn't realise was that some journalist was in on all this and the next thing I know there's stuff about ex-rock journalist Chrissie Hynde singing with a band called the Moors Murderers, and the whole thing had a very nasty flavour to it. No one bothered to ring me up and ask me what was going down or anything. That's the rock press for you."

Then she met Tony Secunda, enfant terrible of the Westbourne Grove rock scene and, at the time, manager of Steeleye Span.

"At this point some of the punk rock ideology had rubbed off on me, and I remember going into his office for the first time with a big sneer on my face, put my feet on his desk and started bad-mouthing everything in sight. And he was very cool about the whole thing, he just said 'How can I hear you? So I told him I had a guitar and an amp, and he said he'd get a car to come and pick me up the following morning and bring me over to do some songs. I thought 'Wow, someone's going to pick me up in a *car*, the big time at last!

"Anyway, I got there and knocked out a couple of chords from 'The Phone Call' and I was still being pretty off-hand and obstinate about the whole thing, glaring at him when I was playing and stuff. But he said, 'Yeah, great!' –, and I went. 'Wow!' cause he was knocked out and wanted to do something for me right from the start. And the fact that he'd been involved in all these projects like the Move and Marc Bolan gave me a great boost to my confidence . . . I'd been writing songs for years by then and sometimes I got to wonder, 'Well what's it all worth?' "

Secunda had faith in the Chrissie Hynde songbook, promising to arrange studio time and to procure session musicians so she could cut some demos. But this was an offer she could, apparently, refuse.

"I rejected all suggestions about using session people cause what I really wanted was to get my own band together. Eventually, though, I figured that Tony really *did* need something he could get people to hear, and he was being very good to me, paying me a small wage and helping me with the rent an' all."

So she went into a studio with Nigel Pegrum from Steeleye Span and Fred Berk from John Moped's band – now *there's* a hot combo for you – and recorded a version of "The Phone Call."

"The trouble was that a lot of time had passed by that point, and Tony was getting very involved with other projects. One day I was having a conversation on the phone with him which got quite heated, and I said something stupid and he hung up on me. That was it. C'est fini. So I just went back to being a bum.

"The next thing that happened was that I met a friend of mine from Ohio, who didn't know anything about the business but always had a lot of good ideas and wanted to do some music. When he heard the tape I'd done, he said he'd manage me.

"After a couple of months, I don't think he could deal with me. Neither of us had any money and when you ain't got the dough, you have a lot of problems . . . One day he was on the phone to me saying, 'Look, I don't need your bullshit any more', and hung up.

"As it happens, this was the day before we were going to see Dave Hill, who was at Anchor Records at the time, to play him the tape. So I had to ring Dave and say 'Er, well, look Dave, I was supposed to be coming in to see you tomorrow but, er, I don't have a band and my manager just told me to kick it in the head. So sorry, man.' But he said, well, come on down anyway, we'll try and get something sorted out, rent some gear, whatever.

"So I was working with this guy Malcolm on bass, and I got Phil from Motorhead on drums, and we went down to Studio 51 and the results were very rough indeed. And I thought, for sure, Dave Hill's going to say, 'Well, it's got a lot of potential, but why don't you come back when you've got something more concrete together, like a band?' But he didn't. Instead he asked me to go to see him at his office the next day.

"So I went in and he suggested that I get the guys together again and we try and do some demos. When we got into the studio it was really like a rehearsal, and after about an hour of it Dave Hill was looking pretty, um, *nervous*. We finally agreed it wasn't a good idea and I guessed that this time he was really going to tell me to forget it. But no, he asked me to go and see him again in his office.

"The upshot of this second meeting was that Dave Hill came down to have a look at my rehearsal room and I said, 'Well, look, I'm 70 quid in the hole for this place,' and right there on the spot he pays off the debt and something like two months' advance rent. And of course I thought 'Far out!' I never withdraw my paw when it's empty, it's just not gracious!"

THE plan was to audition people until Chrissie found the right guys to form a band with. She decided that what she needed was a drummer: "I wanted to make sure I had a backbone in the thing first."

Several were tried, and eventually she found one who seemed right, name of Gas. He said he had a friend who'd just got back from touring Australia with a folk band, which didn't exactly knock Chrissie out, but she said, "What the hell, bring him along."

Enter Pete Farndon.

"So on the way over to the rehearsal room I picked up a copy of King Floyd's 'Groove Me', which has a pretty remarkable bass line on it. When we get down to the studio we're running through the material, and all the time Pete's not saying anything – he probably thought I was just another heavy, loud-mouthed American chick. But then he picked up his bass and he just started playing this riff on the King Floyd record, and he wasn't holding his bass on his knee or using a pick – he was playing like I figure it should be played. And I thought 'Great, I'll go with him'."

She was lucky. Farndon almost became a full-time layabout, having been humiliatingly punched out by eminent Herefordian bassist, Jet Harris, for the cardinal sin of "looking at his girlfriend".

HEREFORD is the last stop for migratory hippies en route to the cheap and verdant pastures of Wales and its attendant promise of self-sufficiency. Sunday afternoons at Hereford railway station, you can watch the college girls jumping the train back to London after a hot and heavy weekend with their hippie boyfriends, most of whom live in country cottages on allowances from their businessmen fathers . . . and sharp-eyed dope dealers making the weekly shuttle back to base with big wads of money down their Y-fronts. Hereford is all long hair and wellies and I like it well enough. But to Pete Farndon, it lost its sparkle after the mod era.

"In Hereford you were either a mod, or you were too young to ride a scooter, so you had a pushbike . . . but still wore a parka. But in those days there was a very solid gig circuit, a place called the Hostel was the place to play. I remember seeing the Stones there in '64, right? Everybody wanted to go and see groups, but the thing was that Hereford was so isolated, like 50 miles from Birmingham, 60 miles from Bristol and so on – that all the bands were local ones. There was a lot of work around – we had it all to ourselves."

Despite the insularity of the Hereford rock scene, Pete never played in a band with the remainder of the Pretenders, Jim Honeyman-Scott and Martin Chapman, until Chrissie became their unsuspecting catalyst.

"First time I met Jim was when I was walking down some street in Hereford carrying my guitar case and looking like a big deal, I guess. And I notice there's this spotty bloke creeping along behind me. Eventually he builds up enough courage to come up to me and says, 'Excuse me, what's that? It's not a guitar is it?' 'Well, actually, son, yes it is.' I don't think I ever saw him again after that."

Jim Honeyman-Scott says this is because he didn't like the look of Farndon's teeth which, in those days, were a mite rotten.

However, Jim got himself a guitar, studied Bert Weedon hard and became something of a local speed-freak guitar hero. One musical combination he was involved with was called the Cheeks, and included Martin Chambers on drums. This little lot were allies of The Temperance League, committed to getting Hereford's wayward youngsters out of the boozers and into the YMCA. Naturally, Jim and Mart drifted out of the Cheeks before their souls actually got saved.

IN the meantime Farndon was playing with a band called Cold River Lady who, when I saw them at a village hop many years ago, were pretty awful but who eventually made it to London.

After an abortive audition for A&R men at a girls' college in Twickenham, Farndon dumped Cold River Lady, and whilst pacing the streets of Earl's Court one day, looking for dog-ends, he came across a chum who was playing with a folksy outfit called, yes, the Bushwackers. Naturally they were just off to tour Australia, by way of Germany, and needed a bassist.

"It was the summer of '76, the Pistols were playing the 100 Club and I was watching all these punks in their pre-record company days and starting to think seriously about trying to get a band together. It was difficult, because I knew I could play better than most of them, but I was really excited by the energy and the atmosphere.

"But then this Bushwackers thing came along and the money won me over. A year later I woke up in someone else's bed in Sydney and wondered what the hell I was doing there. The Bushwackers were a top band there, TV shows and everything, but I had to get back to England."

SO here are Chrissie and Pete in a rehearsal room with a drummer who turns out not to be quite what they had in mind and no lead guitarist. After a lot of argy-bargy, Pete remembers the spotty-faced kid who's since acquired a big reputation in Mott the Hoople country and hauls him up to London.

"I saw this wide-eyed fresh-faced lad for the first time" (the Clearasil had done its stuff) "and thought 'Christ, who is this hick?' But when he got into the studio and started to play, he was just excellent. His personality started to come through and I thought, 'Yes, indeed!' "

By this time Martin, too, had been lured by the gold-plated pavements of London, and was hanging out with Pete and Jim whilst he auditioned for various second division bands. Of course it wasn't long before he was brought to rehearsals and, whammo, ladies and gentlemen, the Pretenders.

Except they weren't.

"We couldn't think of a goddamn name," explains Chrissie. "I used to wake up in the morning, look at the ceiling and think 'Yeah, the Ceilings! Ah, no!' Then I'd go into the kitchen and think, 'Wow, the Kitchens!'

"In the end it'd got as far as the record actually being pressed and Dave ringing us up the day the label was being printed and asking us what the hell we'd decided on. The Pretenders was a last-minute job, but it's good."

AND so are they. It occurs to me, this late in the game, that the world is not universally aware of the Pretenders – or of the fact that in the MM cabal there are those who consider them to be likely rock 'n' roll icons of the Eighties.

Their cover of Ray Davies' "Stop Your Sobbing" is steadily climbing the shaky scaffolding which passes as the Top 100 in this country, Top Of The Pops benefits from their company tonight (Thursday), and a lot of people in the industry are getting very excited. All of which leaves them all somewhat nonplussed.

"We've only done a few gigs," says Pete. "It's great that people like us, but we need to work on our act a lot more."

"Yeah," interjects Chrissie. "At the moment, people mainly know about us 'cause of the single, but the stage act's rather different. A lot of the songs have been around for quite a while, and I'm now writing stuff that's a bit . . . well, there's a thing we do that's close to a Barry White number, another that's reminiscent of Otis Redding material, and another that's straight country and western."

UNFORTUNATELY, the system has a tendency to single out any girl in an otherwise male group, making her the star of the show (Tina Weymouth of Talking Heads being the only exception that I can immediately think of). But things are a little different with the Pretenders because (a) Chrissie Hynde is a damn fine guitarist in her own right, and thus an integral part of the band rather than a stage-front siren, and (b) because she won't let it happen.

"I think everyone in the band", she glances around at them for confirmation, "will have to depend on each other when we're rehearsing or playing. We all

"

respect what each other is doing and, unlike a lot of bands who hate each other's guts, we're very friendly on a social level."

"The reason it's taken me so long to get a band together is because I've been unable to find musicians who can suss my music, and these guys can . . . I mean I got really sick of people coming up to me and saying, 'Hi Chrissie, what're you up to', and I'd tell 'em I was trying to get a band sorted out, and they'd say 'Oh yeah, weren't you doing that last year?'

"We all work on the arrangements together and the guys alter bits or add bits . . . it's not a case of me going in and saying 'Look here, you guys, here's the song and this is how I want to do it,' it's a joint effort."

Anyone who's been to one of the handful of Pretenders gigs will attest to the band's tenacious drive, their individual musicianship and the originality of their material. Further reckless claims I'll leave to more eloquent scribes, but once you've come to terms with how good they are live, check out Chrissie's lyrics. Lack of space obviates their inclusion here, but the point of this story is to illustrate that here is one very sharp, very amusing young lady, who's got a lot of experiences on which to draw. Finely-drafted observations are the result.

And any smart-arse quips about her being the black-haired Blondie are likely to get you a swift knee in the nuts.

Mark Williams

12

Banging on the White House door

THE CLASH
February 24 1979

CLEVELAND squats untidily, like a ragged child on a street corner begging for relief, beneath the bleak winter expanse of Lake Erie. A lunatic February wind whistles up its skirts; a blizzard of snow whips relentlessly down upon the frozen municipal heart.

The TWA Boeing out of New York bucks and shudders in the virulent turbulence as it circles above the city in a nervous orbit. Cleveland grins with callous indifference to our distress: a city as attractive in the chilling dark as a hare-lip, as thrilling, potentially, as an elbow in the throat.

Cleveland! Cleveland! Home of the Rockefellers and Standard Oil. Home of the Hanna Mining Corporation and Republic Steel and the Consolidation Coal Company: economic dynasties which for two generations have controlled, with imperialistic authority, the industrial heartlands of America.

Cleveland! Hey, home – home, too, of the Cuyahoga: a river so polluted by the waste of Ohio's industrial expansion that it once exploded into flames.

Burn on, big river, burn on!

Lisa picks me up from the airport in her battered Pontiac cab – a rusted, scarred relic of some former affluence, it now seems a tired apology for Cleveland's present economic disasters. Cleveland used to be a *great* city, Lisa says. Now it's on the edge of bankruptcy, already in the throes of an urban crisis more severe than that of virtually any other city in the United States.

The city owes more than 15 million dollars to six Ohio banks. The banking interests are demanding either the money or financial control of the city. Cleveland's young mayor, Dennis Kucinich, is fighting for the city's independence and for the welfare and future of the poor whites and blacks lingering helplessly in the slums and ghettoes of Cleveland's inner boroughs. The affluent white middle class has long since retreated to the suburbs.

Lisa throws the cab into a slow motion curve across the highway. Its tyres spin wildly, clamouring frantically for purchase on the ice. I roll around in the back of the Pontiac like a midget in John Wayne's coffin.

We drive on through derelict downtown areas. Cars pass us in a somnambulant parade, creeping and sliding through the treacherous slush. Ice and snow are banked high on both sides of the highway. Lisa says Cleveland is enjoying a mild winter. I shiver and chainsmoke. The streets through which we are skating are illuminated by the dull, exhausted glow of neon signs, flickering from pool halls, bars, porno cinemas – "Eroticinemas" – and assorted lowlife dives.

A drunk stumbles down the sidewalk like a newsprint yeti, wrapped in old newspapers. He collapses head first into a snowdrift and does not move. Groups of bored men gather in windswept doorways along the route. They stamp their feet, pass around bottles. Their breath is frozen on the night air like signatures of disaffection.

Lisa says on a night like this there ain't no one on the street who ain't up to something *ba-a-ad*.

Unemployment and crime are partners here in an unholy marriage. Lisa says it ain't so bad in the winter. People are too cold to kill. The summers, though, that's when it gets *real* heavy. You pack artillery for your own protection, or you go home via the hospital.

"In the summer," Lisa says. "It's like someone declared war, you know, but forgot to tell the other side. There's so many unemployed, they get drunk, they get restless, they kill people. There's a lot of dope murders, a lot of drunk killing. They say the unemployment ain't so bad no more. But I don't see *my* man in work. No sir. Times like this, though in the winter – it don't get so bad. People don't get out so much, you know. Mosta the guys who get killed know each other, you see. . . they hang out together in the bars and they got no one else to fight. . . they get intoxicated and argue and start fighting, and *bang* – someone's dead. I'm just surprised there's enough of them to go at it again after other folk when it gets to be summer again. . . . I'll drop you around the backa th'hotel. It's kinda *safer*."

THE Clash, according to the schedule so kindly provided for me by CBS, are by this time meant to have checked into Swingo's Celebrity Hotel. The Clash, however, are lost somewhere between Oklahoma City and Cleveland.

Their tour opened on January 31, in Vancouver. They then travelled to San Francisco for two gigs (one promoted by Bill Graham, who left the city almost as soon as they arrived, and the other a benefit concert for a new venue, whose promoters, ironically, are attempting tò break Graham's stranglehold on SF's rock promotions). There followed a concert at the Santa Monica Civic. Then, while the roadcrew drove directly across the Midwest to Cleveland, the band lit out for the Southwest, on a three-day trip through Arizona, Kansas and Texas, travelling in a coach hired from Waylon Jennings.

"We wanted to see America," Mick Jones later tells me. "It wasn't entirely successful. I kept falling asleep. It was a long drive. . . ."

When I arrive at Swingo's, they are winging in from Oklahoma. The bus had clapped out at some point during their trek. It's now in Nashville being repaired. I am, however, presently indifferent to any problems encountered by the Clash. At the hotel it's a definite Bethlehem vibe. They don't have a room for your exhausted correspondent. How typical, I think, of the efficiency of CBS Records! The fellow at the desk suggests I try the Holiday Inn on East 22nd Street.

"It's not too far," he advises. "You can go out the back way. That's quicker. But, if I were you, I'd go out the front. It's a longer walk, but there's more light – you'll be able to see anyone coming at you. . . ."

I thank him for his consideration and trudge on out into the cold embrace of the blizzard. I am three blocks from the Holiday Inn when a large black geezer steps out of a doorway, a smile like a half-moon dissecting his face.

"Carry your bags, man? Where you goin', uh?"

I thank *him* for his courtesy, but refuse his polite offer. I walk on, head down, teeth clenched, eyes shut tight, fearing the absolute worst. I open my eyes a fraction and see, my heart leaping, a police car cruising down the street. I look back. The freelance bell-hop has vanished.

I check into the Holiday Inn, still in one piece.

I WAIT an hour for a call from Swingo's telling me that the Clash have finally arrived in Cleveland. It doesn't come. I decide to investigate the city's nightlife alone. I don't however, feel inclined to wander too far from the hotel, and settle finally into Bumper's, a bar adjacent to the Holiday Inn.

One of the cops from the hotel ambles in for a drink. "You're new," he letches at the waitress. She smiles indulgently, and avoids his groping, fat arm. "Kinda *cute*, too," smirks the cop. "I'll have a shot of Bourbon. . . The name's Don. What's *yours*, uh?" The waitress scurries off, a look of bored anguish on her face.

A pianist on a dais next to the bar begins to play. "My Life." No one is listening. He tries to attract the attention of a couple of women sitting across the room from him. One of them, a blonde with makeup on her face so thick it resembles an aerial photograph of the Colorado mudflats, smiles back at him. There is a cage hanging from the ceiling behind her. There are two parakeets in the cage. They begin to squawk hysterically.

"*Shut those fucken birds up,*" someone yells.

A passing waitress smacks the bars of the cage with a plastic tray. The birds scream and fly about the cage, smacking into the bars. Feathers float down into the drinks of the two women. The pianist begins a soulful version of "Help Me Make It Through The Night." He smiles, suggestively, at the blonde. She turns away with exaggerated coyness. Outside a police siren is serenading the moon above Lake Erie.

So this is Cleveland. I feel an immediate nostalgia for my safe European home. I return to Room 607, carrying my jetlag like a haversack full of bricks.

An hour later, Caroline Coon – who took over the management of the Clash last year when they sacked Bernie Rhodes – calls from Swingo's. The group have arrived. They had been detained for five hours because of fog at Oklahoma airport. They're in the bar at Swingo's if I want to meet them. I decline the invitation. I can hear drunken laughter from the street below; I don't relish the idea of being turned over on my way from the Holiday Inn to Swingo's. I tell her I'll meet them in the morning. She tells me nothing will happen until the group meets for the soundcheck at Cleveland's Agora club at 4.30 the following afternoon. I say goodnight.

JOE Strummer comes tumbling into the cocktail bar at Swingo's, resplendent in a fluorescent pink jacket, his hair in a Brylcreemed quiff. He hides behind aviator shades. His face is swollen from a visit that morning to a Cleveland dentist. He has a abcess on a tooth, which he refuses to have extracted. He is suffering, too, from the prolonged after-effects of the hepatitis he contracted last year. Furthermore, he has a savage gash on his lower right arm. He cut it on his guitar during the Clash's first North American concert in Vancouver.

"I keep ripping it open," he mentions. "I have to bind it up in Gaffa tape before a gig. . . I think it's turning septic . . ." I wince as he rolls up his sleeve to show me the weeping wound.

The gig in Vancouver had been especially memorable, I learn. The audience, from all accounts, went berserk. They'd refused the Clash an easy exit, demanding three encores before the band had been able to leave the stage. Then they canned the road crew as they attempted to clear the equipment. To prevent a riot, the Clash reappeared to play another number.

"Trouble was," Topper Headon recalls, "they didn't stop canning the stage. Bottles kept bouncing off us as we were playing . . . It was like England." Headon finished the gig with his head split open in three places.

Strummer has an amusing anecdote about the Clash's gig at the Santa Monica Civic in Los Angeles.

It seems that to celebrate the Clash's introduction to America, CBS (or to be precise, Epic), had decided to fly over to Los Angeles many of its most influential personalities.

"Everyone deemed important enough," Strummer continues, with a bitter disgust he makes no attempt to disguise "to get a return ticket and an expense account weekend in Los Angeles was flown out to see us. . . ."

There were, he estimates, about 40, maybe 50, executives in California to see the Clash: vice-presidents, area vice-presidents, regional managers, regional vice-managers. . . the kind of crew you might recall were at the CBS Convention two weeks ago in Dallas. Hey, ho – have a successful day and keep thinking platinum. . . Strummer was having none of it.

"I was disgusted that they were there. . . they've done nothing for us. And there they were, pouncing about backstage with their slimy handshakes and big smiles. I just ignored them, you know. . . I don't have any time for it. All that record company bullshit. . . .

"Like, I heard that they'd been taking the journalists who were coming to see us out for, like, nine-course meals before the gig. *Nine-course meals.* I've never had a nine course meal in my life. I can't even imagine what a nine-course meal is like. I mean, what kind of person eats a *nine-course fucking meal* before a *rock'n' roll show?* I think it's disgusting . . . a *disgrace* . . . that we should be even associated with something like that."

The Clash played the gig. The audience, again from all accounts, went berserk. The group, exhausted, fell into their dressing room.

143

It was full of executives from Epic. They were escorted by Susan Blond, from the Epic press office in New York. She organised the beaming, sycophantic executives into a neatly defined group, for a photograph with the Clash. The group, sweating and tired, were hustled into the front row and asked to pose, happily, for the camera . . .

"There were these four seats and they told us to sit on 'em," Strummer recalls. "This was right after the gig, right? We'd just come off stage, right? We were worried about how we'd played, right? We were worried about whether we'd given a good show, right? We were wondering what those people – *the ones who'd paid for their tickets* – had really thought about us, right? We'd wanted to give them the best fucking rock'n' roll show they'd ever seen, right. . . and these. . . these people come in from the record company . . . and they want their *photos taken with us*. For *Billboard* or some crap like that.

"We don't care, you know, if it's some fan with an Instamatic backstage at the Glasgow Apollo. We'll pose for the picture or whatever, sign autographs, talk to him – you know, that's part of the reason we're *there* . . .

"But these creeps, you know. . . so they're all lined up, and we line up in front of them, smiling, like the good little boys they want us to be . . . and just as they're about to take the photo we just walk out, all four of us. And they're all looking at us as we walk out with their mouths open. 'Cos they've flown right across America to, like, have their photo taken with us. They haven't come to see us play. . .

"And this guy comes out to us, where we're standing in the corridor having a beer, and he says, 'If I was you guys, I'd go back in there and apologise . . .' We told him to fuck off. We ain't cattle.

"And we were just standing there when all those guys came storming out. They didn't even look at us. Didn't say a word, you know. Just walked straight past us. You could see them *fuming*. It was *great*. It's the *only* way to treat them, you know."

Caroline Coon later verifies Strummer's account of the incident. "Susan Blond came up to me and begged me to get the group back in. I told her I couldn't that they'd only come back in if they wanted to. She told me that the group had *humiliated* the people from Epic.

"They deserved worse than that," Paul Simonon commented.

It is to be presumed that the aforementioned, humiliated Epic executives are no longer "thinking platinum" where the Clash and "Give 'Em Enough Rope" are concerned.

"I don't think they ever believed we'd sell more than ten copies of the record over here," Strummer will counter. "They don't want us here. They think we only want to cause *trouble*. We only wanna play some *music. They* cause all the trouble . . ."

THERE is some truth in Strummer's assertion. As we drive to the Agora, Caroline Coon informs me of some of the difficulties the Clash encountered when they first began to prepare this tour.

"Give 'Em Enough Rope" was released in America at the same time as it hit the racks in Britain. The reviews were more than favourable; Greil Marcus in Rolling Stone and Lester Bangs in New York's Village Voice, in fact, eulogised the album in the most flattering manner.

From the reviews and the past interest in the Clash, which had grown around the import sales of their debut album (never released by Columbia in America), it was clear to the group and their manager, at least, that an American tour could only be beneficial to the future of the Clash.

The majority of their contemporaries had already made brief appearances in the States; and the major competition (the Boomtown Rats, Elvis Costello) were planning exhaustive Spring campaigns. They couldn't afford to miss the chance of cutting in between the Costello tour (already under way), and the Rats' offensive later this month. A hit and run, seven-date tour was suggested, taking in Vancouver, San Francisco, L.A., Cleveland, Washington, Boston and New York.

These were all areas in which the Clash believed (correctly, it would transpire) they could be assured of maximum audience attendances. They told Epic of their determined intention to tour America.

Epic were not enthusiastic.

"Basically," Caroline Coon recalls, "they told us not to come. They said the album wasn't getting any airplay. We told them we didn't care, we were coming anyway. They told us they had the *Fabulous Poodles* and *Toto* on the road and that they wouldn't, therefore, be able to look after us properly. We told them we didn't care, we'd look after ourselves. They said they didn't think they could afford to subsidise the tour. We'd worked out a budget of 40,000 dollars – which is relatively cheap, because we were bringing our own crew – which they said they couldn't give us.

"By this time, I'd spent £3,000 of my own money, flying over here, organising the tour, talking to promoters, finding Bo Diddley who we wanted to support us . . . they said they still didn't want us to come.

"I said they couldn't stop us, we were coming anyway. That was a bluff, really . . . we couldn't have afforded to come . . . they said they didn't want Bo Diddley. Even the promoters who were enthusiastic about the Clash didn't think it would be a good idea to tour with Bo Diddley. They said that he'd be bottled off stage or something. That audiences wouldn't listen. I said that if Bo Diddley got bottles thrown at him at a Clash gig then the Clash wouldn't play . . .

"It was getting absurd. We were all set to come. Epic still wouldn't give us the money we wanted. Then they agreed to a budget of 30,000 dollars. So we agreed. Now we're having difficulty getting *that* out of them."

But the Clash *are* here, despite the obstacles, and they are here on their own terms. They have with them their own crew (John Green, their tour manager, Ace Pina, their American tour manager, a four man sound crew and their own DJ, Barry Myers – "spinning the current English hits between sets" as Rolling Stone would have it).

"One of the principal reasons," Caroline Coon explains, "we were so determined to come was to prove to Epic that *they* could sell our records and *we* could sell out our shows." So far, the Clash have sold out their shows (the Palladium in New York was sold out in three days). Epic have yet to match that with record sales.

"It's about time they started," is Strummer's succinct comment on *that* one.

THE gig in Cleveland is at a benefit concert for a Vietnam veteran, Larry McIntyre. Mcintyre got his legs blown off in Vietnam while serving his country, his flag and his God. He recently moved into a new apartment in Cleveland. The apartment block had, for the use of its occupants, a swimming pool, Mcintyre likes swimming. It's one of the few recreational sports in which he can participate.

One day he wheeled himself up to the pool and plunged into the water. His neighbours were horrified. They called the owners of the apartment block. There's a man *with no legs* swimming in our pool, they cried. Larry was banned from the pool because the sight of him swimming around with no legs was more than his neighbours could possibly tolerate. They thought it distasteful. Larry's now suing them all. The benefit is to raise money for his legal fees.

Caroline Coon and I arrive at the Agora to find the Clash mid-way through their soundcheck.

The club has the look of a more salubrious 100 Club. It's much larger. It has carpets, even. A games room, too, full of pinball machines. Two long bars, flanking the stage. There are potted plants hanging from the low ceiling. There are oak beams, and chandeliers hanging above the tables. There are mock Tudor arches and heavy oak doors.

The band complete their soundcheck and skip on out, back to the hotel, leaving the stage to Alex Bevan, a rather boring local folksinger who'll later be opening the show. I hang about the gig with Caroline Coon. She complains about the lack of any promotional display in the club's foyer. There's all kinds of paraphernalia for the Ramones, who'll be playing here within the next week. There is only the sleeve of "Give 'Em Enough Rope", loosely pinned to a wall, to advertise the Clash. She curses the local Epic marketing man. "He said it wasn't his fault," she will later say. "But he's on the list, anyway."

Bo Diddley, a massive man whose mood swings unpredictably from high good humour to exaggerated, almost theatrical pessimism, stops to talk with Caroline. I sit in some awe as he enquires after Strummer's health. He has heard about his inflamed tooth.

Bo Diddley has had personal experience of toothache (like almost everything else) on the road, as he informs us with an obvious flair for melodrama.

"Ah wuz on tour one time. Got this sunuvabitch tooth playin' hell, man. I wen' ta this den'is, yeah . . . he tol' me Ah'd be fine. Ah wuz half way 'cross Texas when that dude *went*. Gave me no warnin' . . . Jes' hit me. Sonuvagun. Ah made mah driver pull over right there . Got tah th' neares' den'is' an' got him outta bed. Made him chisel that dude right outta mah head. Yah tell that boy tah watch hisself. Get s'me oila cloves," he adds, revealing a characteristically practical turn of mind.

"An' tell him not ta worry. If he can mek th' gig, he's doin' awright," he continues. "Ya mek th' gig, you got the money. Tek it from an' old hand. Tek that dollar. 'N fuck the res'. As long as you got that dollar in yo' hand, yo' doin' awright. Y' needs th' dollar. Cuz when yo' *finished*, that's *it*. Ain't no one gonna come nowhere wi' money for' you' when yo' finished. When a bucket loses its bottom, *everythin'* goes, man . . ."

And Bo Diddley laughs his Bo Diddley laugh, which is both startling and infectious "*Yeeeeuch*," he laughs, a deep chuckle in his throat, rising to an hysterical shriek, "*yeeeuch*."

I reflect, as Bo Diddley heads back to his dressing room, complaining of a cold settling on his chest, that the Clash's idea of having him open their American show has been taken in some quarters as an insult. It seems like another instance of the Clash's good intentions being unfortunately interpreted as a mercenary or insensitive manoeuvre.

Caroline Coon explains that the group wanted him as their opening act to remind American audiences (who were the first to forget) where their music came from.

Certainly, they went to enough trouble to secure his presence on the Pearl Harbour '79 Tour. Caroline finally tracked him down in Australia. He wanted to know, what the group was like. Then he wanted to know how much money they were offering him. She told him. He didn't care any more what the group sounded like. I was unable to discover how much exactly Bo Diddley is being paid for the tour. I do know that he'll come out of it with substantially more than the Clash though.

"He's doing it for the money, basically," Mick Jones will tell me, backstage at the Ontario theatre in Washington. "But I don't mean that to sound rude or anything. . . I mean, he's being going, you know, for so long. . . and people have ripped off his music and his money and everything else. . . so, you know, he's not going to do anything unless, he's decently paid for it. He doesn't have to be here with us . . . he didn't have to drive with us from Cleveland, and spend, like ten hours on a bus. . . he gets as much as he deserves. . . but the thing is, really, that he really seems to be enjoying himself. He's really well into it."

There's nothing at all facetious, either, in Strummer's clear adulation of Bo Diddley, which he openly confesses.

"I can't," he says, "look at him without my mouth falling open."

BO Diddley's pick-up band in Cleveland – "cats everywhere can play mah music" – wouldn't exactly set the earth on fire with their playing. They latch onto the beat and doggedly hang in there to the bitter end, but they have difficulty keeping pace with the leader's sprightly imagination. Time and again, he leaves them stranded (and seems to amuse himself considerably by so doing), as he scoots off during the middle of a familiar tune into some musical territory entirely unfamiliar to them.

The set is dedicated entirely to history. To the Beat. To the legend of "Bo Diddley." He struts and hollers, and hollers and struts. He tells the audience how much he loves them; how much he appreciates their support over these last 23 years. I look around. I feel like I'm the oldest person in the audience, and I was barely out of the cradle when Bo Diddley first started playing and recording.

He holds aloft his guitar (a new, custom-built job, made in Australia, it cost a mere £28,000). "Ah love you," he tells the audience. "Ah come up here tonight.. . Ah got the mos' terrible cold, y'hear . . . but that's how much Ah love yah. . . Ah come'n play mah music – even though Ah feel as poor as hell. . . thank you."

DURING the short break before the Clash appear, I mince around the audience. It's a sight that would have alarmed the Sunday People two years ago – "they've definitely caught up with the spirit of '77," Mick Jones observes – they're all done out in dog collars and safety pins. The girls have green hair. The guys wear their tears like medals.

I stand against the sign advertising a forthcoming appearance by Elvis Costello.

"You, uh, commen t'see Elvuss?" one Cleveland stereotype punk asks his chum.

"Nah. . . *everyone's* seen Elvuss. . . Yah can't go *anywhere* Elvuss ain't played, man. I jes' wanna see *Ultravox*, man. That's *my only fucken dream* . . . To see Ultravox . . ."

THE Clash are waiting backstage at the Agora. They are impatient. They want to *play*. Mick Jones sits slightly apart from the rest of the band. "Comeoncomeoncomeoncomeon," he keeps repeating. Paul Simonon has his bass plugged into the practice amp; he plays the same nagging riff over and over. Strummer prowls around, running a comb through his hair. Topper Headon practices his martial arts poses.

I hadn't seen the Clash on the boards for a fair old time. Since the shambolic Mont de Marsan punk festival in the summer of 1977, as it happens. We hadn't parted on the best of terms, as I remember. And I certainly didn't know what to expect from them in Cleveland.

The reports of their last London shows (from the Clash Sort It Out tour) didn't help at all. Many of the reviewers seemed to spend most of their time attempting to deny that they had ever seen anything in the band. They were mostly smug putdowns, accusing the Clash of having wilfully exploited the naivety of their original audience with all that sulphate-waffle about high-rise nightmares and the sound of the Westway and stenguns in Knightsbridge. Most took the view that the Clash myth was dying in its combat boots.

Fair enough, I thought, never having been known for giving them a good notice myself, and prepared myself for a far slicker version of the Clash storming the gates of heaven than I'd previously encountered. I imagined, really, a kind of gross heavy-metal onslaught, the slogans intact, but the passion threadbare.

I was surprised that they sounded no different, really, than they had two-and-a-half years ago at the 100 Club.

The sound quality may have improved slightly, but I wouldn't bet my life on the thin edge of the improvement. Strummer's vocals are still buried, the lyrics almost entirely lost (but, then, maybe, I'm one of the people who was NEVER meant to be able to decipher them). And, looking at him, all criticism of his increasingly stylised performance seems so much waffling on the old Adler; he looks and sings and jerks and stares with no greater premeditation than ever he did with the 101ers.

He still can't sing and successfully change chords on the guitar, he still sings with more conviction (even when, to some ears, it's misguided or confused) than most of his bleating contemporaries; though he still resorts to merely bellowing when his passion gets the better of his control.

The rough edges of their collective performance remain untutored and blatant. Mick Jones may adopt the familiar poses of the guitar hero, but such a mantle sits awkwardly upon his shoulders . . . it all gives the illusion, however fleeting, of a rough-house spontaneity that I find quite becoming.

They begin (predictably, perhaps, but it's difficult not to smile at their cheek) with a raucous "I'm So Bored With The USA", and already the fists of the audience are punching the air as they clamber hysterically about the front of the stage, climbing upon one another's shoulders, gobbing – yes! – at the group.

A surprisingly powerful version of "Jail Guitar Doors" (which always sounded so *weedy* on record), is followed by a brief announcement from Strummer thanking the audience for "the bits of information and bits of paper in envelopes you managed to smuggle backstage . . ."

They play "Tommy Gun", the final passage of which, with Strummer screaming like an epileptic being electrified, sends a cold shiver up the spine.

"Glad you've all come tonight," Strummer shouts, "and been so free with your money for this guy wot's got no legs . . . and, uh, fuck you lot at the back with the American/English dictionaries . . .

The words to the next number are in Japanese . . ."

The next number is "City Of The Dead" . . .

WHEREVER we go," Mick Jones says backstage at the Ontario theatre in Washington, "we're always given these bits of paper that say, 'From the City of the Dead'. They all think *they're* living in the City of the Dead . . . I got this one tonight, I got some more in Cleveland. . . actually, I think they were probably *right* in Cleveland . . . it was a bit *awful*, wasn't it?"

THE next number, Strummer is telling Cleveland, "is off our first LP, released in 1965 . . . "Ate 'n' Wah'," he screams as Mick Jones hops across the stage to take the lead vocals. How quaint it sounds! It's rather like listening to "Masters Of War" or "Eve Of Destruction" or, perhaps more accurately, Hedgehopper's Anonymous's "Goodnews Week"! The Clash, it seems, are becoming as an anachronistic as any of the bands they sought to replace, having replaced one system of cliches with another.

An indifferent "Clash City Rockers", with a weak guitar solo and garbled vocals, redeemed from inconsequentiality only by Headon's robust skinwork, relieves none of the doubt. "White Man In Hammersmith Palais," is interrupted by the flow of bodies being bowled over the footlights and passed backstage – the crush at the front is murderous – much to Mick Jones' concern; his face is washed with anxiety.

Then they hit the audience with "Safe European Home", which really is (next to the overlooked "The Prisoner", the B-side of the "Hammersmith" single) one of the few *complete* and distinctive songs they've ever written. They pursue the climax of their set through "Stay Free" (much more virile than the vinyl prototype), "English Civil War" ("what are you on – stilts?" asks Strummer of someone trying to get on the stage, via someone else's back). "Guns On The Roof" (more propulsive drumming here from Headon), the obligatory "Police And Thieves", "Janie Jones" (more instant nostalgia), and "Garageband". They commit the final chords of the song to Cleveland's memory and split. . .

"Sex Pistols! SEX PISTOLS!" the guy behind me begins to chant, reviving a yell he had begun much earlier.

"When did you ever see the Sex Pistols?" I ask him.

"SID!" he shouts, his eyes wild, his girlfriend staggering on his arm.

"You *ever* see the Sex Pistols?" I ask again for some reason angry

"Naaaah, man . . . never saw 'em . . . wish to fuck I had man, I'd throw *tables* to see the Sex Pistols . . ."

The Clash race back on the stage, whip through an uninspiring "Julie's Been Working For The Drug Squad" (easily the weakest number in their repertoire), "White Riot" (flying the banner of '77, again), "Complete Control" and "What's My Name", which is a weak climax (no nudge, as Simon Frith might say).

But the audience is ecstatic.

I talk to a guy called Eric Schindling backstage. He and six friends have driven from Lawrence, Kansas, to see the Clash. It had been a 20-hour drive – it's 900 miles from good ol' Lawrence – and it's taken all their money to finance the trek.

"Hell. . . yeah. . . sure it was worth it, man. We saw the Pistols in Tulsa. And after the Pistols there was only one other group to see. The Clash. . . Nah – it weren't too much of a drive. Like, people drove right across the States to see the King Tut exhibition. Us coming to see the Clash is just like them driving across America to see King Tut, "And at least the Clash are still alive. . ."

The next morning, in the lobby of Swingo's, no one looks too healthy (there had been a bit of a party after the gig at the Agora).

The original tour schedule had the Clash leaving Cleveland at noon for

Washington in Waylon Jennings' bus. Two hours later we're sitting around in the lobby of the hotel.

It turns out that the Clash, at the moment, are financially embarrassed: they can't pay the hotel bill. Caroline Coon has been on the telephone all morning to Epic in New York, demanding that they wire out enough money to Cleveland to cover the bill. The Epic person to whom she must speak to authorise the payment of the bill has been in a meeting, she is told. It looks at one point as if the group will have to do a runner.

"I told Epic," says Caroline, "that they could meet us at the State border. We'd be the bus with the Highway Patrol chasing it . . ."

Topper Headon appears. He has been watching a local news programme on the television. There had been a feature on last night's benefit at the Agora. It had stated that Bo Diddley headlined the gig. There was even an interview with him. There had been no mention of the Clash.

"Which channel was it on?" I ask.

"Channel 8."

"Which network is that?"

"I dunno – probably CBS," Headon replies sarcastically.

"It is CBS," a local fan confirms.

"*Whaaaat?* cries Headon, incredulously. "Fuckin' typical. What a circus."

The bus finally leaves the cold clutches of Cleveland at 3.00 p.m. and we settle down for a 10-hour drive across America to Washington D.C. It is snowing as we hit the highway. . . "It's gonna get a bunch worse, too," says Bo Diddley, pessimistic to the last.

Strummer, Simonon and Mick Jones have retired to the rear lounge of the coach; the rest of the party sits up front in the main compartment listening to tapes and watching television and videos.

The countryside spreads out on either side of us; a vast plain of ice and snow, frozen lakes and rivers, isolated farmhouses, truckstops. . . I begin to wonder whose movie I'm in, as the view through the windscreen begins to resemble the opening credits of How The West Was Won. Darkness falls as the giant Exxon signs light up and snow piles down harder, freezing on the windscreen. We have to stop regularly to chip off the ice.

"Maaaa-a-aan, it's gonna be a baaad night," Bo Diddley intones gravely, rolling his eyes like white marbles beneath the brim of his stetson. "Ah wuz drivin' this way once," he recalls, and we all listen, "th' road jes' wen' from unner me. Wen' straight over th'hill, whhhoooosh . . ." His large hand glides through the air.

I ask whether he's suffered much trouble on the road. This cracks him up even more. He literally *howls* with laughter.

'Yoah a *comic* sonuvabitch," he laughs. "Lissen – Ah'm 50 years old. Ah'v lived all mah life in the United States, travelled in every goddam state, an' Ah'm *black*. An' you ask me whether Ah'v eveh been in trouble. . . . *sheeeeit*. Yeeeeeeuch. Ah been in th' kinda trouble. Ah don't care even t' remember. Ah'v had dudes come up to me and put a *gun* to mah head. An' they'd say – 'Nigguh – we gonna blow th' *shit outta youh brains*.' An' Ah'd allus be very *polite* an' say 'Yessuh, sho' you are.' An' then get th' hell on outta there."

I ask which areas he found most troublesome and dangerous.

"Texas," he replies. Then, after a pause, "An' Alabama, an' Kansas, an' Virginia, an' Mississippi, an' Georgia, an' Tennessee, an' Missouri. . . *America*, you know. Yeeeuuuch."

IT is close on 2 a.m. when the bus drives into Washington. We stop on the outskirts of the city for something to eat. Wearily, we pile out of the coach and into the truckstop. Topper Headon looks around at America.

"When it all comes down to it," he remarks, "it's really all just *Finsbury Park*, innit?"

I don't have an answer for him.

THE Clash book into the Americana Hotel at 2.30, after a brief skirmish at the Barbizon Terrace, where they had originally been booked. For some of us, the night is not over. John Green, Simonon, Strummer, Jones, Barry Myers and I make our way to a nearby Italian restaurant for a meal.

Simonon tells us about his trip last year to Moscow; he had been intrigued by the attempted obliteration of the memory of Joe Stalin from the nation's consciousness.

"You won't find his name *anywhere*. In none of the history books, on any of the statues . . . they pulled all his statues down. They even dug up his body. They renamed Stalingrad. . . ."

"You know," says Mick Jones, diverting the conversation towards the group's erstwhile manager, Bernard Rhodes, "I think it was always Bernie's ambition to have a city named after him. . . ."

"Yea," says Strummer, "he was gonna re-name Camden Town. Call it *Berniegrad*."

They are still in litigation with Rhodes, Strummer says, but no date has yet been fixed for an official hearing.

"We haven't spoken to him for a while. He doesn't answer the phone. I suppose he finds it a bit difficult since they took him off to the hospital and put him in a straitjacket . . ."

153

Mick Jones has a map of Washington. He decides he would like to go sightseeing. Now. It is 4.00 a.m. Jones wants to go to Arlington, the military cemetery, where there burns an eternal flame dedicated to the memory of John F. Kennedy.

"*Great*," says Strummer, "let's go and piss on it and put it out."

It is decided, finally, that we'll visit the White House.

It is deathly silent as we drive down Pennsylvania Avenue in search of Jimmy Carter's gaff. We eventually stumble upon the building and slide to a halt across the road from it. The White House looks small, unimposing, almost insignificant.

"*That it?*" asks John Green, disappointed. "Looks like a toilet. It's a garden shed. Don't tell me they run the entire bleedin' world from *that* . . ."

"Just think," says Strummer, "If we had a mortar or a bazooka or some machine guns, we could blow it all away. Just lob a few grenades over the garden wall and wipe them all out. It's worth thinking about. . . ."

"Can we go, please? I'm getting nervous," says Mick Jones. "I can *feel* them looking at us and loading the guns. I don't want to be here when the bullets start flying . . ."

STRUMMER and Headon are sitting in the back of a limo outside the Americana Hotel the next afternoon.

They have been persuaded to drive out to the radio station at Maryland State University to be interviewed. Strummer is furious.

"I hate doing this. It's just so much arse-licking. I'm not prepared to do it. It's the worse thing in the world. I'm here to do a job. And that job is to play the gig, not spend all afternoon poncing about Maryland in a limo talking to idiots . . . I just wanna get on with my job. . . ."

I tell him that Geldof and Johnnie Fingers on their recent radio promotion tour of America visited three or four stations a day for a month.

"They must have been out of their heads, then," he replies tersely.

We drive through the campus of "Maryland State, Strummer's mood darkening as we make our way through groups of dufflecoated students. We arrive outside the radio station building Strummer gets out of the car and walks up the steps to the entrance.

He scoops up a massive block of ice from the steps. He flings it viciously at the glass doors. It shatters with an enormous crash. The glass remains intact, but the impact draws inquisitive faces to the windows of the buildings around us.

"Place looks like a dog ranch," Strummer mutters as we step inside.

STRUMMER and Headon are being interviewed by a fresh-faced girl called Audrey. It is clear from her opening remarks that she knows little about the Clash. Strummer and Headon are in no mood to offer any pertinent information. They act dumb, answering her questions monosyllabically, with terse replies and occasional mumbles.

Audrey asks Strummer how the Clash got together.

"We all met in the street one day," he replies.

"I bumped into him, and he knew the other two," Topper adds, not very helpfully.

"Me and him were odd-job merchants," Strummer says. "The other two were at art school. . ."

"How does an art major get into music?" Audrey asks.

"Because art is so *boring*, init?" Strummer says.

Audrey wants to know whether there was some concept behind "Give 'Em Enough Rope". Strummer thinks it over.

"Concept . . . mmmm . . . no."

There was no message the Clash wanted to get over to their audience?

"I just want to educate the world on how to speak Japanese," Strummer says.

"Yeah . . ." says Audrey, fascinated. "I didn't hear a whole lot of Japanese on the album . . ." She is sure, however, that there was something more to the record; some significant message.

"Maybe," says Strummer. "But we don't like to brag about it . . ."

"How did you guys break into London?" Audrey asks.

"We *kicked* our way in," says Strummer.

"*Literally?*" asks Audrey, astonished.

"IT was a pathetic waste of time. We should never have done it. Caroline told me that radio station reaches 40,000 people. More like 40. If that station has 40,000 listeners, I'm Bob Geldof.. . It was like a hospital radio, where you go in and speak to all the cripples. . . I've done that in my time, too. . ."

We are sitting in the restaurant of the Americana Hotel, Strummer, Mick Jones, Paul Simonon, photographer Bob Gruen and I. Strummer is still complaining bitterly about the radio interview. We are joined by Caroline Coon. Joe turns his complaints against her. I don't mean to eavesdrop, but I can't ignore their conversation.

"We shouldn't have done it," Strummer repeats for Caroline's benefit. She looks a little exasperated, but tries to be patient. "No one told me what it would be like. I shouldn't have to go driving around half of Maryland with some pansy journalists. I shouldn't have to go to these radio stations and talk to these morons.. . no one told me it was gonna be like this."

"I know how you feel," says Caroline.

"No. You don't. *That's* the point," Strummer argues. "You should sit down and think about it before you arrange these things. It would have been better to spend the afternoon in my room, reading a book or watching TV or something. We're here to do one job – play the gig. *That's* what we should be concentrating on. What we should be doing is going out and playing the best rock'n' roll show these people have ever seen and piss off . . ."

"That's what we *are* doing," says Caroline. "But at the same time I *know* that radio stations are the key to America. I'm sorry. I *thought* you wanted to get through to as many people as possible. I was wrong."

"*Spare* me the sarcasm, Caroline, will you," says Strummer bitterly, ending the conversation.

THE television lights cast a harsh glare on the drab walls of the dressing room, back stage at the Ontario theatre, which is a converted cinema in downtown Washington. The television crew, cameras and sound equipment strapped to their backs, follow Bo Diddley around the room.

Mick Jones and Paul Simonon look on in amusement as Diddley performs for the cameras. Strummer, whose mood has brightened considerably since the afternoon, watches in some awe.

"How do you feel," asks the television interviewer, "about all these people who've copped your licks over the years, Bo?"

"Hey, ma-a-an," laughs Bo Diddley. "Everybody does it. Look at the Japanese. They cop *everybody's* licks. Can't do a thing abut it, though."

"Why are you on tour with this group, the Clash; Bo?"

"Cuz they *asked* me. An' it's an honour an' Ah'm happy t'be here. They're nice dudes. Everything's goin' beautiful. The shows are sold out. The kids go wild when they see this band. It reminds me of the Fifties."

JOE Strummer is sitting on the bus after the Washington gig; people clamber over him, settling down for the overnight journey to Boston, another 10-hour drive.

"I don't feel *un*happy, you know," he tells Mick Jones. "But I don't feel particularly *happy*, either. I just feel sort of *good*, you know? I'm just glad that it's over . . ."

"I thought it was a good gig," says Mick Jones. "I thought it was all right in the end. . . smashed the neck right off my fucking guitar though. . . 'sfunny, I used to *hate* bands that smashed their instruments . . ."

Jones had smashed the neck of his guitar during the final onslaught of "London's Burning"/"White Riot", as the Clash's set roared to a furious climax.

There had, earlier, been hints of disaster. The vocal mix throughout much of the first half of the set was a soggy blur; and often the group's musical thrust had lost its impetus, with only Headon's drumming urging them forward.

"Hate And War" had collapsed into chaos, probably the lowest point of the show. "City Of The Dead" – "this one's for Sid," Strummer declared – revived the tempo, and "Safe European Home" continued the improvement. They lost touch again with the rising momentum after a ragged "Police and Thieves," but a powerful "Capital Radio" (soon to be released on an EP alongside "I Fought The Law" and "Groovy Times", incidentally) had set up the audience for the climax and the encores. Strummer was even smiling as he left the stage with a rose in his teeth. . .

"I thought we played fuckin' great," says Topper. "Why be bashful?"

The weather forecast on the radio predicts snow and ice and sleet and all kinds of horrors on the highway to Boston.

Bo Diddley rolls his eyes and tucks into his bag for his bottle of Rock & Rye (a lethal concoction that tastes like marmalade and paraffin). "It's gone be a muthuh of a ride. It's gonna be another baaaaaaad night," he declares, as optimistic as Cassandra with the Greeks coming over the walls of Troy. . . "We'd best be goin' before we're frozen . . ."

The engine of the bus starts ticking over.

This is where I leave them. I stumble off the bus, into the snow. The bus draws away slowly on the icy road, and is lost in the night.

I walk back to the hotel. With Jimmy Carter in Mexico City, there seemed nowhere else to go.

Allan Jones

13

Fear of flying

BLONDIE

March 3 1979

NEW YORK. SUNDAY: Picture this (if you can): Deborah Harry, pin-up Empress of the Lipstick Vogue, stands alone in the kitchen of the modest penthouse apartment she shares with friend and business associate Chris Stein. She wears a bright red sweater and a bewildered look.

She seems to be studying intensely some form of literature. A closer examination reveals that she grips an empty pumpkin pie tin in her left hand while perusing a volume titled The Joys Of Cooking.

"Aw . . . shit!" Debbie sounds mildly irritated. "It doesn't say if it should be served hot or cold."

She moves towards the cooker, where a pumpkin lies in a pot. She adds a pint of milk. I examine the result and fail to suppress a brief chuckle.

"I wouldn't laugh," she snaps. "*You're* gonna be eating this."

The blonde head with the black streak stoops. Debbie opens the oven door to reveal a roast duck. She stabs it in the breast. "D'you think it's ready?" But before an opinion is offered, the bird is cooling on the sideboard.

"Right," she mutters. "I gotta go out an' look at some clothes." She puts on her Supergirl outfit and slips out into the New York cold. Dinner will be served when she returns. I mean, can you picture this?

SATURDAY: Realising Harry and Stein's preoccupation with psychic phenomena ("sometimes we don't have to speak to know what the other's thinking") I was sure that they'd appreciate that "Heart Of Glass" is playing, loud and proud, on the radio in the cab which ferries me from La Guardia Airport into New York.

"Phone us soon as you get in," Chris Stein had instructed me, and Debbie's voice welcomes me when I check in.

"Hold on a minute. I'm just scrubbing the bath." This introduction to the domestic Debbie Harry comes as a shock. It seems interestingly at variance from our usual vision of the lady photographed licking a record on the sleeve of "Picture This".

Subtitle this: breaking down the walls of fantasy.

Debbie summons her mate to the phone. He has, she tells me, risen from his bed this minute. Over the next couple of days, Stein's attachment to the mattress becomes very apparent. "C'mon over," he drowsily blurts. "Dunkley'll be here too." Dunkley? The way he says it implies my knowledge of the person. Andy Dunkley? The Living Jukebox? Nah, couldn't be.

I jot down the address and hit the streets of New York, aiming for the Harry/Stein residence on Seventh Avenue.

4.30 pm: I enter the apartment. I don't know what I expected (it being a penthouse "suite", and this being Seventh Avenue), but what I saw persuaded me that "penthouse" does not necessarily equal "de luxe". Luxurious this was not. Comfortable and homely it is.

On the left is a neat, compact kitchen – the tidiest room in the house, in fact. It would have looked perfectly normal, were it not for the five-foot statue of a nun ominously lurking in a corner.

"Uh? Oh, *that*. Chris bought it somewhere for ten dollars," Debbie explains. "See those marks on it? What happened was that we used to share a place with Tommy and Dee Dee Ramone, and they were so freaked by the presence of the nun that they kept attacking it with daggers, trying to kill it. Eventually Chris had to cover the thing with a blanket."

Next to the kitchen is the living room, which isn't really the living room because it doubles as Chris-and-Debbie's music room. Papers, books and tapes are thrown about the place. A battery of reel-to-reel and cassette machines is flanked by two guitars, a Fender bass and a six-string, on their marks and ready for action should Stein and Harry wish to record demos for the next Blondie album. With studio time booked for the next week, the music room has been used a lot recently.

No, if you want the living room you must advance to the bedroom, which, apart from serving as the sleeping quarters, is transformed in the daytime into Chris Stein's office.

Stein's business acumen has increased considerably in the past year, following management mistakes in the early part of Blondie's career, so as often as not he's holed up in the bedroom, telephone to ear, conducting conversations with record company, promoters, management, publicist and whoever. Occasionally he even conducts business meetings in the room.

In the evening, it reverts to the role of leisure-room, where friends from a very tight circle meet to talk and watch television.

Again, the sparseness of material effects is striking: the furniture is confined to a couple of chairs, a double-bed and, of course, the TV – the main source of entertainment in the household.

So this is the home of Blondie's celebrated sweethearts, an unassuming pad which employs a double lock to hold the madness of the music business at bay, and to ensure that they stay out of the in-crowd. It was once occupied by Hollywood actress Lilian Roth, during a particularly heavy drinking spell in the Thirties. Its present occupants are very different. In a rare unguarded moment, Debbie will express a wish for more of this life. "I'd like to spend more time fixing up the place. There's so much to do. But we just don't have that kind of time yet."

The relationship between Stein and Harry is an intimate kinship that touches whatever they become involved in. Stein has unselfishly accepted that his partner will always hog the limelight, and understands the reasons why, to the degree that he is constantly seeking new avenues to explore her strengths and potential. Rock music was an obvious choice to exploit both the voice and the looks. Now he's encouraging a parallel career for Debbie in movies. For her part, Harry is forever hinting that it's a joint venture; beyond question, she realises that her fortunes turned when she struck up a relationship with Chris.

"That's cos there's nowhere to hang out any more," Stein will reply when I suggest that this life with Debbie in New York seems somewhat reclusive. "We used to hang out in places like Max's and CBGB's, but now all we see there is strangers. Also, we got all these people pestering us all the time. But we don't just sit around. Most of our free time is spent working on side projects. Boredom is what causes a lot of hanging out."

WHEN I arrive, Debbie is soaking in the bath, preparing for a photo session later in the evening with Mick Rock. Chris, as is his wont, is prostrate on the bed. Sure enough, perched next to him like an attentive psychiatrist, is Andy Dunkley.

Dunkley has dropped into New York en route to South America for a month-long holiday. Somebody must be pumping more than 5p into this livin' jukebox.

Stein, meantime, insists on demonstrating the versatility of his TV set by flipping through a string of channels via a remote-control unit on a bedside cabinet. America is famous for its multi-channelled television system, but Stein gets double the normal number of stations because he subscribes to Manhattan Cable Television.

This afternoon, though, it's pretty boring fare, so, in an unprecedented burst of energy, he struggles off the bed and opens a cupboard to show Dunkley and me a couple of pieces of art. The first exhibit is rolled up like a poster, but Chris calls it "the only real piece of art we have in the place".

He unfurls the roll to reveal an Andy Warhol *copy*. Not an original, mind you. A copy. What I see there is a cow, just like any cow. Except that *this* cow was photographed by Andy Warhol, who has signed it with a dedication to Chris and Debbie. Dunkley – and I don't care what he says – looks as dumb and apathetic as me. "Great, ain't it?" Stein enthuses. "Yeah," Dunkley tentatively agrees. "Great." I maintain a dignified silence.

The second exhibit is a rough of the album sleeve Stein has photographed and designed for the new Robert Fripp release – "a supernatural album".

Stein and Harry have built a solid friendship with Fripp since the ex-King Crimson figure made his home in New York two years ago, and were probably instrumental in reactivating the guitarist at a time when all sorts of stories about his withdrawal from public life were sailing across the Atlantic. He's jammed with Blondie a couple of times, and made a guest appearance on "Parallel Lines", with an off-the-wall solo on the album's strangest track, "Fade Away And Radiate".

Stein is justifiably satisfied with his stab at graphic design on the Fripp cover, especially as it looks certain that it'll see the light of day. He had a couple of dummies (i.e. rough versions) drawn up for the last Blondie album, but they never got past the planning stage. The graphics and photography are part of the "side projects" he referred to earlier.

"Photography is easy to pursue because I'm already set up to do that," he says. "And I went to art school and studied graphics, too, so I'm just utilising what's at my disposal. My mother was a beatnik painter; I've been around artists all my life."

As Chris collects his scraps and puts them away, Debbie makes her first appearance of the day, resplendent in kimono and dripping hair. She is frantically waving a note allegedly carrying a personal message from Gene Simmons of Kiss.

"Meet me for a drink and talk," Gene pines in the note. The girl of his dreams does a crude parody of his vile tongue-wagging role in Kiss. "A phone number for the black book," she mumbles through a rolling laugh. Chris takes it a little more seriously. "You'd better not call him . . . or else." The number goes into the book all the same.

By early evening, the Harry-Steins are preparing for the photo-session. Decisions, decisions. Debbie is having a furious argument with herself over what to wear, but eventually settles on a beige mini-dress/maxi-jumper with matching wool tights and black heels. Chris has his suit ready, and pulls on a pair of boots that might be described as hob-nails without the nails. Debbie is wide-eyed with disgust.

"Jesus, Chris, you're not wearing *them*, are you?" she screams, staring at his feet in horror.

Chris, lethargic as ever, remains unruffled. "Sure. He's not shooting our feet."

"I hope not," sighs an exasperated Ms. Harry, and we set off downtown to Mick Rock's studio.

It's a strange sensation, standing with Debbie Harry in a main thoroughfare in Manhattan. Stars should not be ignored in the street, but that's what's happening here. In the freezing cold, Debbie shuffles towards the shelter of a shop front, seeking warmth.

Meanwhile Chris is stranded out in the iced road, fruitlessly waving for a cab. They motor past. There are a few close things, but Chris loses out every time. Debbie is fed up, and barks: "C'mon, Chris, for Chrissakes." Stein explains his predicament, but Debbie remains unsympathetic. "Ya gotta be aggressive. That's the only way you'll get a cab. Be fuckin' *aggressive*."

A few minutes later a cab is driving us towards the photo-session.

THE rest of the group, plus girlfriends, are already at Mick Rock's studio by the time we make it. Rock, who used to work for David Bowie, speeds about the place organising the set, having earlier despatched his juniors to collect as many old radios as they could find.

The changing room looks like Take Six in Oxford Street, the boys in the band having brought along their Sunday-best. Nigel Harrison has resurrected clothes from his glitter days with Silverhead. "Mark my words," he warns in a suave English accent, "glitter is returning." After primping and preening, the members of Blondie look so smart that they could pass for models in Freeman's Catalogue.

"Heart of Glass" can be heard on the radio. Clem Burke loses no time in pointing out to me: "Hear this? This is New York's *number one* disco station."

The significance of that, of course, is that "Heart of Glass" has attained credibility with the disco buffs. Who, a year ago, would have dreamed that a new wave band would have a number one *disco* single?

The song was written by Stein and Harry and was born out of their fondness for R&B and soul material – plus the influence of the disco phenomenon itself.

"To us, it sounds like Kraftwerk," Debbie maintains. "It's certainly influenced by them. It's just a syncopated sound. It's disco, yet at the same time it's not disco. It's neither. We really like Donna Summer and the Bee Gees. That stuff is good if you're open-minded about it and you don't make a big political deal outta it."

"With me, it's a psychic thing," Stein continues. "It has to do with the beat. The 4/4 rhythm has a calming effect on the listener. It's that heartbeat beat. That's why it's so popular, whereas rock, which has an erratic off beat, creates excitement. It's a physical thing. It's biological.

"I like some disco songs, and I don't like other disco songs. It's sorta like an alternative to punk rock. It's a gut emotion. I can't really see disco as being the death knell of live music. Not at all. I think what people object to about disco is the dumb straight people in suits makin' out that they're John Travolta goin' to discos, listenin' to disco muzak and thinkin' they're him. I find that very distasteful, but that side of it is just bullshit and has nuthin' to do with it. I mean people were doin' that to Jefferson Airplane too . . ." Listen out for another couple of disco-orientated tracks on the next Blondie album.

THE session completed, Debbie and Chris, not usually noted for painting the town red, decide to leave for home; Frank Infanti heads for Max's Kansas City, where the Heartbreakers are staging yet another comeback (or is it farewell?) gig; Burke and Jimmy Destri are Broadway bound to see their former buddy, Gary Valentine, play at a relatively new NY club, Hurrah's.

Hurrah's has been acquiring a healthy reputation with kids and bands alike. It merges rock with disco so subtly that neither audience loses credibility by hanging out there. Its trendy mirrored architecture makes it a safe place for the more fashion-affected kids to visit, while the wide range of bands – the Only Ones made their New York debut there – attracts the earthier audiences.

It wasn't a particularly inspiring night for Gary Valentine, though one wonders why he ever left Blondie in the first place. This gig proved that he is neither a guitarist nor a singer, but there were a couple of good songs that could have been done justice to by a singer of Debbie Harry's style. You may remember that Valentine wrote "Touched By Your (Presence Dear)". You wouldn't if you heard him sing it. If Gary would realise that his vocation is writing songs, and not performing them, he might find a more fulfilling path.

"Yeah, I know what you mean," Harry later agreed. "There were a lot of ego clashes with Gary, within the band, and that's what led to him leaving. He was always wanting to change things. The difference between us is that I know how to sell a song."

SUNDAY, 4.30 pm: Debbie is sweating over the cooker while Chris conducts a business meeting – in the bedroom, of course – with a representative from Shep Gordon's office. Gordon is interested in taking over Blondie's vacant management. He has a lot of clout in the States, but Stein is being very cool. Twice bitten, he's third time shy.

Back in the kitchen, waiting for the duck to roast, Debbie pulls out a few Polaroids from the previous night's session with Rock. They look impressive, the boys bunched around their singer in their high-street suits, holding the radios that the photographer had liberated from market shelves, all set against a striking red background.

"At least we've already got a cover for the next album from that session," Debbie says, noting her own sensuous pose in the shot. "Get out the cheeseboard! The record company wants me to sell my body again."

While she batters the living daylights out of the pumpkin pie, Debbie reveals that she, too, is working on a "secret project", and then is slightly taken aback when I tell her that I know it's a film – and it's not Alphaville.

The project is, indeed, shrouded in secrecy, and both Stein and Harry are unwilling to divulge too much information about it. As the day wears on, I learn that it's a psychological thriller, that it's a low-budget production, that it will only take a week to make (which was instrumental in Debbie's decision to accept the part), that shooting starts the next day . . . and that she will play a "tortured housewife".

She has, it appears, been offered a host of movie roles. She turned down ("Thank God!") a part in Stigwood's Sgt. Pepper's Lonely Hearts Club Band, and is frequently plied with scripts. This one was accepted because of the brief schedule, and because it had an exceptional script that appealed to both Stein and Harry. They also see the venture as a comfortable introduction to acting, which will serve her well when it comes to filming Alphaville, probably some time later this year.

The Alphaville project has come to a temporary standstill, after the introductory blaze of publicity sparked off by an MM front page picturing Harry and co-star Robert Fripp. Stein and Fripp had used the publicity to attract financial backers, and now they're considering the offers. It hadn't, however, originated as a movie project. Stein, having secured the rights to the book wanted to record an album based around it, until a close friend, former Interview editor Glenn O'Brien, persuaded him to go a step further and put it on celluloid.

While Stein views the move into films as an exciting new frontier, his other half remains sceptical about her future under the lights until she feels the temperature.

"It's a whole different sense of timing and pace of working," she muses. "I guess it's much drier, and it's certainly more personal. You don't *need* to have an audience response. You just do it, and if you do it good, you get turned on. It's *that* personal. The director is there, and the crew, but everybody is, like busy, busy, busy.

"I haven't really done any acting before . . . just a couple of underground videos. Not like this, not like . . . ah . . . official. An' it's really complex. You have to choreograph. You have to time. It's the same thing with music – but with music, you have the music to carry you. It's a challenge, and I'm looking forward to it.

"It's so different from rock 'n' roll. There's a lotta things about rock 'n' roll that I don't like. I love being on stage, and I love the excitement, but I don't like the business that much. For some reason, the rock business hasn't *dignified* itself. After the movie industry was around for 20 years, it was dignified. They *forced* themselves to become dignified. They were protected. They could work in certain ways. In rock 'n' roll, a lotta people get misused physically – and a lotta times mentally. The movie industry has all these unions, like the Screen Actors' Guild. Those things are very strong. Your working conditions have to be of a certain calibre. But in rock 'n' roll you get constantly faced with very fuckin' wild conditions, y'know. Like, for me a lotta times they seem really rugged – freezin' cold theatres, stuff like that. I dunno if that happens to actors or not.

"Anyway, this is my first experience of doing a movie. If I like it, I like it. If I don't, I'll knock it on the head."

WITH dinner almost ready, Debbie excuses herself to pop out and check out her wardrobe for the impending seven days on the film set. Which leaves me in the company of Mr Stein, who has now completed his informal talks with the aspiring manager.

Stein is content to spend a lazy afternoon waiting for dinner – a full-scale meal of this sort doesn't happen too often in this household – watching TV, this time switching between sport and films on the cable channel.

On the bed lies a copy of UFO, the magazines which brings up a discourse on one of Chris's many eccentric theories. For instance, he believes that the CIA (who else?) have extra-terrestrial beings captive in the White House, an opinion encouraged by an article in this month's copy of UFO.

"The CIA have been involved is so many weird cover-ups," Chris will argue earnestly. "I wouldn't put it past them."

While on the subject of radical theories, it's also worth adding that Stein believes that Crosby, Stills and Nash were planted on an unsuspecting population by the government in the early Seventies to calm the increasing political consciousness and activities of the Sixties. And who'd argue with that?

It turns into an amusing afternoon of TV and Stein philosophies. The peace is shattered, though, soon after Debbie returns, when she receives a call from a friend who's just finished reading Tony Parsons' and Julie Burchill's The Boy Looked At Johnny and wishes to point out the observations made by this other odd couple concerning Stein and Harry. Debbie calmly puts the phone on the receiver and explodes. Chris wanders out to discover what all the fuss is about. He lethargically returns and flops on the bed, casually reporting: "She wants to sue Tony Parsons."

After a few minutes' thought, he returns to Debbie in the kitchen. She will not be placated.

"I didn't say those fuckin' things," she cries. "He's tellin' lies."

Stein's voice is so soft and controlled that I can't hear his reply. Debbie is outraged by his diplomacy, and attempts a more direct approach to stir his anger.

"Did you see what he said about your fuckin' photographs? He said you're a lousy photographer!"

Chris is stirred, but only because Debbie's outburst is irritating him.

"So what? I don't give a fuck what he says."

Stein again returns to the bedroom, giving no clue of the proceeding battle. "Some fuckin' friend that was on the phone," he murmurs.

THE incident emphasises Harry's mistrust and suspicion of the Press. She is loath, these days, to be roped into an interview, and though she was usually the picture of charm in New York, she became decidedly cagey and unsettled if a discussion moved towards any seriousness.

Blondie's relationship with the papers, and particularly the British papers, has deteriorated rapidly over the last year, the rot ironically coinciding with the band's outstanding success in Britain. Stein, for instance, puts the recent

166

rumours of a split down to "one of our enemies spreading malicious gossip. A lot of stuff that's written about us has a high percentage of inaccuracy."

Nevertheless, Stein is the more tolerant of the two, showing an implicit appreciation of the power of the media, and an anxiety to exploit it whenever possible.

"Some of them have obviously turned on us cos we're too successful. We're outta the grasp of power-mad critics. It makes them very nervous when they know they can't make or break you any more. The bigger you get, the more imaginative the lies they'll print. It isn't that we get misquoted a lot. It's just that it's taken out of context. It's different here, though. The American press is less opinionated, on the whole, and more musically analytical."

Debbie cools down and, while carving the duck, doubtless thinks only of Tony Parsons.

DURING the evening, it should be reported, Debbie's hair changes colour – from blonde to light brown with the first rinse, to slightly darker brown with the second. For the movie, you understand. Stein is impressed.

"Hey, that's really good," he raves. "It makes you look younger."

Debbie doesn't know what to make of that one.

MONDAY 7.30 am: "Make-up call for Ms. Harry."

7.30 pm: At the home of Debbie Harry and Chris Stein.

Harry: "Nervous? This mornin' I was scared shitless. I was gonna call you up. I was almost in tears."

Stein: "Why? D'you think you couldn't do it?"

Harry: "Yeah, I thought 'Oh shit. Here I am. I can't do it.' Like, I was really freakin' out. That was it. I was really fucked up."

Stein: "An' what happened? You did it, didn't you?"

Harry: "Well, y'know, I would feel how freaked out I was and then I would just say to myself 'You can't let this happen! You gotta do it. What're you gonna do? Quit?' An' I just had to talk myself back into doin' it."

Stein: "So then what happened? Didn't you do it? Whadda you worryin' about?"

Harry: "So then in the afternoon I just beat the words into my head. I just studied the script."

Stein: "What couldn't you do? Remember the lines?"

Harry: "Yeah. Like, I was havin' terrible trouble. I couldn't choreograph the words an' the movin', put the endin's at the right time or the beginnings. I was so fucked up."

Stein: "You were a little nervous. What's the big deal?"
Harry: "*Dennis* could do it right away."
Stein: "Well, he's done movies before."
And it goes on.

IN the course of the evening, with Debbie completely exhausted after a hard day's work, we talk more about the "side projects". Debbie says that she was interested in producing a group, the B-Girls, but the plan was abandoned when the lead singer and guitarist had a fight. Movies now take care of Debbie's spare time.

Stein, however, is taking on as much as he can handle. Apart from photography and graphics, he's also been producing an album for a friend, violinist and electronic musician Walter Steding, and at the mention of his name heads for the tape deck to play a result of the collaboration. It's a rather far-fetched version of "Hound Dog", with a solo by Robert Fripp.

Steding, according to Stein, is the antithesis of Blondie's pure pop. They first met a couple of years ago, when he supported Blondie at places like CBGBs and Max's Kansas City.

"Producing him is great because there are no preconceptions whatsoever, and there are no references to music or anything else that I can think of except to jazz and that isn't deliberate. It's sorta like psychedelic jazz. It has a good sense of humour, too, which appeals to me. It satisfies my desire for abstraction. Blondie's music is much more regimented and mapped out carefully.

"I should say, too, that there's a definite trend now towards free-form rock and jazz in New York. Even the B52s, who play tight, have these weird abstractions on top of the driving rhythms. It's a backlash against the regimentation of punk rock. It's like you play faster and faster – and finally you can't play any faster, so you just play erratically."

Other members of Blondie, too, have been involving themselves in solo projects. Jimmy Destri has been producing an excellent local band called the Student Teachers, as well as working on his own material, while Clem Burke was recently playing with Chris Spedding. Within the framework of Blondie, Stein sees it as a very healthy practice.

"It's easier for me to create things now, because I feel like there is really an audience and people will look or listen to whatever I do. We always wanted Blondie to be a multi-media commune. It's not supposed to be just a band. Actually, we're gonna go into religion pretty soon . . .

"We view it as a long-term thing. You see, if I'm bald I can't appear on an album cover, but I can still *produce* records and stuff. All the boys in the band are worried about their hair. I'll bet Joe Strummer would worry if he was bald. Some people can pull it off, like Eno can do it gracefully. Actually, Debbie should shave her hair off. That'd be great."

Framing Harry and Stein within Blondie can be a delicate matter, especially when the issue of internal conflict is raised. They argue that most of the problems have been eradicated now that the various members have settled into their own apartments, and now that they are looking for a new manager. They claim to be in complete control of the situation.

But I'd guess that there's still a certain amount of friction within the band. In some ways, Harry and Stein have a different outlook on rock 'n' roll than the rest of the band. For instance, some of the band are anxious to get out on the road gigging, while Stein and Harry are reluctant to drag their bodies across the United States.

They don't deny that there are problems. "All these projects act as a valve and give us a lotta satisfaction," Debbie says. "There are so many strong personalities within the band that you have to find a channel to release the rest of the energy, otherwise you get a lotta bickerin'."

Stein once stated, in a Rolling Stone interview, that touring is "for morons".

"That was misconstrued. What I meant is that if a band has to tour incessantly, it's not really for morons but it's just for people who don't have the right kind of hook that can be grabbed by the media. Bands like Kiss and Rush *have* to tour constantly, because they can't get the right type of media coverage. That doesn't necessarily mean it's moronic, but it's a lifestyle that we don't adhere to. We want to use the media – which is there to be used, after all.

"Being on stage is great. What I don't like about touring is the rest of the day. You spend an hour having a good time, and you spend 22 hours sleeping or lazing about a bus. That's a real drag. I mean, you're never not tired on a tour. You're always tired because you always gotta get up too early."

Maybe they didn't like the lengthy tours because their relationship is one which doesn't allow for participation in the on-the-road raving that many bands maintain keeps them sane.

"Well, it makes it a lot easier when you have somebody to bounce off. Now that we have a little more money, when we do tours of the States the boys take their girlfriends with them, too. It's more fun. It's a better atmosphere."

Many bands think that it's taboo to take girlfriends on tour.

"Yeah," Stein says. "But everybody has cool girlfriends in Blondie."

BEFORE I leave, Stein has one more treat in store, a visit to an underground television programme that's beamed on cable TV. He's genuinely excited by the prospect. TV Party, as it's called, goes out every Monday night at 11 pm, and is masterminded by Glenn O'Brien. It is, truly, Alternative TV.

Chris explains that it's a sort of community venture and that the studio, off East 53rd Street, can be hired for 40 dollars an hour. It's available to any crank who has some message for the nation; one night there was a woman so in love with her goldfish that she acquired the studio to tell Manhattan about them. She had a potential audience of half a million.

A couple of weeks back, Debbie – who decides tonight to rest at home – went on TV Party and gave lessons on pogo dancing. It's that sort of programme.

When we arrive at the studio, the audience and artists are mingling. They come in all shapes, colours and sizes – the lunatic fringe, Stein calls them. As the hour approaches, the studio is a scene of unrelenting chaos, with the calm O'Brien presiding, but when the clock strikes 11, a loose band of Stein, Walter Steding, a bassist, a percussionist, a sax player and a singer play and sing the first thing that comes into their head. So *this* is free-form jazz.

O'Brien launches into his introductory spiel. Michael Aspel he is not. "Cold enough for ya? Welcome to the station that doesn't say 'cold enough for ya?' "

And on it goes, with spontaneous anecdotes and a guest appearance by Peter Hammill, who looks as if he's just stepped into another planet (which, of course, he has).

Stein is called upon by O'Brien to give a few words. He imparts his theory of extra-terrestrial beings at the White House. Steding calls for more venues in New York, mentioning that CBGB's has gone downhill (an opinion with which the audience vociferously agrees).

The hour flies by, and Stein dismantles his equipment in a corner of the studio.

"You were asking about the people we hang out with," he says, casting an eye over his eccentric court.

"Well, *these* are our friends."

Harry Doherty

14

Can't stand losing

STING

September 22 1979

I t's a basement flat in Bayswater, just beyond the casbah rowdiness of Queensway. Sting is in the small front yard when I arrive. He's leaning against the whitewashed wall of the house, his arms folded across his chest, the telephone receiver cradled between the side of his head and his shoulder. Beneath the open window of the living room sits a movie director's chair. The red canvas is stretched loosely over a wooden frame. Sting's name is printed boldly in large white letters across the back. Sting continues his telephone conversation. Two shy school-girls pass. One looks down into the basement yard. She recognises Sting, giggles. She shouts to him, waves through the iron railings.

Sting barely notices. The telephone is ringing again. He apologises for the interruption, takes the call. It's someone from the Police office. The band's new single has been voted top of Capital Radio's Hit Line. Sting conveys the news with glee. A roadie arrives with plane tickets. The Police are flying out to Holland the next morning for a television show at the weekend. They'll be back in London the following Monday to finalise preparations for their British tour. There's another telephone call. Sting smiles again. He's just been told that "Outlandos d'Amour" has gone platinum in Holland.

The afternoon is full of such distractions. Sting enjoys the bustle. He seems to come alive, to thrive on the constant activity. The attention is, after all, another kind of flattery, a further acknowledgement of the Police's success.

The flat is not especially grand, certainly no ostentatious advertisement for Sting's recently won affluence. It is tastefully, almost soberly furnished and decorated. There is a colour television in one corner, a stereo in another. Prints, photographs and paintings hang from the walls. Shades of brown dominate, giving the room a comfortable warmth.

Sting falls back into a luxurious velvet armchair, immerses himself in its embrace. He has strong, handsome features: a broad forehead, high, perilous cheekbones that give him an imperious look. The mouth is wide; it could be cruel, but he is quick to laugh. His laugh is a sandpapered chuckle and its softness finds an echo in his voice, which is seductive, coloured by his Newcastle accent. It seems to float you into its confidence.

He's relaxed here; clearly, he enjoys the security of his home. It is, one suspects, a retreat whose privacy he defends zealously. He lives here with his wife, Frances, and his three year old son. The air of domesticity settles easily on him. He seems unselfconscious about it. He relishes it, in fact, and makes no secret of it.

"As you can see," he says, waving a hand around the room. "I do want things around me that I wanted as a kid. I wanted a house of my own. I wanted a car. I wanted to send my kids to a good school. I don't think there's anything phoney in those aspirations. There's a humourous side to it, too . . . I mean, I'm aware of the middle class caricature – the ducks on the wall, you know. But I haven't got them yet.

"But all this is part of me. I try as far as possible not to disguise the fact that I am a home-loving, average house-husband. I have a wife. I have a child. I do have a family life that is quite normal. And I don't see any point trying to disguise it. I don't see any profit in trying to promote an image of myself as a kind of rebellious playboy."

He chuckles at the idea. "I mean, someone like Phil Lynott has this wonderful playboy image – you know, a girl in every bed and all that. I think it's very funny. But people eventually start seeing through it. One day the world catches you with your hair in curlers and there goes the image, blown away."

He pauses for a moment, then smiles, teasing.

"I really do feel rather ordinary," he says. "Sometimes."

WHISPER the name: Mont de Marsan. It was at the second of Marc Zermati's mad punk binges in the south of France that I first met Sting. The Police were so far down the bill at that festival in the summer of 1977, that their name barely made the posters.

The festival headliners – the Clash, the Jam, the Damned; the London punk elite – were all flying into Mont de Marsan from Blighty. The supporting cast of English bands – among them the Police, the Boys, the Maniacs and the Tyla Gang – and a detachment of intrepid rock hacks travelled by coach to Mont de Marsan. The journey took 37 hours. In Paris, 16 of us shared what was basically a single room divided by hardboard partitions. The hotel was so dreadfully seedy it brought tears of disbelief to our tired eyes.

The drive from Paris the next day was horrendous – 17 hours in a clapped-out old banger of a coach driven by a speed freak. There was no air-conditioning, less food and a drink was out of the question. We arrived in Mont de Marsan feeling like a ragged platoon of boat people. And the worst thing about reaching the village was the terrible knowledge that two days later we'd have to suffer the same appalling conditions on the weary journey home.

Sting can recall that terrible adventure now and savour marvellous ironies that fate held up its grimy sleeve. The Police were virtually unknown then, they were disliked and frequently dismissed. Their future was as bleak as a gravestone on a Yorkshire moor and without any sign of immediate promise. Two years later he has gold records hanging on the walls of his lavatory and a bank balance that must send his bank manager into paroxysms of delirious delight.

"It's undreamed of," he says. "Just this last year we've been presented with financial problems that are just bizarre. Shall we become tax exiles? Shall I buy an estate in Ireland? It's fun, I must say. I mean, I'm not complaining. It's just that because we're a small group we've been able to keep costs down and make an *extraordinary profit*.

"People criticise us for being a nice little business. Well, we *are* a nice little business. We're a damned good business. And we've made money because not only are we a great band, but we're also very intelligent. We're not in debt up to our eyes, like most groups. The mindless spending of £100,000 on one album is something we avoided because we recognise that it's so mindless.

"Most bands just don't make money. They just squander it on producers and cocaine and lots of other bullshit, and it's disgusting. There's so much idiotic excess. It goes beyond enjoyment, you know . . .

"Like, I heard this absolute horror story about X (drummer with a multi-platinum heavy metal band). He apparently has this huge bag of cocaine on stage and at each gig, at the start of each number, he'll reach down and dig up a handful of coke and just sort of spray it all over his face. Just to get through the number. So at the end of each gig the roadies are crawling all over the stage, sniffing the Persian carpets which have got, like, thousands of dollars of cocaine all over them . . . The waste is appalling."

"

STEWART Copeland had been nursing the idea of the Police throughout most of 1976, but his idea only began to assume a coherent identity when Curved Air – whose drummer he was then – played a concert in Newcastle. Phil Sutcliffe, a local journalist and a contributor to Sounds, took Copeland to see a Tyneside band called Last Exit who were playing at Newcastle Polytechnic. The story has been told before, but a little elaboration will do no harm.

"It was a terrible gig," Copeland remembers. "The band was a sort of sophisto Newcastle Chick Corea affair. Everybody was in their mid-thirties and balding, and taking it all very seriously. And the numbers were all seven minutes long and very intense. They'd moved the venue from a small hall to a smaller classroom and everyone was standing at this bar wondering where the band was supposed to be playing. There was no stage. There were two reading lamps on a desk – that was the light show. Everytime somebody walked into the room you could hear their footsteps echoing on the floor. It was absolutely, incredibly awful.

"But they went down a storm. Just because of Sting. Because of his raps with the audience. Because of his singing. Because of his presence. The group was dire. They'd do these really jazzy numbers that started with little swishes on the piano or the cymbals . . ." He holds his head in his hands and laughs loudly at the memory. "But Sting," he continues, "had then what he has now. This fantastic presence. It was really pretty obvious that he had enormous potential."

The commercial emergence of punk – of which Copeland was an early champion – allowed the drummer the opportunity of liberating himself from the redundant confines of Curved Air. He found a young guitarist, Henri Padovani, and persuaded Sting to move down to London to join the Police. Padovani, whose musical talents were restricted, was subsequently sacked. Andy Summers was enlisted in time for Mont de Marsan.

I don't remember anything specific of Sting from that nightmare excursion, though we were introduced by Andy Summers. I'd known the guitarist for two years, as a member of Kevin Coyne's band, and, more recently, as a Kevin Ayers sideman. I was more bemused by Summer's unexpected appearance in what I took to be just another group hopping on the punk bandwagon than I was interested in Sting. The Police had just had their hair dyed blond, I recall, and frankly I thought Summers had lost his marbles.

"A *lot* of people thought I'd lost my marbles," Summers reflects. "I think when I first announced to a circle of friends that I was joining this new wave group called the Police, there was definitely a certain amount of sniggering behind my back. Especially when the dyed blond hair appeared. That really was the big snigger. They might have laughed, but I didn't give a shit. And, obviously, I'm having the last laugh now. At first there were a lot of jokes. Now there's actually a bit of cap-doffing. I think we've earned it, actually."

Summers surrendered a secure career as a session guitarist and freelance musician to join the Police. There were times, he now admits, when he doubted the wisdom of his commitment. The first year was especially depressing, he remembers. The Police played a mere dozen gigs in the six months that followed his arrival. He recalls gluing up posters in the freezing snow for their gigs at the Red Cow. The group was starving and he was being supported by his wife.

"I felt like I'd just put my balls in my mouth and taken a big bite," he says.

What pulled him through that period of desperate uncertainty was the conviction and confidence of Stewart Copeland and Sting. He was impressed and carried by the sheer force of their personalities.

"Stewart's great enthusiasm and drive was immediately conspicuous," he observes. "He and Sting were overwhelming in their preoccupation with the Police. You just don't meet that many people with that kind of drive and energy."

Miles Copeland, Stewart's brother and manager of the Police, also remarks upon the extraordinary conviction and self-confidence displayed by Stewart and Sting during those grim, unfortunate months.

"Sting on his own, but especially under the influence of Stewart, was not about to be put down by anybody. Sting has a very strong opinion of himself. I don't mean he's wildly egotistical, but he has tremendous self-confidence. Stewart is exactly the same. And with the two of them, the confidence in the group was doubled. It didn't matter to them that people were putting them down, that they were unfashionable, that most of the other punk bands looked down on them. They knew that one way or another they would survive, that they would come through.

"Sting always knew that he was good, and if someone came along and said that he was a talentless sonofabitch he thought there was something wrong with them, you know. If someone came along and said, 'Hey – you're a loser, you're full of shit . . . ' he'd feel sorry for that guy, because he knew that guy must be an idiot. He knew that he had the ability.

"Sting always knew he was going to be a star. Like he knew and Stewart knew and I knew that the Police were going to be successful. Anyone could have seen that Sting was a person of obvious talent. An idiot could have seen it. But the trouble with this business is that it often takes the idiots a lot longer to open their eyes."

STING was born in Wallsend, a working-class district of Newcastle. His recollections of his childhood there are mostly affectionate, but never sentimental.

His earliest memories are of a street dominated by the Tyneside shipyards. He remembers his amazement as a child watching the skeletons of ships rising above the streets, gradually taking shape above him.

“We'd watch them being built,” he says, a faint taste of incredulity still apparent in his voice. “Then, after about six months, they'd fall into the river and sail away.”

His father was an engineer, ambitious and eager to improve his family's fortunes. When Sting was five the family moved into a better, middle-class, neighbourhood. “I knew we'd taken a step up the social ladder,” he smiles, “because we had a house with a garden.”

If the move took him away from his earliest friends, his parents' ambitions took him even further away from his original background. They encouraged his academic promise. He was a bright pupil, one of two students in his class to pass the 11-plus and qualify for grammar school.

“Immediately,” he says, “all your friends and contemporaries were shaved away. Your friends considered you an outsider because you went into the town to the grammar school and you wore a different uniform. They were at secondary school, you weren't, so you were different. In a way, I grew up not having many friends. They didn't want to know – they were all preparing to leave school and get jobs. Down the mines. In the shipyards.

“I was totally bewildered, caught on this academic treadmill. I wished that I was at a technical school – somewhere where they taught you something practical. Iron work or metal work. Then I would have had something obvious to aim for. I could've gone to work in a factory, or become a draughtsman. Grammar school was so nebulous, you know. It was just a good status symbol for my parents, having their son at grammar school, going to university.”

He recalls feeling jealous of the freedom his friends seemed to enjoy. They were all working, earning money, buying flashy suits, riding motor bikes and scooters. He was still in his school uniform, taking more exams, trying to win a place at university.

“I felt less mature, less sophisticated. I was really tempted to leave school, to get a job.” He didn't. He passed more exams and went to Warwick University to study English. He was there for a term.

“I was lost, totally lost,” he confesses. “I decided that it just wasn't for me – I mean, I thought that leaving school meant getting rid of your uniform, I thought it meant freedom. Being at university wasn't freedom at all. It was more of the same in a different uniform. So I decided to leave.”

He returned to Newcastle, worked for six months on a building site and then joined the Inland Revenue. He clutches at his hair in mock desperation at the memory. His career in the Civil Service was not illustrious. He was threatened with the sack and decided to leave gracefully. He enrolled at a teachers' training college in Newcastle.

"It was a total lack of imagination on my part that took me back to college," he says. "I just didn't know what else to do. My life was falling apart around me."

THERE was, he thinks, one central focus for his life at this time: music. An uncle who had emigrated to Canada had left behind a guitar. When the uncle returned to Newcastle five years later he found that Sting had requisitioned the instrument. He taught himself to play, strumming along to records.

"I'd listen to the Beatles, the Stones, the Kinks. Learning the chords to 'Dead End Street' was a major breakthrough," he laughs.

He was determinedly catholic in his listening. When he was 14 he borrowed some jazz albums from an older friend at school: "I didn't like any of the records, but I thought it would do me good. I'd listen to album after album of Thelonious Monk piano solos and I thought – this must be doing me a world of good because it's just so awful. Gradually it grew on me. It was the same with blues. I'd listen to loads of blues albums, and I just didn't like them. But I persevered because I thought they were doing me good. It was like having to take some kind of medicine.

"Eventually I grew to love things like that. But at first it was a real effort. I just endured them because I desperately wanted to be hip, you know. There was an elite group of us in the sixth form. Very snobbish, we were. We knew who John Fahey was. We'd heard of Thelonious Monk. We'd heard Jimmy Witherspoon. We were *horribly* precocious."

He didn't start playing in bands (at least none that he will admit to) until he was 18, after returning to Newcastle from Warwick University. By this time he was thoroughly disenchanted with rock music. He often found himself drinking at a pub called the Wheatsheaf. Newcastle, he explains, has a tradition of Dixieland jazz. The bands play in the clubs and pubs, and the musicians used to congregate regularly at the Wheatsheaf for informal sessions. He remembers all these old guys sitting at tables with their drinks and instruments, swapping solos, getting drunk. There was a resident rhythm section in one corner. The bass player's name was Ernie and occasionally he'd allow Sting to sit in with the band while he went off for a quick jolly-up.

"He had this big double bass. I used to get up, play two numbers and get blisters that wouldn't go away for three weeks. Eventually I got the hang of it, learned to play."

One night Ernie failed to turn up. The group asked Sting to play. He brought along his electric bass and plugged in. "The band jumped into the modern world that night. It was the first time they'd ever played with an instrument that worked on electricity. They went crazy."

He was subsequently invited to join Newcastle's premier traditional jazz band, the Riverside Men, which he regarded as a considerable honour. "It was great. They all wore blue suits. The band had been together for about 20 years, which was the same age as the suits. They were a great band. Trad jazz is regarded as a bit of a joke, I know, but it can actually be very exciting. Especially really fast rags. I really loved it."

He felt little sympathy for the current mood in rock. Led Zeppelin and heavy metal and hard rock dominated at the time. He thoroughly abhorred such music. In many ways, he says, he was a musical snob. He disliked all the local Newcastle bands, who were all surrogate HM dervishes.

"They all had long hair and flared trousers, looked terrible and sounded worse," he says. "I was only 20, but I didn't have any time for them. I was mixing with much older musicians, people who'd worked for years at their craft. I felt really proud to be playing with them. It was a great experience. If I'd been in a rock band with long hair and loon pants I wouldn't have learned anything like as much as I did.

"I was conscious that there was some sort of apprenticeship being served. I learned to read music, worked hard practising every day. I was very enthusiastic. I was still a student at the teacher's training college, but I was earning a fortune every night. I had a brand new car. I was," he says, laughing, "very definitely the face of the college. Everyone used to come and see me play . . . There was, uh, a ratio of seven girls to one guy at the college . . . You could say that I was well looked after."

AFTER graduating from college, Sting worked for two years as a teacher at a primary school in Cramlington, a small mining village outside Newcastle.

"The kids in my class," he recalls, "were about nine or ten years old. You might laugh, but they were real delinquents. I loved them, though. They were lovely."

The affection he felt for them is implicit in his voice as he recalls taking instruments into the class for music lessons. Few of them had ever seen a saxophone or a trumpet; they were all thrilled.

"I'm not sure they ever learned anything from me," he says, "but I'm sure they had a good time. I never gave a fuck about teaching them maths or logarithms. I just wanted them to enjoy themselves while they still had time.

I'm not sure what I accomplished as a teacher, but if one kid in that class becomes a musician or plays in a group somewhere, I think he'd have to be thankful to me for encouraging him."

"Actually, when I was on teaching practice once at a secondary modern school in Newcastle, I got one kid really heavily into the guitar and another kid really heavily into the clarinet. They used to write me letters when I went back to college, telling me how they were getting on. Their parents had bought them instruments of their own, you know. I think *that's* the most useful thing I accomplished as a teacher."

He was not often enamoured of the approach of his fellow teachers, though. Especially those he encountered at the secondary school in which he briefly taught. "It was just a job to them. They didn't care for the kids at all. I felt really frustrated there. It was a very reactionary school, very conservative. It was hell, actually. No way were the kids there going to feel anything but resentment for school. I felt the same. I hated that school as much as they did."

He was still teaching at Cramlington when he formed Last Exit. The members of that band were young, but had served the same kind of musical apprenticeship as Sting. They were all accomplished musicians, with aspirations toward jazz-rock sophistication. For the first time Sting started writing and singing.

"I was listening to female singers like Cleo Laine and Flora Purim," he says. "I had a naturally high voice with a wide range – I tried to model myself on them. I never tried to disguise the high voice. I never felt embarrassed about it. I used to love voices like that. McCartney has that kind of voice – I loved him. It just cuts through everything. Slices through the whole band. It doesn't matter if the band is playing at a thousand decibels – it's the kind of voice that cuts straight through."

The local success of Last Exit encouraged him to bring the band down to London, in an attempt to win the attention of a record company. They played a series of support gigs at the Nashville and the Red Cow, supporting groups like Plummett Airlines – "I remember we blew them off stage at the Nashville." They also managed to secure a gig at the LSE with Kevin Coyne and John Stevens' Away. He remembers that gig especially, because it was the first time that the group ever received a review in one of the national rock papers.

"Karl Dallas reviewed it in Melody Maker. I remember there was a sentence about us in his review. I was thrilled. I remember thinking – 'At last we're a tiny microcosm in the rock business, at last we've been recognised!' I've still got the review. I've got loads of press cuttings now, but that was the breakthrough."

Last Exit touted their tapes around the companies. No one seemed overwhelmingly interested. Virgin, though, offered Sting a publishing contract. He accepted. "It wasn't a good deal, but I was so excited that I took it. I thought, 'I'm a real songwriter' – it was like a trophy that proved I was a songwriter. I could talk to people about *my publishers*. It was another great thrill."

Last Exit were forced to return to Newcastle through the lack of interest and available work in London. They were making a reasonable living as the most popular and respected group in the North East. They were offered the support gig at most of the prestigious gigs at the Newcastle City Hall and once played on the same bill as the Manchester Symphony Orchestra, who performed the orchestral version of "Tubular Bells". The MSO was conducted that night by David Bedford. Mike Oldfield was understudied by a guitarist called Andy Summers. Oh, sweet irony!

Sting wasn't satisfied, however. He had been to London and wanted to return. His ambitions had been fired, he was convinced he could make it in the capital. He tried, unsuccessfully, to persuade the rest of the band to accompany him. They were reluctant to forsake the security of the North East, but he decided to go.

"I packed in teaching. Packed everything I owned into a car and drove off. I'd just got married. The baby was six weeks old. It sounds dramatic and it was. My life suddenly just turned over. I said, 'This is it.' It was the only way to do it. We were all in this car with the dog and we didn't have anywhere to go. We had a friend who had a flat in Battersea, so we went there. We slept on the floor of his living room for two months. It was awful.

"The only thing that looked hopeful was this group that Stewart Copeland had called me about the week before we moved. I told him I'd see him in London."

STEWART Copeland was living in a two-storey apartment in Mayfair at the time. He had a small rehearsal studio there, and he and Sting and Henri Padovani would meet and discuss the musical strategy of the Police.

Sting, Stewart Copeland remembers, was initially dubious about the project. "He was a typical provincial boy," Copeland says. "He thought he was going to get ripped off by everyone. He wasn't at all sure about the music . . ."

"Musically, I thought Stewart's ideas were shit," Sting recalls. "But the energy, the dynamism of the guy really affected me. I thought straight away – this is the bloke for me. Yes, I suppose I did see something of myself in Stewart. He's very egocentric. Very, very energetic. Very determined. Very intelligent. He realised what was happening at places like the Roxy. He's an opportunist. Like me."

Copeland admits that he was concerned that Sting's background in jazz would alienate him from the kind of raw aggression he was intent upon harnessing in the Police's music. He remembers coaching Padovani before Sting came down from Newcastle to join them.

"Henri only knew about three chords. I used to say that in the very early days, when we first started gigging, that we had a 20-minute set and a 20-minute guitarist. He had a nice feel but he wasn't technically very proficient. I knew that Sting was a sophisto jazz musician and was going to freak when he met Henri. Henri had never played in a group before, and here was Sting about to turn up having played for years with all these old jazzers. God, I thought he'd go crazy. I don't know how we managed to pull it off, but we impressed him enough for him to come back to rehearse the next day."

Copeland, by this time, was fully immersed in punk; in its music, and its attitude. Sting wasn't so quickly impressed.

"He was a dreadful reactionary," Copeland says. "And it really showed in the early days. Which was one of the reasons we were never accepted by the punk elite. One of the first gigs we did was at the Nashville. Everybody on the punk scene turned out for it. And Sting . . . Sting did this thing where he said, 'Alright – we're going to play some punk now, which means that the lyrics are banal and the music is terrible . . . ' He just totally blew it. He didn't understand what he was doing then. God knows what he thought he was up to."

"I was reactionary," Sting agrees, "but that was just because I wasn't sure where we stood with all these punk bands. It took me a while. Stewart's enthusiasm carried me along for quite a while, until I actually started to contribute something to the group."

"I knew it was going to take some time to acclimatise Sting," Copeland says. "For those first few months Sting hated everybody he saw. We did some gigs with the Heartbreakers, I remember. Sting hated them. We'd wander down to the Roxy and he'd be going, 'Jesus Christ, what the fuck is this all about? Who are these people?' And a band would come on and he'd be totally freaked out. But the crucial thing was that he was immediately competitive. He'd see these guys and say, 'Look at these guys – they're causing all this media attention and they are shit. I can do better than this fucking lot.' And he'd get wilder and wilder. He became very aggressive, very determined."

Both Miles and Stewart Copeland became antagonistic when the hostility and indifference of the Police's punk contemporaries is mentioned. Miles, especially, rants belligerently at the audacity of the group's early critics who condemned them for being merely opportunistic. Stewart is more reasonable. Sting says that it never really bothered him, though he was aware of it.

"I met a lot of those punks . . . Joe Strummer, Paul Simonon. Rotten. We were never incredibly chummy or matey. I don't think we ever had much in common with those people. I never got to know them very well. We were sort of untouchables as far as they were concerned. We weren't allowed to mix with the in-crowd. There was an inner circle which we didn't belong to, and which we didn't try to penetrate. I wouldn't have minded being part of the in-crowd. But at the same time I wasn't going to lose my temper if Dave Vanian refused to speak to me one night at the Roxy."

It becomes clear, though, that he does allow himself some small grin of self-satisfaction, having now become considerably more successful than those individuals who once shunned the Police.

"I like the irony of the fact that we've stuck to our guns and eventually won through. Our success in America is especially ironic. We were forced to turn to America, because here virtually every door was locked to us. And then we went there and we did it, where all the elite bands from England totally failed. And will continue to fail, I think. They have nothing to say to America that America wants to hear. They don't want to hear the Clash. There's a minority on the coasts, maybe, who think it's very fashionable to like the Clash. But the heart of America is the Midwest. That's the reactionary, conservative, Ted Nugent territory. That's the area you have to break to break America. And they don't want to listen to bands like the Clash out there.

"You know," he says, warming to his theme. "I really think groups like the Clash and the Sex Pistols had it too easy. They had such an easy victory. It was a walkover for them. I'm sure it's not as satisfying as having been right down there and then swimming up to the surface through all the shit like we had to. In many ways that's probably why the Sex Pistols split up. It was all too easy for them. They were just catapulted up there without any problems. They were their own biggest problem. They just couldn't cope.

"We've been through it all and we've grown with it. We crawled and then we walked and now we're running. And we'll keep running until we fall."

STEWART Copeland says that his principal difficulty with Sting in the early days of the Police was simply keeping up his morale. They were playing gigs at first for a fiver a night, the press was against them (they say), they were without a following. It was like one long shout into the dark.

"There was only one real crisis, though," Copeland mentions. "Sting was offered a job with Billy Ocean for 90 notes a week. We were starving at the time. We were playing with Cherry Vanilla for a fiver a gig and sometimes she couldn't even pay us that. But I really put her over a barrel. I forced the money out of her. Just to keep Sting. He would have gone, I know. Cos he's a real breadhead. And he goes for the money. If it had looked to him like the Police was about to fold, he would've taken that job.

"I'm glad that happened, cos whenever he now says, 'Shit – I wrote "Outlandos", I'm the Police' – I can say, 'Oh, yeah? If it wasn't for me, mate, you'd have joined fucking Billy Ocean.' The guy who turned him on to the gig actually joined Billy Ocean. The gig lasted four months. So, four months later Sting could've been back in some pub in Newcastle in a jazz group."

The tenacity of the group – and Stewart's overriding determination that they would succeed despite the odds stacked against them – carried them through those months of doubt and disappointment. And slowly the circle began to turn in their favour. Andy Summers joined. Sting realised that the songs he had been withholding from the Police because of Padovani's lack of technique could now be played. He would no longer have to compromise his more sophisticated inclinations to accommodate a musically backward guitarist. And, just as important, he made a significant connection with reggae.

"I'd always wanted to make a connection between the energetic music of punk and more sophisticated musical forms," he explains. "There was this amazingly aggressive music full of energy on the one hand, and I wanted to take it and bridge a gap between interesting chords and harmonic variations and this wild energy. And what eventually allowed me to do it was listening to reggae. Bob Marley, especially. I saw a rhythmic connection between the fast bass of punk and the holes in reggae. I got interested in trying to write songs that combined these apparently diverse styles. I think we succeeded with 'Roxanne'."

Andy Summers has touching memories of the afternoon that Sting presented the Police with the song.

"We were rehearsing in this piss-awful cellar in Finchley. It was freezing cold and the rehearsals were going dreadfully. I knew that Sting had had the chords for 'Roxanne' for ages. I remember him playing them for me once in Paris. We weren't really getting very far with anything, so we said 'let's have a go at that song' . . . Sting had written the lyric by this time and he sang it and we messed about with the chords. We changed it around, played it backwards and thought, 'Mmmm. Not a bad song. Rather good, in fact.' Then Miles came along to see how we were getting on. He had had this real punk-religious glint in his eye. So we played him all the more obvious songs and he told us that mostly they were shit. Then we played 'Roxanne' and he flipped."

"I thought it was one of the fucking great classic songs of all time," Miles Copeland says now. He took it on to A&M who picked it up and released it. The group felt very pleased with themselves. It was a minor hit. The profits enabled them to fly to America. The circle continued to turn in their favour.

Each member of the band refers to a specific gig, a specific moment when they realised that they were, after all, going to find success at the end of the water-chute. Stewart remembers a gig at the Marquee, Sting thinks it was probably discovering reggae and finding a form for his songwriting. Andy Summers probably thinks it was when he joined Sting and Stewart. But Miles Copeland has the most intriguing memory.

The Police had just started their first American tour, were driving eight hours a day across the continent, chasing good fortune and headlines. They played a gig in Syracuse. There were four people in the audience.

"Most groups," he said, "would have said, 'Shit – fuck this.' The Police went out and played one of their best gigs. Sting actually introduced the audience to each other. And one of the people in the audience turned out to be a deejay who was really blown away. The next day he started playing the Police really heavily on his show. That gig turned out to be one of the most important they've ever played. That's why I think their success is such a tribute to their conviction – they play each gig as a challenge. They'll play anywhere, to anyone. They're prepared to do anything for success."

And so their audience began to grow. In America. In Britain. Sting became the obvious focal point. He didn't flinch from the spotlight.

"And God he loved it," Stewart Copeland smiles. "He took to it naturally. Comfortably. One might say casually."

I asked Sting later how he felt on stage at Reading in front of 30,000 ecstatic fans.

He smiled.

"I felt like God, and I loved it," he said.

STING is the public face of the Police," Stewart Copeland says. And, of course, it's true.

Sting is the one to whom journalists rush most eagerly for interviews. It is toward him that the photographers gallop, shutters clicking like frantic dice. It is his face that beams from the front pages of the music press. It is to his bank account that most of the royalties from "Outlandos" and "Reggatta de Blanc", the new album, will be credited. The small miracle here is that such attention on one member of the band doesn't precipitate all manner of internal warfare.

"I don't care how much money Sting earns," Stewart Copeland firmly declares. "I'm really proud of him. It doesn't surprise me that he's turned out to be a great songwriter. It doesn't surprise me that he's turned out to be a fucking superstar actor either, the bastard.

"I don't resent him his success. I was prepared to hand over the group to him, remember. I wanted him to write. I wanted him to sing. I wanted him in the group. The main thing is to have good songs and to be a successful group. Fuck the arguments.

"I've seen a lot of groups where the bass player is buying his first apartment out of the royalties from the first hit record and is feeling great . . . then, hey, he sees the fucking guitarist buying some fucking mansion cos he's got twice as much from the publishing alone cos the songs on the album were his. So the next album comes along, and the bass player says, 'Hey – I've got all these songs and I'm leaving unless we record them.' There's a million stories about groups being ripped apart like that. And I'm determined that it won't happen to the Police. So I don't care how much money Sting makes. I hope he makes lots and lots and lots of money. I'm more interested in safeguarding the future of the group."

Sting, equally, would not like to think that his diversification might in any way threaten the internal stability of the Police. At the same time he is anxious to dispel any suggestion that because Copeland and Summers so politely tolerate his activities outside the Police the group is therefore run on the lines of a garden party at Buckingham Palace.

"We're a tough band," he says. "And I can be very ruthless. I mean, we sacked a guitarist we all liked. We all loved Henri as a person, but because he stood in the way of our musical progress we sacked him. It was ruthless. But it had to be done. We sacked him in pieces. I started it and Stewart finished it off.

"I do think that work should come before friendship. We're all friends, obviously. But if I'm angry about a work situation, I won't let friendship get in the way. I'll be very angry. Stewart's the same. We really do fight a lot. It's a very hard, committed relationship. It's not always nice or polite. It's often very, very tense."

STING tells a rather crucial story about himself at one point during our conversation. We had been talking about his childhood in Newcastle, his youth, his schooldays. He mentioned that along with music his other great passion was athletics. He had been the Northern Counties 100 metres champion. He had raced in the national championships. He came third. He never raced again.

"You're either the best or you're not," he said. "I realised when I came third that there were two people in my age group who were better than I was. And there was no possibility of me beating them. So I just stopped running. I didn't want to be part of the pyramid. I wanted to be on the top. I like to be the best. I only want to be the best. I enjoy being the best. I am an egoist. I wouldn't get on stage and do what I do if I wasn't. I'm supremely self-confident about everything I do."

"One thing I'll say for Sting," Miles Copeland had said, "he never fails at doing anything. Every single audition he went to for a movie or for a part in a commercial – he always got the part. Either he's got luck or he's got a winner look about him or something. He just succeeds.

"I think part of it is his conviction that he is great, and he knows what he's capable of. And he's also got the right credentials as far as looks go. That always helps. Generally, he's lucky. He's also talented. He's also a good person. It's a rare combination. And usually those combinations are very successful."

"I'm not really surprised that Sting has been successful in movies," says Stewart Copeland. "He always looks so great, anyway. He has a real rapport with the mirror. He enjoys being looked at. But only when he's being Sting. Like, people say that he's not wild, that he doesn't party after gigs. That's because he can only keep up that kind of intensity of being Sting for a limited amount of time. Then he has to switch off. And he can only do that when he's alone in his hotel room. He won't even come down to the hotel lobby if he thinks there might be a photographer there. He has to be Sting in front of the camera. He'd have to keep up the persona. That's his career. His whole art form is down to the way he looks. That's why I'm not surprised by his success in movies. Everything about him you can see is part of his art form, and he really gets uptight if you try to get around behind it. Because he really does put out a lot all the time. He gives people plenty to look at and conjure with. And that should be enough.

"He's not exactly two different people, but there are differences . . . let me put it like this: when he shows up he's on stage and when he's not on stage he doesn't show up."

STING, perhaps fortunately, is less abstract when it comes to discussing his movie career. He finds it amusing, in fact, that so much emphasis has been placed on it.

He has, he reminds us, appeared in only two movies (having been excised from the Sex Pistols' epic) – Quadrophenia and Radio On. His wife is an actress, he explains. Her agent suggested that he might possibly find some work in commercials to help subsidise his career in music. He went along to his first audition. He got the job.

"It was incredible," he says. "Do you know how many jobs there are for actors? Do you know how many actors are out of work? To go for your first job and actually get it is virtually unprecedented. And then to go on and get seven more in succession is unbelievable. With each one, I went in and said, 'Hi, I'm Sting.' And they said, 'The man for the job!' So naturally my confidence blossomed. I was ready for anything."

He was reluctant, though, to audition for Quadrophenia. He thought he was too old. He knew that both Jimmy Pursey and Johnny Rotten had been tested for the part. He was eventually persuaded to meet the film's director, Franc Roddam.

"I washed my hair, went down to the studio, met him and sat around discussing Herman Hesse – The Glass Bead Game, I think. Suddenly, he said, 'You're perfect. You look perfect.' I got the job that day. It transpired during the conversation that followed that I was going to appear in a two-million dollar movie. And I'd never even been in a school play."

The cameo appearance in Radio On came about in the same manner. His agent sent him along to meet Chris Petit, the director, and he was offered the part.

"I just sing 'Three Steps To Heaven' and sit in a caravan," he says of his role. "It's not exactly Ben Hur."

He has just turned down the leading role in the Rock Follies movie (which has just been abandoned). He didn't want to become associated with rock movies, he says; he doesn't want to do another film with any overt connection with music, though he would like to pursue a career in films.

"He won't do anything unless he thinks there's a good reason for it, though," says Stewart Copeland. "He's ambitious. He wants to be huge. But he won't do anything that he thinks is beneath him. He's playing for higher stakes. He's turned down the Russell Harty show – or the Parkinson show, I can't remember. Something like that. He just won't do it. I mean, it's the kind of thing that Elkie Brooks would break an arm to get on. Sting just doesn't want to know."

THERE is a part of Sting's personality that appears to react frivolously to the success he is presently enjoying. Everyone will tell you how much he enjoys the attention of his audience and the media. He'll tell you himself how much he delights in the idea of being a sex symbol (his own description). He loves being recognised, he says. He loves being stopped in the street and asked for his autograph.

"It means that I'm doing my job well," he says. "It means I'm successful at what I do." He wants to remain accessible, he doesn't want to turn people away. As Miles Copeland says, however, he might soon find the pressure greater than he imagined. "Talk to me this time next year and I'll tell you whether I'm still enjoying it," he says, grinning.

He is aware, though, that with success comes a certain responsibility.

"I'm in quite a responsible position. A lot of people will read what I say and take it seriously, so I have to be very careful. But I'm prepared to accept the responsibility. If you have a coherent opinion you shouldn't be reluctant to express it. If you have nothing to say, keep your silence. But on some issues I do have views that I want to express, given the opportunity. I want my voice to be heard. But without abusing the position I'm in. I mean, it's not going to sell any records – it's divorced from all that. But it's still a part of being successful. I accept it.

"It's hard, though. It's one of the pressures. But I enjoy it more than being looked at."

THE POLICE, Miles Copeland had told me with characteristic modesty, could prove to be "another Who, another Rolling Stones. I think they could be a legendary force in music for the next 10 to 15 years."

I wondered whether Sting thought he would be happy with the status of a Jagger or a Rod Stewart.

"I really don't see myself becoming a playboy, you know. I'm a family man. I'm very down to earth. I have a wife and a child and I'm very happy, we have a nice flat in the centre of London. I can't see my life changing that radically.

"I don't take drugs. I don't even smoke dope. I don't even smoke tobacco. I drink occasionally . . . I don't mean to sound boring, but the avenues of excess aren't actually open to me. I don't have any habits that vast amounts of money will exaggerate.

"I know I'm arrogant. But it's largely a professional arrogance. It's a useful tool for me. If I wasn't arrogant, I wouldn't be as successful as I am.

"I think it would be false for me to be modest. I'm a great singer and I know it. I'm a great songwriter and I know it. Largely because the competition just isn't there. There's very *little* competition, actually. Of course, this kind of arrogance will antagonise some people. But I don't think it's a vicious arrogance. There are people who don't like me, obviously. I'm not beloved by everybody, for God's sake.

"But a lot of people," he says with a thoroughly disarming smile, "still think I'm really rather a nice bloke."

Allan Jones

15

The only flame in town

U2
January 5 1985

IT WAS the night they turned on the Christmas tree lights in
Rockefeller Plaza. Stars glittered cold and bright over the crisp
winter precipices of Manhattan. Channel 4 News kept cutting back
and forth between studio and Plaza to catch the moment of illumination, but in
the end they bungled it. We flashed back, but the muffled and scarved spectators
were clapping the already-lit tree.

Anyway, the event had been overshadowed by the horrific murder of a
young actress on an apartment block roof way up on the West Side. A fairy tale
of New York? A couple of hours later, U2 went onstage at Radio City Music Hall.

*". . . the band has expanded its vocabulary to incorporate jittery funk rhythms and
a stuttering high-powered rock beat that recalls The Who's Sixties standards. The rhythmic
broadening has helped turn U2 from a good into a great band whose passion is matched
by its technical resourcefulness." – New York Times 6/12/84*

EVEN from where I was standing, you could see that look come into Edge's eyes. Larry Mullen was already on his feet behind his drumkit, one stick outstretched in the direction of the incident. A kind of darkness crossed Edge's face, and he dashed forward into the ongoing melee at the foot of the stage. "I Will Follow" ceased abruptly.

I couldn't see what happened, but it was the first of several incidents which brought U2 to a series of chaotic halts. Edge had a favourite guitar smashed in the first bout. In "Gloria", Bono darted forward to pull a simian security man off a punter who he was efficiently re-landscaping. Bono was flung backwards across the stage, whereupon U2's trusty road crew and manager Paul McGuinness ran onstage to form a protective cordon round the band.

"There was a veritable blood-bath on the way there, honestly," said Bono afterwards. "When security men turn on the band, then you start to wonder what you're doing on a stage. As it happens I won't have 'em turning on the audience, and that's what started the row." He grinned ruefully.

It was a small miracle that U2 finished their set at all. With Radio City operatives standing by to pull the plugs on the show, Bono had stood his ground and pleaded for some calm. The show is likely to remain a blot in the group's memory, but they forced the result they wanted. Just.

Cynics among you may argue that occurrences like this are merely U2 reaping the whirlwind of their own devising. After all, runs this argument, do not zealous men bearing flags and singing songs about religion and massacres in Ulster get the audiences they deserve (by implication, a horde of born-again stormtroopers)?

Certainly the Radio City crowd verged on the unsightly. I stood next to the 'Maker's dauntless New York correspondent David Fricke and his wife. Fricke is tall but Susan isn't, and as yet more teenage drunks clambered over us and each other to stand on seats and play invisible guitars Nugent-style, Fricke grew surly. He allowed his hand to fall heavily on the shoulder of the oaf dead ahead. "*Siddown*," he snarled. The oik obeyed. "Unfortunately I think it's illegal to *throw* them," Fricke growled. Before long, our view was obliterated by multiplying layers of dorks. Imagine what it's like for Iron Maiden.

After the show, U2 locked themselves away in their dressing room for a lengthy post-mortem. Much later, Edge and the infallibly sociable Adam Clayton put in an appearance at the huge liggers' gathering which is apparently obligatory for any sizeable act playing in New York. Duty was seen to be done, but their hearts weren't in it.

A couple of days later in Washington DC, Edge and Bono had managed to fashion a rationale from the Radio City shambles. After all, they'd had to face semi-riots in New York before. Once at the Palladium, someone had thrown a box of white mice onstage. A lot of them died instantly of heart attacks as the others scampered into the shadows. On another occasion, a hired American crew-member (and Teamster organiser) poured a torrent of abuse onto the band, then pulled a gun on a horrified Bono when the vocalist tried to argue about it.

"But wouldn't it be boring if they were all, y'know, the *perfect pupil?*" asked Bono. "I had to stop our last show in New York because I was in the middle of 'Sunday Bloody Sunday' and there was a party of people giving it this 'eff-the-British' line. I stopped the show and said, 'okay, it's all over. You're completely misreading the group'. There's times in the show when I have to say that.

"At the time it may not sink in maybe, but afterwards as they take the train home, as they walk through the streets and they're talking about it . . . you know my feeling on this, I believe that in the mass there is a collective understanding of what we're doing. There are exceptions to that."

Edge chipped in. "It's something that's getting better in New York, but for a while I don't think our New York audience really had that sort of insight into U2. New York is such a large market that a lot of people were coming along and they didn't really know the band. Whereas in say Boston, where we get a lot of radio play and there has traditionally been a lot of support for the band in the media there, the audience have a far better understanding of what we're trying to do. There's not really a lot you can do about the variation except maybe make sure it doesn't affect you and make you adjust to the crowd, in a sense. You're not compromised when you discover the audience are expecting something else from you. You don't bend towards that."

Over lunch a little earlier, Clayton had forcefully voiced quite the opposite point of view to Edge and Bono. Clayton had disliked both the violent scenes and the New York protocol which demands a guest-list several feet long for a bunch of unknown industry insiders. He wouldn't be sorry, he said, if they didn't play New York again.

"So you'd let a handful of trouble-makers spoil the whole thing for 6,000 people, would you?" demanded Bono, while Edge resignedly pointed out that New York was traditionally the place where people who'd helped the group on their way up the American ladder were thanked and generally made a bit of a fuss of. Hell, nobody ever said it was *easy*.

THE Muzak rippled softly in the background. Bono, Edge and I were hidden in semi-darkness at a corner table in the hotel bar, nursing a couple of beers. We were circling round the topic of the misunderstoodness of U2. After my piece on them from France recently, people had been coming up to me and saying "are they *really* like that?" This intrigued Bono.

"The reason we had backed off from the press over the last three or four years was because we wished to separate ourselves from a lot of the other groups around who were only too glad to appear on the cover of the teenybop press, and as soon as they had a single out they were in the Melody Maker talking about it – it was a very predictable production line thing.

"We pulled away and we knew that our fans respected our position on this, but I see that in some ways it backfired because it looked as if we were removing ourselves, not just from the business but from our audience. And I think at one point the only voice being heard was the voice of our critics, and the portrayal of the group was a cartoon world and we were the characters in the cartoon. I would look at the person that was supposed to be me, and I didn't recognise this person as *being* me.

"The real people that were involved in the group, The Edge, myself, Larry and Adam, we were lost in all this, and that's why I suppose we're rethinking our situation and saying 'hold on a second'. It is a kind of character assassination.

"I think a group like us need a good clip round the ear, a good kick in the pants. Rock 'n' roll groups need it. But you know what I'm talking about."

Yeah, I think so. What do you think, Edge?

"It's actually because we come from Dublin and never became part of the whole system of things that exists in London, and we are removed from that and we don't play the game that a lot of bands do . . . and fair enough, it is part of it. I'm not suggesting that you can actually not have anything to do with the press. But there are certain things that everyone understands about, and everyone uses the press and manipulates it to a certain extent. We have made a decision not to do that, and to really treat the press with respect in a sense, and only do interviews where we felt there was a good reason for doing them, not just do them ad hoc. I've read a lot of interviews with people like Nick Cave, and you just know that the guy's almost planned out every statement he's made."

"Let's not get into knocking Nick Cave," said Bono, who has an infuriating habit of choking himself off when on the brink of sordid and scurrilous revelations.

"I'm just using that as an example," said Edge.

"Edge can knock Nick Cave if he wants to," I said hopefully. But he didn't.

SOMEWHERE behind this tangle of fears about self-projection, worries about audience identification, agonising self-examinations about musical direction and qualms about faith (what to say about it) or politics (what to do about it), beats the human heart of U2.

My first impressions were of a self-contained group of people with a clear picture of their goals and procedures for achieving them – shrewd undoubtedly, careful of course, determined to do it on their own terms, though not ruthless as far as I could tell. That was in Europe. In America, where the pressures are different and bigger, more revealing perspectives could be discerned.

Bono can talk an excited mob out of an impending riot and will rattle through an interview with the Washington Post almost as smoothly as one of the smartly-pressed congressmen who haunt the bars and restaurants of Capitol Hill's Hyatt Regency hotel, but his armour is far from flawless. I'm not sure why this should come as a surprise. Perhaps I shouldn't believe everything I read in the papers.

The point that needs to be absorbed is that "The Unforgettable Fire" isn't simply a different sort of record for U2, it's the tangible evidence of a radically changed collective frame of mind within the band. If their music has had some of its hard, overbearing corners removed, so have other aspects of the group's public personality. Faith, for instance ("We've seen a lot of the falsehoods and rejected them, so I think we're probably more *temperate* than we were a while ago" – Edge), or their attitude to the press, and thus by extension their attitude to their audience. They are still unreasonably paranoid about photographers.

The first time I ever saw Bono in the flesh, he was holding court to half a dozen friends in the bar of the Portobello Hotel. Given half a chance, when the tape recorders have been stowed away for the day, he'll fall into streams of reminiscences about the group's formative Dublin years, when Bono's best friend was Guggs from the Virgin Prunes (Edge's brother Dik is also in the Prunes) and U2 was still just a glow in the corner of his mind's eye.

Officially, he'll say something like this: "It's hard to get into the folklore, cos it seems like it's all over now. The Virgin Prunes wallpapered my car on my birthday . . . I've always felt elitism is next-door to a kind of fascism-type thing. It's a we-know-better-than-anyone-else type attitude, and I think we were guilty of that, where we came from." Here we go, the automatic self-editor back in action . . . "We did sneer and mock a lot of the people round us."

Edge: "But the funny thing was that we mocked pomposity and we mocked people who couldn't laugh at themselves. We laughed at each other – we derided and took the piss out of one another, and that was part of it. It wasn't as if the only people who got slagged were the outsiders. Bono, for instance . . . the name was a direct slag in a sense, even though it doesn't mean anything."

Of course, these formative days had a direct bearing on the way both U2 and the Virgin Prunes chose to pursue their divergent careers. Bono: "Y'see, at this time what happened was a lot of us were getting interested in the spiritual side of life, and reading up and finding out and sticking your fingers in the fire and getting burnt.

"We'd a lot of bad experiences there with the positive and the negative. The negative side was the occult and the whole black magic and mysticism thing, and we were severely burnt by that. We were never involved, we removed ourselves from that, and there was a lot going on. Really it's more than you could talk about in an article. What was going on in people's lives at that time really does defy description and it could come out in the most horrific way . . . honestly, because there were really wild incidents and nerve wracking things."

The embracing of Christianity followed from here. "One of the ways we reacted towards the positive was because of our experience with the negative, you could say," said Bono.

But this much-publicised "faith" of U2's is difficult to detect when you're around them. Outward trappings don't seem to exist.

"If you were on the road with us for a long time or if you saw us in a crisis situation or if you saw things happening around us . . ." said Bono. "You know what they say, there's two houses built, one's built on sand, one's built on rock. It's only when a flood comes that you find out which is built on a rock. And so sometimes . . . there is something we've had to fight for in the group and it's there.

"We all know it's there. Adam knows it's there and it's a real love of each other and love of what we do, and it is a flame y'know, and that's the song 'Indian Summer Sky' – 'to lose along the way the spark that set the flame to flicker and to fade on this the longest day'. There's times when it feels like it's nearly been blown out, but it's still there. You might not see it but it's there and it can ignite into a forest fire or whatever, depending on what's happening around us."

Edge is particularly scathing about what he calls "the faith industry", a business which is booming in America. "I think people in the States have been subjected to some of the most appalling sides of faith, and therefore it's so easy for them to kind of cast aside the whole thing, to throw out whatever baby there is with the bathwater, because it's been so appallingly exploited in this country.

"We tend to try not to justify anything of a spiritual nature in interviews because it's so dangerous to try to explain it or to talk about it. But at the same time it's nice to be able to say that we don't agree with this sort of spirituality or supposed faith."

"Can you imagine how it feels to believe in Christ and be so uncomfortable with Christianity?" asked Bono. "The church is an empty, hollow building. It's the edifice. The established church is the edifice of Christianity. It's as if when the spirit of God leaves a place, the only thing that's left are the pillars of rules and regulations to keep its roof on. And we are more and more uncomfortable and claustrophobic around organised religion.

"I used to think I could walk into a Protestant or Catholic church or whatever and just be at one, you know, myself and the surroundings. But we are . . . it's as if the way we are outsiders in the musical scene, we're outsiders on every level. We get flak from everyone. We seem to be walking this line, and whenever we cross it either way it's a long way down, on either side, to fall. And I don't know how we're still there, but . . . it takes away from it to talk about it."

Edge: "You see these guys on TV and you understand why people are suspicious and therefore you apply that to your own situation. At this stage I think my line on this is that it's really down to actions, and words will never substitute for actions, really."

Bono: "We don't talk about our personal beliefs because there's too much talk, y'know? You turn on the television in this country and you have this guy who looks like a neo-Nazi with a Bible in his hand, and his fist is virtually coming out of the TV screen and into the room where you're sitting and watching him. The credits come up and the call for cash comes.

"Can you imagine how that feels? For me, it's as much as I can do to restrain myself from throwing the television out of the top floor of the hotel. It's taught us to shut up. Let's not be the band that talks about love, let's be the band that loves its music and the people that are attracted to its music. And even the ones that aren't maybe, as well (*chortle*). But even that sounds pompous. It's such a claustrophobic position to be in, being in this group, in some ways."

"You couldn't have asked for a better example of U2's magic last night at Constitution Hall" – Washington Post 6/12/84

WASHINGTON DC's Constitution Hall is owned by the Daughters Of The American Revolution, and of course the revolution in question was not a Marxist one. The hall is small, neat and seated. There seems to be a security man for each customer the night U2 play there.

After the New York traumas the show is smooth and often impressive, though it falls short of becoming incandescent. They're still playing basically the same set they took around Britain and Europe, though "Unforgettable Fire" and "A Sort of Homecoming" have now been moulded into shape, not least by Larry's hard, whiplashing beat.

After "Electric Co", with Bono's crafty deployment of "Amazing Grace" across its middle section, he talks to the audience about his vision of "the two Americas". Bono's fascination with the natural forces of the North American

195

continent continues to grow, and he tells the Washington audience that they are the mythic, resonant America, not its bigoted and violent darker side. They seem to understand, and cheer resoundingly.

Later, after the group had spent some time meeting acquaintances and well-wishers backstage, they went outside to catch the bus back to their hotel to find a further knot of fans waiting patiently for them in the rain. Earlier, they'd been singing choruses of "how long to sing this song?" from "40". The band paused to get wet, talk and sign autographs.

"They were really nice," said Larry appreciatively once he'd gained the safety of the bus. "Very *civilised*."

I guess you're still not doing interviews, Larry?

Larry grinned. "I explain meself through my drumming. I don't see the point in doing interviews where you just repeat yourself and turn yourself into a cliche. I decided I wasn't doing myself justice, so I stopped doing them." Thanks Larry, very good interview.

"U2 is perched on the brink of superstardom" – *Washington Post 5/12/84*

" 'THE Unforgettable Fire' is a record of brokenness," said Bono. "I mean 'record' in the sense of a document. Its images are fragments. 'The Unforgettable Fire' itself, I wrote that high up in the Keio Plaza hotel in Tokyo. As I was looking out of the window to the silver and gold of the city and the skyline – because Tokyo really is like a Christmas tree at night.

"In the reflection in the window I could see myself and the room and I had been going through a very depressed, down period, and the room was just in a mess and everything in it was turned over. I wasn't . . . I wasn't, er, well. I told you the other day that a bottle of wine would put me on my back. I wasn't up to much.

"So that whole song, you know, 'carnival, the wheels fly and colours spin, through alcohol red wine that punctures the skin, face to face in a dry and waterless place'. It *is* a record of the broken side."

Well, I know what you mean about the Japanese house red.

"I don't understand why people don't see that even 'Gloria' is a song of . . . it's about *failure* to express oneself. I try to sing this song, I try to stand up but I *can't* find my feet. 'I Fall Down', 'October' – 'kingdoms rise and kingdoms fall'.

"See, this is why when I see myself being described as some sort of high priest or prophet standing up there, erect and proud, white flag in my hand, you know . . . I *know* who I am, and I know that if there's any triumph it's the triumph of being able to face yourself as you look at yourself. That's what the songs are about, and that is where the real thing comes from.

"All those images, they're images of brokenness. Like here, here's the man in a fist fight with his own audience, supposedly this man of peace. I mean, it's a joke. It's a sick joke actually. Because the reason I'm attracted to a man like Martin Luther King who as it were could turn the other cheek is because I *can't* turn the other cheek. I'm the very person who'll nut the guy next to me, I'm the very person who in a rage will . . . do the things I don't want to do.

"Humanness is what I'm interested in, not being superhuman or subhuman. There's as much fear on our records as faith. Maybe we've walked ourselves into it. Our first record, we had a boy's face on the cover, the whole perversion-of-the-innocents thing. Maybe we've dug our own grave. That was just one of the dimensions of it. I more than any other member of the group have been responsible for digging the bigger hole. We actually don't talk about it very much."

PEOPLE in rock groups are on duty, and worst of all on parade, a lot of the time. The strain is undoubtedly greater than the cynical hack would normally allow, especially with a group like U2 which would like to be remembered for being a little more than a Eurovision no-hoper. Their responses are varied. Larry won't give the press an inch, Edge keeps calm and plays a straight bat, and Bono wants to explain everything (*almost* everything, at least) and occasionally looks as though he might split open under the pressure.

Meanwhile there's Adam Clayton, cheerfully laconic at all times and perfectly happy to toe nobody's line but his own. At school, his headmaster finally agreed with him that he was ineducable and expelled him. Bono and Edge have a fund of Clayton stories, in which he undertakes such feats as selling paintings to nuns and driving cars up people's back gardens without warning. He is also renowned for flatulence of a high order.

WHEN he sang "Wire" in Washington, Bono rolled up his sleeve, clenched his fist and wrapped the microphone lead around his arm, just like Lou Reed used to do in "Heroin".

"A lot of the people on the street where I grew up at the age of 15 or 16 got into scag, heroin," he'd told me earlier. He'd read Art Pepper's harrowing auto-documentary "Straight Life" a few weeks before, as it happened.

" 'Wire' for me is an image of a hypodermic needle. That's its subconscious value to me. I'm intrigued that often imagery that is for me subconscious is actually quite conscious to other people. A guy, somebody in the music business in London, came up to me in the Portobello Hotel and told me he had nearly died last year. He had three cardiac arrests, three overdoses. He got involved in Narcotics Anonymous and sorting his life out.

"He told me that our music was a real soundtrack to a change in his life. And – this completely bowled me over – he knew everything I was on about on 'The Unforgettable Fire'. He knew what 'Bad' was about, he knew all the feelings, he knew what 'Wire' was about. He knew the two songs that related directly to what he'd been through.

"That, to me, if ever I was worried about my words being impenetrable, I felt that okay maybe they are on a surface level, but from deep to deep they actually do cut through. And this guy was telling me, he says that line, I just said it to myself over and over again, 'I'm wide awake I'm not sleeping – I'm not going back into that sleep'. That drug-induced sleep. And the times he'd wanted to. And that said a lot to me. Of course, the song is about so many other things."

There was a big hiatus for U2 after "War". There was the "Under A Blood Red Sky" live album as an effective stop-gap, but it was the best part of two years before any new material appeared with "Unforgettable Fire". There was a crisis in the band, wasn't there Bono?

He laughed quietly. "We broke up the band. We literally broke up the band, and formed another band with the same name and the same band members. That's what we did. We had all those teething problems that you have when you start a new band." He chuckled again.

"Yeah, it was really difficult, that period. It was awful. I was a *madman*. You know what they do to terrorists in Northern Ireland? They put brown paper bags over their heads, they put them in rooms where they can't stand up or sit down with their legs stretched out, they keep the light on 24 hours a day so they don't know what time it is or whether it's night or day. When you become a piece of luggage . . . when you're on the road you can sometimes lose track of yourself. Completely and utterly. You become lost in time and space.

"You walk out onto a stage, you give of yourself for an hour and a half, and the applause that comes back is uplifting but sometimes it's anonymous. You leave the venue and I need to talk to people afterwards, I need for that applause to be personified in some way so I can get a grip on what's been going on. But if you don't, you end up going back into this empty space which is your hotel room, and this constantly is a bit like this guy with the paper bag over his head.

"I think I lost myself at various points, and became an utter madman I think. That's when I started doing all those things. That US Festival thing. Have you ever seen that on television, when U2 played the US Festival? I climbed to the very top of the stage, it was like hundreds of feet up, and walked across the top of it on the canvas, and the canvas ripped.

"God! I can't watch that. I don't know who the person is. I don't know who it is, climbin' up there. Cos I'm afraid of heights anyway. Y'know, the adrenalin is a drug and it can go right or wrong in you, and I have to learn to deal with it, that's all."

Did that period include the festival at Phoenix Park in Dublin, August '83?

Bono paused for a moment before answering. "There was 15 minutes of the Phoenix Park gig that was an extremely important moment between U2 the Irish band and our Irish audience. When I said 'no more, no more' in the middle of 'Sunday Bloody Sunday', and the response 'no more, no more' came back, something *went up outta there*. I dunno, a message to the Gods y'know, 'get off our back . . .' I don't mean that! I don't mean that! I'll be screwed for that! But something happened that I don't think anyone else understood, but yes, that whole period . . ."

I didn't enjoy your set at Phoenix Park. The band sounded ham-fisted and the fanatical audience reaction was a bit frightening, frankly.

"But y'see we were an Irish group and they were Irish people, and they had a voice to speak out the way they felt. Everyone felt it. And yeah, I could understand the fear there. We are a very Irish group. That's another thing, another part of the misunderstanding."

In New York, after Bono had filmed an interview for a local Irish TV station, we'd dropped into the Russian Tea Rooms for fruit salads and vodka, served by smooth-talking men in moustaches and Cossack uniforms. The off-duty Bono is a fund of information, anecdotes, advice, praise and slag-offs, all delivered with remorseless energy. The man still has it in him to be star-struck too. Ringo Starr and Barbara Bach came into the Tea Rooms, whereupon Bono sent them a note via the waiter and invited them to any future U2 shows in New York.

"It's really embarrassing isn't it?" he giggled. "Me turning round and looking at them like that."

And when all the soul-searching has been done, that remark strikes me as being as pertinent as most.

Adam Sweeting

16

Legend of a loner

NEIL YOUNG

September 14 1985

L OOKING back 10 years or more, Young can now put his well-documented bleak period into a longer perspective. After "Harvest" had clocked up sales running into millions, Young's fans were horrified first by the release of the double album "Journey Through The Past", a bitty and meaningless "soundtrack" for Young's rarely-seen film of the same name. After the album came out, the film company refused to release the movie, to Young's continuing disgust.

Next came the nerve-shredding live album "Time Fades Away", a dingy and macabre affair notably devoid of the pure melodies beloved of his soft-rockin' afficionados. Young, feeling boxed in by commercial success, had steered away from it. The chart performance of "Heart Of Gold" had brought him a lot of things he found he didn't want.

"I guess at that point I'd attained a lot of fame and everything that you dream about when you're a teenager. I was still only 23 or 24, and I realised I had a long way to go and this wasn't going to be the most satisfying thing, just sittin' around basking in the glory of having a hit record. It's really a very shallow experience, it's actually a very *empty* experience.

"It's nothing concrete except ego-gratification, which is an extremely un-nerving kind of feeling. So I think subconsciously I set out to destroy that and rip it down, before it surrounded me. I could feel a wall building up around me."

To add insult to injury, his next studio recording was the harrowing "Tonight's The Night", though with a perversity that was becoming typical of him the latter wasn't released until *after* the subsequently-cut "On The Beach". Both albums stand up strongly to this day. Both use the rock format as a means of redemption and rejuvenation, the very act of recording (no overdubs) serving as therapy.

" 'Tonight's The Night' and 'On The Beach' were pretty free records," Young pondered, lighting another unfiltered Pall Mall. "I was pretty down I guess at the time, but I just did what I wanted to do, at that time. I think if everybody looks back at their own lives they'll realise that they went through something like that. There's periods of depression, periods of elation, optimism and scepticism, the whole thing is . . . it just keeps coming in waves.

"You go down to the beach and watch the same thing, just imagine every wave is a different set of emotions coming in. Just keep coming. As long as you don't ignore it, it'll still be there. If you start shutting yourself off and not letting yourself live through the things that are coming through you, I think that's when people start getting old really fast, that's when they really age.

"Cos they decide that they're happy to be what they were at a certain time in their lives when they were the happiest, and they say, 'that's where I'm gonna be for the rest of my life'. From that minute on they're dead, y'know, just walking around. I try to avoid that."

One of the key tracks from "On The Beach" was "Revolution Blues", a predatory rocker in which Young adopts the persona of a trigger-happy psychotic, eager to slaughter Laurel Canyon's pampered superstar residents. Reflecting on the song prods Young into some unsettling areas.

"That was based on my experiences with Charlie Manson. I met him a couple of times, and er . . . very interesting person. Obviously he was quite *keyed up*."

Gulp. Before or . . . *after* the Sharon Tate killings?

"Before. About six months before. He's quite a writer and a singer, really unique – very unique, and he wanted very badly to get a recording contract. I was at (Beach Boy) Dennis Wilson's house when I met Charlie. Coupla times.

"The thing about Charlie Manson was you'd never hear the same song twice. It was one of the interesting things about him. He had a very mysterious power about him which I'm hesitant to even fuckin' *think* about, it's so strong and it was so dark, so I really don't like to talk about it very much. I don't even know why I brought it up."

Young stopped talking for a moment. Thought we'd lost him, but he continued.

"There is a saying that if you don't look the devil in the eye you're alright, but once you've looked him in the eye you'll never forget him, and there'll always be more devil in you than there was before.

"And it's hard to say, you know. The devil is not a cartoon character, like God is on one side of the page and he's on the other. The devil lives in everyone and God lives in everyone. There's no book that tells you when the devil said to God 'fuck you' and God said (makes raspberry noise). All those books that are written are just one person's opinion.

"I can't follow that, but I can see these things in other people. You can see it and feel it. But Manson would sing a song and just make it up as he went along, for three or four minutes, and he never would repeat one word, and it all made perfect sense and it shook you up to listen to it. It was so *good* that it scared you."

A couple of years later, then, Young wrote "Revolution Blues" – "well I'm a barrel of laughs with my carbine on, I keep them hopping till my ammunition's gone" . . . So how did the superstar community take it, Neil?

"Well, see, I wasn't touring at the time, so I didn't really feel the reaction of 'On The Beach'. Then when I went on the road I didn't do any of it, so . . ." He did, however, perform the song on the Crosby Stills Nash & Young reunion tour, to the discomfiture of the others.

"David Crosby especially was very uncomfortable, because it was so much the darker side. They all wanted to put out the light, y'know, make people feel good and happy and everything, and that song was like a wart or something on the perfect beast."

WHEN it came to the release of "Tonight's The Night", Young again incurred the wrath and disbelief of people who thought they knew him fairly well. The album had been recorded with a Crazy Horse reconstituted after the death of songwriter and guitarist Danny Whitten, a close friend of Young's who'd given him early encouragement in his career.

Whitten had been due to go out on tour with Young, but was too heavily dependent on heroin to cope. Young sent him home. The same night, Whitten died of an overdose. "Time Fades Away" documented the subsequent tour, while "Tonight's The Night" was made in memory of Whitten and Bruce Berry, a CSNY roadie who also died from heroin.

Young remembered the day he'd taken "Tonight" into the offices of Reprise, his record company at the time.

"It was pretty rocky," he grinned. "I would describe that as a rocky day. They couldn't believe how sloppy and rough it was, they couldn't believe that I really wanted to put it out.

"I said 'that's it, that's the way it's going out'. It's a very important record, I think, in my general field of things. It still stands up. The original 'Tonight's The Night' was much heavier than the one that hit the stands. The original one had only nine songs on it. It was the same takes, but the songs that were missing were 'Lookout Joe' and 'Borrowed Tune', a couple of songs that I added. They fit lyrically but they softened the blow a little bit.

"What happened was the original had only nine songs but it had a lot of talking, a lot of mumbling and talking between the group and me, more disorganised and fucked-up sounding than the songs, but they were intros to the songs. Not counts but little discussions, three and four word conversations between songs, and it left it with a very spooky feeling. It was like you didn't know if these guys were still gonna be alive in the morning, the way they were talking. More like a wake than anything else."

Why did you take it off, then?

"It was too strong," said Young slowly. "It was really too strong. I never even played it for the record company like that. We made our own decision not to do that. If they thought 'Tonight's The Night' was too much the way it came out – which they did, a lot of people – they're lucky they didn't hear the other one."

It was here that Young hit the lowest patch, spiritually, of his career, probably of his life. His impatience nowadays with the hippy generation, and his endorsement of a right-wing President, believed by many to be a dangerous lunatic, can probably be traced back to the traumas around the time of "Tonight's The Night". Until then, the ride had been more or less free.

Was it, I queried, a case of Whitten's death being not only a personal tragedy, but a metaphor for a generation and a way of life? Or death?

"It just seemed like it really stood for a lot of what was going on," Young answered. "It was like the freedom of the Sixties and free love and drugs and everything . . . it was the price tag. This is your bill. Friends, young guys dying, kids that didn't even know what they were doing, didn't know what they were fucking around with. It hit me pretty hard, a lot of those things, so at that time I did sort of exorcise myself."

Did you feel guilty that perhaps you and people in your position had encouraged that?

"Somewhat, yeah, I think so. That's part of the responsibility of freedom. Freedom to do what you want with not much experience to realise the consequences. I didn't feel *very* guilty, but I felt a little guilty."

IT'S fitting that Young's latest re-emergence in public with yet another shift in musical direction should coincide with a wave of new groups who acknowledge a debt to his past work. Green On Red's Dan Stuart freely admits that their "Gas Food Lodging" LP was heavily influenced by Young's epic "Zuma" collection ("if you're gonna steal, steal from the best," as Stuart puts it). Jason & the Scorchers play "Are You Ready For The Country", the Beat Farmers turn in a welt-raising treatment of "Powderfinger", and Pete Wylie's just cut a version of "The Needle And The Damage Done" as an anti-heroin gesture. And Dream Syndicate's Steve Wynn will reminisce about Young and Crazy Horse any time you like.

With half the material for a follow-up album to "Old Ways" already in the can, Young is in the middle of a renaissance of sorts. Not even the AIDS terror can dent his confidence.

"It is scary. You go to a supermarket and you see a faggot behind the fuckin' cash register, you don't want him to handle your potatoes. It's true! It's paranoid but that's the way it is – even though it's not just gay people, they're taking the rap. There's a lotta religious people, of course, who feel that this is God's work. God's saying, y'know, 'no more buttfucking or we're gonna getcha'." Young cackled dementedly.

"I don't know what it is. It's natural, that's one thing about it. It's a living organism or virus, whatever it is. I hope they find something to stop it. It's worse than the Killer Bees."

Young obviously isn't making a play for the Gay vote. They probably don't hold with that sort of thing in the country. But his conception of the entire universe is, to say the least, unorthodox.

"I'm not into organised religion. I'm into believing in a higher source of creation, realising that we're all just part of nature and we're all animals. We're very highly evolved and we should be very responsible for what we've learned.

"I even go as far as to think that in the plan of things, the natural plan of things, that the rockets and the satellites, spaceships, that we're creating now are really . . . we're pollinating, as a universe, and it's part of the universe. Earth is a flower and it's pollinating.

"It's starting to send out things, and now we're evolving, they're getting bigger and they're able to go further. And they have to, because we need to spread out now in the universe. I think in 100 years we'll be living on other planets."

On a more earthly plane, Young's excited about the prospect of playing a benefit for the people of Cheyenne, Wyoming, whose houses and land have been devastated by a freak sequence of natural disasters. Young's band and equipment will be airlifted in for the show, by National Guard C130 transport aircraft and by private jets loaned for the occasion by some giant corporations.

"There's something different about it," Young mused, "having the government help us get there so we can help the farmers. The National Guard's gonna help us load and unload, get in and outta the place, help us set up the stage. It's interesting."

But it's something else, above and beyond his this-land-is-your-land preoccupations, that gives Neil Young his lingering aura of menace and strange purpose. You can feel it when you talk to him, and it permeates all his best music. He sees it something like this.

"I've got a few demons, but I manage to co-exist with them. The demons are there all the time y'know, that's what makes you crazy, that's what makes me play my guitar the way I play it sometimes. Depends on the balance, how strong the demons are that night, how strong the good is.

"There's always a battle between good and evil in every second in your life, I think. In every judgment you make both sides are represented in your mind. You may hide the bad side, but it's there."

Adam Sweeting

17

Welcome to the occupation

R.E.M.

September 12 1987

" **Y**OU can't tell anyone you came here."
Michael Stipe mutters this as we pull up in the drive of his house, the humid night air alive with the chatter of crickets, brown recluse spiders and rattlesnakes.

Stipe has learnt the importance of protecting himself from the inquisitive glare of the unhappy, imbalanced and downright undesirables who turn up on his porch from nowhere, seeking words of wisdom or comfort from someone they see as the closest we've got to an Eighties rock 'n' roll guru.

For that reason the house is now strictly off limits, and, if it *is* possible to *hint* f*** off, then a notice, pinned on the door does so with characteristic Stipean charm.

Once inside it's easy to see why. Common courtesy and respect for his privacy forbids any description of the interior – suffice to say it's a magical place. An R.E.M. LP cover brought to life.

THE last train to Disneyworld left the station just as R.E.M. guitarist Peter Buck was waking that morning. Blinking his way across the bedroom he switched on the TV and was, once again, confronted by the Reverend Ike, who, as usual, was frothing at the mouth.

"I *want* you to send me your money! And I don't mean that *jingling* kind cos that only makes me *nervous*. I want the folding cash! Cos I need a new Cadillac. God *told* me, I need a *new Cadillac!* I don't want my pie in the sky – *I want my pie now*!"

That was when Buck knew that R.E.M. had to make an album about America, 1987. America '87 and its surreal madness. Its attempts to revive the spirit of McCarthyism, its clandestine operations in Nicaragua and the blatant ones in the Gulf. The insatiable desire for money, murder and madness – everything that, to him, a young American, meant one thing – Disneyworld.

"It's a sideways look at the world and us. It has a kind of Orwellian wry humour. It's not that we're making light of America, it's just that I can't look at it the way Bruce Springsteen does. To me, America in 1987 *is* Disneyworld."

Buck pulls apart the slats on a Venetian blind and peers out into the Athens sun which is nudging 100 degrees. He surveys the quiet streets around the R.E.M. office, a last bastion of sanity in a country gone bonkers.

The evening before we arrived in Athens, R.E.M. had played an unannounced gig at the neighbouring 40 Watt Club – rumours of which had shot round the close-knit community like a synapse, ensuring that the club was overflowing by the time they took the stage. According to eyewitnesses, they tore through a selection of new material and just one old song "Begin The Begin" from "Life's Rich Pageant".

The experience had left them excited and obviously eager to talk. Even the infamously hard to pin down Stipe appeared relaxed, almost *eager* to please, if somewhat distracted by his friend's dog Joey, who he was looking after for the day.

R.E.M.'s last studio LP, "Life's Rich Pageant", was characterised as much by the directness of the songs themselves as by Don Gehman's lushly textured production. The man behind John Cougar and the Blasters, Gehman grabbed R.E.M.'s intangible, intransitory meanderings by where their balls should be, and sculpted them into something very nearly approaching pop. Surprising, then, that "Document", the revised title for "Disneyworld", should be an almost complete about face, if anything, capturing the band in even heavier sepia tones than their pre-"Pageant" days. Was this desire to trip it all down and get back to basics a reaction against the highly polished sheen of "Pageant", an unhappiness with a direction they'd not envisaged being pushed in perhaps?

"No, not at all," Buck explains, walking away from the window as the blinds snap shut. "Every record is a process of reacting against the prior one. I was really happy with 'Pageant' but none of us wanted to make that record again. I think we made the perfect record we could in that style and the new songs, because of the way we wrote them, wouldn't have lent themselves to that big AOR thing.

"We always go into the studio with a set idea but it never comes out that way. It's hard to write to order. I think this time we wanted a really big sound with lots of chaotic stuff on top. Big in a way that a Peter Gabriel record would be, but not as clean – full of weirdness, backwards stuff and noise."

"Document" is, at times, both more violent and more whimsical than any other R.E.M. LP to date, yet is less exact in the way it executes its intentions, displaying an almost cavalier attitude to any notion of conventional songwriting or playing.

"Well, we've been trying to write songs lately that are a little less form following," Mike Mills explains. "We're trying to write a little more musically nonsensical."

"Yeah," Buck interrupts, "I'm probably the worst for this, I'm the one who has to have a chorus in each song. But there are three or four songs on this LP which just don't have a chorus in the accepted sense, which is neat. Van Morrison has a lot of songs that don't have choruses and it's hard to work that into a rock 'n' roll perspective, but we wanted the songs to flow a little bit more and be divided less into anything like verse-bridge-chorus. Where's the bridge? Well the bridge is where the verse and chorus aren't."

So there was absolutely no intention of making a commercial LP then?

"I don't have a clue what commercial means," Michael Stipe deadpans as he's yanked into the room by Joey. "To me, commercial is 'Sledgehammer' or Gang Of Four."

Stipe's vocals are pared down almost to a shout on "Document", while Buck's guitars screech and soar against them, defying the gravity of each particular song. In a way, Buck's guitar work plays much the same role on "Document" as Stipe's voice did on "Pageant", and what few layers there are on the LP are stacked by him.

"It *is* our most male record," Stipe says, tongue in cheek as he disappears to fetch a bowl of water for his canine companion, never to be seen again that afternoon. Buck takes up the conversation.

"It seemed that on the last record, there was very little room for guitars because of all the keyboard parts. This time I got a bit greedy." He grins wickedly.

"It was a kind of release," Mike Mills continues. "We were coming out of the winter and we were itching to get it going so we really attacked it."

"Document" was recorded in Nashville with Scott Litt who Buck admired for his "dare I admit it? Big modern drum sound." For all its music biz connection Buck claims that Nashville was essentially a quiet town which soon succumbed to the R.E.M. way of doing things.

"Every night we'd finish at around one, go to a bar and meet the same five people." The band describes the sessions as easy going, a far cry from those for "Fables Of The Reconstruction" which, from a safe distance, they now admit came close to causing a split within the band as well as a personal crisis for Buck.

"I think we were all kind of miserable," the guitarist explains. "I hate to say it, but it was raining every day in England and we were all going through these weird pressures and I think that every band goes through these times when you think: 'Do I want to be in a rock 'n' roll band?' We were at the point where we could feel ourselves getting sucked into the business. I was pretty much a wreck for most of that time.

"I was just drunk all the time. It's not that I didn't care, I was just depressed a hell of a lot and it showed within the band. I think we were thinking 'Why can't we just be hippies and say f*** the record. We don't want to do it we're going home.' In the end we worked through it. If we were to record those songs now, in a similar mental state to what we were in at the time, they would be very different. I *do* like that record. I'm not saying it was a failure. I mean, rock 'n' roll isn't showbiz, we don't have to be happy. F*** it. As weird as that album can get, that's how I felt every day. The thing that sums it up is that bit at the end of 'Feeling Gravity's Pull' where the strings come in and it goes down 'Neargh!' I probably looked like that too."

"Document" shares a similar intensity but, by and large, it's developed into an intrinsic theme rather than a state of mind. From the unstoppable droning folk of the LP's opening tour de force, "Finest Worksong", to the Thirties' WPA-style social realist murals which adorn the cover, its central themes can scarcely be denied. Much later that same night, in his favourite pizza parlour, Stipe puts it all into perspective.

"In America, if you can't make money, they think it's because you're a failure. The work ethic is really intrinsic to American thought and that has a lot to do with this LP. The idea that you can work and work and get what you want and then try for even more. It's the American dream but it's a pipe dream that's been exploited for years. I could get by without money, I've done it before. You can get by in this town without money, it's not a necessity. But it's kinda gross what money does to you. Businessmen say hello to me on the street now. They acknowledge me when I go into a nice restaurant. They let me put my bike in the kitchen at the best restaurant in town. I can wear a smelly tee-shirt and they'll take me to the best table. It's really gross."

The likes of the Reverend Ike and his ilk offering the promised land at a price also meet with due disdain, this time from Buck.

"That whole faith thing is something that goes through American culture like a knife. It has done for years. At the turn of the century I guess it was a big thing. Amie McPherson and Father, er, what's that bastard's name? But he was a crook too. They all were. There's this American evangelical, Huxterism, America's full of religious nuts. They all came here for that reason. They got kicked out of their own countries. My family came over from Sweden because they were agnostics and atheists. They came here to get away from that.

"That's why, when you compare our songs to writers like Flannery O'Connor and Carson McCullers, I'm flattered but don't quite make the connection. Flannery's characters are all struggling to reconcile their faith to a modern world where faith doesn't play any apparent part. In our case I'd say none of us have got any faith anyway. I don't believe in God."

In the past, many of R.E.M.'s finest songs have walked the fine line between patriotism and gentle celebration of certain elements of American culture. Yet, over the last year, Buck claims to have derived most pleasure from the tainted visions held by Big Black and Sonic Youth. Was theirs a view he'd been tempted to share?

"I dunno. I'm certainly not an apologist for America, though it would be a nice piece of land if you could wipe out most of the people. I think Sonic Youth's vision is very tongue-in-cheek. I don't think you can take all this America 1969 blood and Manson stuff at all seriously. I mean, they haven't killed anyone yet. It's real Alice Cooperish. They're probably just a lot more comfortable with that imagery than I would be. I'm not a blood and guts type guy. All the clothes that I like have skulls on them but, if I wore them, I'd look a dork. I just look at it all differently to them."

Nevertheless, the songs on "Document" are more overtly political and damning than anything they've put their name to before. "Welcome To The Occupation", "Exhuming McCarthy" and "It's The End Of The World As We Know It" all rage with a seemingly uncontrollable anger. It's almost as if the passion and poignancy so prevalent on "Fables", stirred by the spread of inhumanity and decay, had festered and boiled over into blind hatred.

"Well, generally, Michael is really worried about this conservative trend that's going on and the way that people in power seem to look at things," Buck ventures. "Right now Russia has the most sensible leader they've ever had and

Reagan is just keeping the door open for more war. Reagan is a moron and that's all there is to it. I get upset when I think about him."

"End Of The World" and "Strange", a cover of the old Wire classic, are also among the most powerful and strange vocal performances Stipe has ever laid down. Both are delivered in a speed crazy rush of emotion.

"I wrote the words to 'End Of The World' as I sung it. When they showed me that song in the studio I just said 'It's the end of the world as we know it and I feel fine.' I wanted it to be the most bombastic vocal that I could possibly muster. Something that would completely overwhelm you and drip off your shoulders and stick in your hair like bubblegum.

" 'Strange' was a scratch vocal. I went in and sang it twice and said, 'That's it.' I didn't listen to it after that. They took it away and mixed it up and put some reverb on it. I just couldn't be bothered with it. I put a whole load of energy into the other songs and that one was just 'Ugh!' It's like spitting – you don't want to get it over your shirt but you wanna get it out and keep walking."

"WE'VE never played before. It's gonna be awful – I can't wait!"

Michel Stipe is musing on the evening's entertainment. Athens' two rock clubs, the 40 Watt and the Uptown Lounge, offer the kind of nightly entertainment and guest appearances that, two or three years ago, would have had the average Brit rock critic salivating for more. Tonight, Stipe and a couple of friends are opening for his sister's band, Cowface. Unfortunately they are awful. Stipe whacking out a guitar drone while two beefcakes bash sheet metal with 10lb hammers – a more testing Test Department.

A tortuous 30 minutes after it begins, an end is abruptly called and Athens' youth drifts back to the bar, unsure whether to laugh or mourn the loss of their eardrums. Only Catlin liked it and Catlin, as anyone who's ever been in a car that he's driving will know, is quite mad.

In the early hours of the morning, in a parking lot adjacent to the 40 Watt, Stipe unveils his reasons for all the recent extra curricular activities. This last year has seen him extending his work with the Golden Palominos as well as producing an LP by Hugo Largo, the bassist of whom he met when interviewed by him in New York.

"As a band, what R.E.M. are capable of is still pretty limited when it comes down to it. There's a very set position where I exist. I could never get a sledgehammer on stage and hit metal with R.E.M. I've done it in the early days when we used to play biker bars. I'd wear this globe as a hat and I'd take it off and pound it on stage. The bikers thought I was insane so they left me alone. I think they kinda admired me cos I was this really skinny kid with funny hair.

"It's not really a frustration with R.E.M. If anything, it's been opened up so wide to us that it's actually dangerous. But we're able to keep things intact and stay on top of each other. R.E.M. now is kinda like the statues that look out on Easter Island." His voice trails away, a trifle embarrassed at the veracity of the comment.

"I don't know why that came to me," he says. "It just did. I can't explain that one. I was trying to make some connection and it didn't happen."

Do you feel there's a responsibility as Michael Stipe to always try and be profound?

"Not really, no. I think my most artesian profundity comes when I have no idea and I'm just rambling. The best time to catch me is when I've had seven cups of coffee and I haven't slept in three days. I just vomit and, if you're there, you can catch the little chunks. I've read some interviews with myself and it's like I *could not believe* that I had said these things, they are so amazing. It's like Kafka or Jung. It sounds so incredible and underneath it says 'Claims Stipe!' And I just go 'Wow! Something's there after all.' "

THE previous evening at a Mexican restaurant the waitress had voiced much the same opinion and had stared in disbelief when we told her we'd spent 10 hours on a plane just to talk to R.E.M.

"We see them in here all the time," she'd said. "Last week Mike Mills left his glasses in here and all the other waitresses were trying them on. It was real funny. Maybe we should have auctioned them."

Athens hardly trades on the reputation of its most famous sons. A tee-shirt here or a poster there modestly proclaiming "Infamous Athenians!" A far cry from the intensity with which Distiples, as they're called in Athens, study the band's output and lyrics, often coming up with the most amazing translations and interpretations.

"I guess I wouldn't have it any other way," says Stipe, slurping at an iced espresso. "If I had a band, I would want people to either love them or despise them. I would hate for them to just go 'Oh yeah.' In a lot of ways, I think people come to the band because they think that I have some kind of answer. I *am* kind of questioning things in a different way but I'm just as lost as everyone else. So when I'm expected to answer these questions and spout forth with humorous and philosophical anecdotes, sometimes it's difficult."

Stipe's reluctance to talk has led to Peter Buck and Mike Mills tackling most of the interview chores which they do with the geniality of old pros. I wondered whether it was the inanity or the intensity of the earlier interviews that Stipe found so repellent.

"Well, I don't dislike *doing* them. It's just actually what comes out of them which is not to my liking. I enjoy talking to people except that it's always me, me, me, which is kinda gross. A lot of times in interviews I come across as very sensitive or very dour because when I talk about myself it's like 'Ugh!' I get too intense. I'm real reluctant to open up."

Does it hurt when people insist on calling you weird?

"No, I don't care. I've dealt with that all my life. I don't think anybody can hurt me really. I think they're disappointed when they find out how normal I really am. Cos I'm not weird."

The memory of a cold night in Glasgow two years ago flashed into my head. An everlasting vision of Stipe careering frantically across the Apollo stage, wearing watches all over his body and with the word "DOG" written in felt-tip across his forehead. This is *normal* behaviour?

"Oh, I was so sick that night," he protests. "I couldn't stand up. I hadn't eaten anything but potatoes for a whole week cos the food is so bad in England. All I could eat was a sprig of parsley before I went onstage and I was vomiting and shitting. It was just awful. I felt like a dog so I took a felt tip and wrote it on my face. But I started sweating it off while I was on stage, which looked weird."

There are other rumours though, sightings of him reading books upside down for one! Could he remember the first time that someone remarked that what he was doing was strange or odd?

"You know my earliest memory as a child was when I was two years old and I had Scarlet Fever. I was hallucinating and I was having my picture taken. I had a sweater on and I was really miserable and there was this guy zooming in and out. To me that was weird but I can't remember people remarking that I was weird. I don't know . . . I think you block those things out."

THE following morning he's up bright and early and already sitting by the phone in the R.E.M. office when we call. A pair of plastic sunglasses sit awkwardly on his head held together with a wad of Sellotape over the bridge of the nose. Along the sides he's glued strips of cardboard giving him the appearance of an Athens Terminator. In a truck parked in the street two storeys below, 18 globes of the world are stacked neatly ready to be burned and bent out of shape in the video for "Worksong" that Stipe is shooting that afternoon. While he's not nearly as sensitive as he's constantly portrayed, Stipe is an incredibly serious and obsessive artist who never stops work, drawing inspiration from every waking moment and, often as not, every sleeping one. Indeed, he cites his dreams as an often frightening subconscious release.

"I was shot in one dream by this assassin who was sent to kill me. But I didn't die. I was shot point blank but he didn't kill me. In the dream, he was hired to kill me, but he couldn't do so until I looked him in the eyes. He tracked me for a long time and I finally got tired of it so I looked him in the eyes and he shot me. But I didn't die. So then I was wounded and went on for a while, got tired, looked him in the eye and he took an ice pick and stuck it in my temple and killed me."

Despite the unguarded descriptions of dreams, Stipe has learnt to hold his tongue on the more mystical side of his nature. He refuses to be drawn into discussing the transgression therapy he is about to undergo, whereby he will be hypnotised and taken back to a past life.

"Well you know it's really outside the band and I think it would infuriate them if I talked about it. We get enough shit about being hippies already, especially now my hair's long again."

That said, R.E.M. don't really care two hoots or too much about how they're perceived by others. Like every good band, they understand what it is they do that is so unique and are now sitting in a position where they can afford to indulge what their conscience tells them is right.

"Every decision we've made that has seemed to fly in the face of common sense has worked for us," Mike had said the previous afternoon. Peter Buck had agreed. "You know, people say that we don't play the game but I don't know. To a certain degree, we do things that are unpleasant to us, photosessions and the like. It's just that we won't do things that we feel are deplorable or are against our ideals. They'd like us to have a glitzy video where we all sing and look sincere and where there's a pretty girl and we have to say 'Wait a minute. If we did that we'd look such pricks.' If you've got something people want you don't have to follow the game plan. Prince doesn't.

"Prince has weird covers and weird records. The new one sounds like a demo to me – which is partly good and partly bad. But at least he had the balls to do it."

Likewise, R.E.M. have turned down a prospective Radio 1 session scheduled for when they hit the UK this week.

"It's not like we *won't* do it," Buck explains, "it's just that we've got better things to do. If things hadn't have been so rushed maybe we would have found time."

Further example of their single-mindedness is the compilation LP, "Dead Letter Office". From a marketing point of view, released dangerously close to "Document", the LP works so well because it includes all the embarrassing bits other bands leave out. It makes you feel that you're listening to something that you shouldn't be which as everyone knows was one of the earliest appeals of rock 'n' roll.

"Yeah well, we didn't have too many illusions that it would sell two million," Buck laughs. "It's a summertime album. Plus, if we put it out now we can have control over what's on it as well as the packaging. If we were to change record companies, we wouldn't have that control. I was gonna leave out some of the ones that were more embarrassing but ah, f*** it!"

What *didn't* make it onto the LP?

"I really shudder to think!"

DREAMS for the future include a re-union with Don Dixon and Mitch Easter, probably after the next LP, an attempt to buy the rights for the soundtrack of a cinematic version of Ian Banks' "Wasp Factory" and more production work for each member of the band.

"Basically, we're trying to learn how to produce," Mike says. "Also it's good to do other stuff besides performing. We can have a secondary career so, if the band should break up, we can always do that."

Horror of horrors, you're not seriously contemplating . . . ?

"Well," Buck sighs, "I've always thought that a band should put out 10 LPs before they split. But the thing that always worries me is that we'll dry up. Everytime we finish an LP, that's what we think. And it's like 'God, this is it guys, it's finishing, enjoy it while you can.' There again, I suppose we could always play Las Vegas. Nostalgia for the early Eighties! Now that I could look forward to!"

Mat Smith

18

Viva hate

MORRISSEY
March 12 1988

ONE **of the best tracks on "Viva Hate" is "Little Man, What Now?", an eerie, enchanted, rather chilling song in which Morrissey ponders the fate of a young TV actor ("a real person** – but I don't want to name names") he remembers from "Friday nights 1969", briefly elevated to the level of minor celebrity before being abruptly dispatched back into obscurity, never to return – except for an afternoon TV nostalgia show, where the panel "couldn't name you". It's another example of Morrissey's unusual awareness of the trajectories of fame, and the ways in which fans use and are used by stars. He's personally experienced the extremes of both sides of the double-monologue that is the fan/star "relationship".

"Fame is the most fascinating subject in the world and I'm keenly interested in speaking to certain people who've had fame and then lost it."

Was there ever a point when you considered that it might all dry up for you, that you might have to go back to being a nobody?

"I do think about it, but I somehow think, with the intensity of the last five years, that even if, through some dramatic personal desire, I tried to obtain anonymity, it would be impossible. One way and another, I will always be *somewhere* just skating about the edges of global fame, pestering people and throwing glasses."

Did you *always* crave fame?

"I always had a religious obsession with fame. I always thought being famous was the only thing worth doing in human life, and anything else was just perfunctory. I thought anonymity was easy: it was easy to be a simple, nodding individual who got on the bus. I wasn't terribly impressed by obscurity."

Did you have a rich sense of destiny and difference?

"I always knew something, shall we say, *peculiar* was going to happen. I think real, true artists do have that instinct."

From the age of what, nine, 10?

"Much earlier. In some form. I saw a multitude of options and the dilemma was just which one to concentrate on. Obviously, I wrote. At the age of six I compiled a personal magazine every week. I was intensely interested in journalism, and all the things around it, whether it was performing or actually playing records. I intensely envied dee-jays. To simply sit on this cushion at the BBC day after day and flip on anything they thought was moving – well, I thought that was the most sacred and powerful position in the universe. To me, it was more important than politics."

You *wanted* to be a dee-jay?!

"At a tender age, I craved that power – to impose one's record collection on people in launderettes and on scaffolding. But now I think it's such a terrible job that dee-jays should be the highest paid people in the country. To have to sit in an office all day playing the same records – all of which are awful – over and over and over again – well, it's not funny, is it?! We shouldn't pick on these people. We should send them parcels!"

About this early magazine . . .

"I was only six, so . . . the art direction let it down a bit, really. It was simply the Top 10, then certain pin-ups of artists of my personal choice . . . sketched, in fact, by the editor himself."

What kind of circulation did it have?

"There was just the one copy, which limited readership somewhat."

So you quickly became an avid reader and writer?

"I very quickly became obsessed by music papers and pop journalism, and collected them ravenously."

So did you turn to music as an avenue for writing, or were you driven by musical instincts?

"By staunch instincts of very brittle criticism. Developed through having had this magazine of my own since the age of six, and listening to the Top 30 every Tuesday only to run off instantly to the typewriter in order to compile my own personal Top 30 which totally conflicted with how the world really was. But in my sense, my Top 30 was how the world *should* have been. It was a Top 30 of contemporary records, but the new entries were *very* unlikely, and obviously I favoured certain artists, like T. Rex.

"I can remember writing an extravagant critique of 'Cinderella Rockefeller'.

I was always a totally dissatisfied consumer, aflood with complaints. It seemed to me that the world of pop music, which I worshipped, was there to be altered and corrected."

THAT feeling – that pop belongs to "us", so how come it's blocked up with all this other people's stuff – has been an abiding feeling on the rock "left" for some 15 years. (Punk had very little impact on the charts, on what sold.) So Morrissey's infantile gainsaying of pop reality, was the chrysalis for indie pop's wistful, wishful fantasies of a "perfect pop" returning to oust the imposters in the hit parade.

"I think it's fact, things have reached an unthinkable state, where things are orchestrated entirely by unsympathetic and unmusical hands and ears. The people in key positions are people who don't consider pop culture to have any serious importance whatsoever."

So you believe pop is, or can be, art – but it's a belief that is only sustained by very rare instances. You seem to have very specific ideas about what consti-tutes art. The other day it occurred to me that there are maybe two kinds of intelligence in the world: one that's very open, that tries to take on everything, and accordingly gets paralysed by choice; another kind that's narrow, that finds strength by focusing on some things and excluding most everything else.

"If I liked everything, I'd be very hard to *understand*. I always found the idea of people who were very hard to please, including journalists who were very critical – I always found they were almost right when they found something praiseworthy. I find people who are unbudgeably fair, quite time-consuming. I find agreeable people immensely disagreeable."

Is that the idea of "Viva Hate" that we need bigotries in order to make sense of the world, make it actionable? (The hankering for a punk-style commotion is for precisely such an *illiberalism*, a taking of sides, a new order.)

"Sadly, a lot of people *need* to be told, rather than asked. Also, I often feel I can gain from venomously critical views of me as an artist, more than I can from dithery, sloppily fawning, supportive views."

GOING back to fame, to your intimate knowledge of the processes of identifi-cation and obsession . . . having been through various manic fixations, *you* have progressed to being a star, the subject of fixations yourself. Most of your fans though, will remain condemned in a lonely monologue with their distant idol . . .

"*Condemned* sounds a bit rough . . . but, nonetheless, I can't help but agree, really."

You encourage the obsessiveness, though, don't you? I remember you once saying you were delighted people sent you underwear, or demands for underwear . . .

"Yes, both! No, I do get lots of very fascinating and fascinated letters, and lots of *fascinating* gifts. I can very clearly understand obsessiveness, and the people who write to me *see* that I understand obsession and preciousness. And I respond in the same way. I still get very nervous when I meet people who I admire . . ."

Like who?

"Avril Angers . . . "

Who?

"Well, exactly – Avril Angers! She acts. I get very nervous when I meet people from the theatre. I think that's a very hallowed, sacred thing to be in. And I still have scrapbooks."

What does it feel like to see *your* proliferated image about, on hoardings, in magazines, to hear your voice on the radio?

"It's very odd. I was in a shop once, buying scented candles, and on the radio came Steve Wright with a collage of Smiths songs, and I got a distinct chill, almost as though the hand of Death was tapping me on the shoulder, saying: 'put yer candles down, it's time to go!' "

ABOUT the split . . . there seems to be a desire, on the part of both you and Marr, to represent the end of the Smiths as though there was little or no acrimony involved. But if a band ends, after a period in which the main protagonists hadn't communicated for some three or four months, surely *some* kind of serious conflict was going down . . .

"I expect it's hard to believe there weren't some elements of hatred slipping in and out. I don't think I'd believe that there was no acrimony. But it became a situation where people around the band began to take sides, and there was even a belief that within the audience there was a Morrissey contingent and a Marr contingent. And critics began to separate, and praise one and condemn the other.

"I *personally* did not find this a strain. But I find acrimony and even dwelling on the final events very futile; although in a sense I feel reportable, in another, more affecting way, I *don't*. And I think explanations create their own suspicions that things were much worse than they were. And that's what happened. Because there were so many people around the group, everyone had their own exaggerations, and stories began to breed."

Was the question of conquering America a problem, Marr being keener to undertake a world tour than you were?

"Once again, this was fabricated. Although I had very little passion to do a proposed world tour, and had less passion than any other member, I always thought my opinion was totally, totally valid. But it's true, if I'd nodded, a world tour would have happened. But I wasn't prepared to become that stale pop baggage, simply checking in and checking out, not knowing where I was or what clothes I was wearing, and quite ritually standing onstage singing."

The other Smiths had more of a taste for that?

"Not exactly, but they were more realistic and adaptable."

It wouldn't have been so wearing for them as for you?

"No."

Do you think Johnny is possibly even *more* into being famous than you are?

"It's very difficult for me to answer that question. People often tap me on the shoulder and ask me that, and it's a general assumption that he must have been. But my general impression is that he wasn't. He had many opportunities to talk to the press, and I was *always* the *only* person who encouraged him to do extra-curricular activities. But I also do become very confused by the *number* of people he does become involved with . . ."

Do you blame Ken Friedman (ex-Smiths manager and now Marr's personal manager) for the split?

"Um . . . I'd rather not discuss that."

IS it hard to maintain a barrier between your inner self and the worldliness of the biz and its machinations?

"There is a lot that's unavoidable. Money is a constantly draining occupation – trying to deal with it, keep it, *get* it. I find the business side very distasteful, harrowing and soul-destroying. I could talk about tax which I find quite frightening. But this always sounds like a soft and phoney complaint. Because even though I'm taxed to an extreme and impossible degree, I still at the end have a lot of money. I do get the sense, though, that it's illegal to earn money in this country."

Surely you're not with Margaret on this one, up there on the guillotine? *Presumably* you believe the disadvantaged ought to be supported and enabled?

"It's very difficult. I always had a very basic view that if you earned money it belongs to you. But that is obviously not the case. People have very slim rights over the money they earn.

"You have to get up very early and concentrate very hard to ever see any of it. The Smiths never earned *any* money touring. We'd come off remarkably successful tours and have to sit down and sign 80 cheques. Johnny and I would just look at each other and all of a sudden get very . . . old."

DID it feel like it was all getting out of control?

"Oh, it got entirely out of control, totally, *totally* out of control. This, if anything, was the cause of the Smiths' death. Especially the monetary side. We were making huge amounts of money and it was going everywhere but in the personal bank accounts of the four group members. Johnny and I would be walking offstage in the Universal Amphitheatre in Los Angeles, after playing an insanely devastating performance, and *instantly* have to sign cheques, while we were still euphoric and dripping with sweat, otherwise we couldn't put our trousers on.

"And finally, I think, Johnny had to back off from that, and put his entire life into the hands of his manager, because there was too much pressure. And there were too many people around the group saying, 'pacify me, say something nice, make me feel needed.' All people surrounding groups are like that, they need to be needed, they need to telephone you at strange hours to find out if they are still liked and still included. And that's very annoying, because the only two people who needed to be supported were Johnny and me."

SO the Smiths: ye olde storie of something unspoilt being strangled by the success engendered by its very novelty, of love crushed by the wheels of industry. It's the tragedy at the core of rock: how can something essentially private withstand the pressure of going public. Morrissey's answer is to retreat still further into his memories.

The Smiths were prime movers in what you could call the depoliticisation of personal life after punk's initial scornful demystification. Remember 1980: "personal politics" was the phrase that tripped off every lip, groups like Gang Of Four ("Love Like Anthrax") and Au Pairs *worked* towards their dream of the equal relationship, liberated from the veils of romantic "false consciousness" – unconsciously mimicking the pragmatism of therapists and counsellors, with their notion of love as contract.

Then 1982: attention shifted to the public language of love, to pop's iconography – the buzzwords were "the language of love", "the lexicon of love", "the lover's discourse", demystification was superceded by deconstruction and ambiguity.

Finally, with Nick Cave's misogynist agonies, the Jesus and Mary Chain's candyskin classicism, and the Smith's eternally unrequited gaze, came the return of romanticism in all its purity and privacy. Pop had returned to what it has *always* been about: the privileging of the personal as *the* realm in which the meaning of your life is resolved. The motor-idea of romanticism – the dream of the redemptive love that will make everything alright, resolve all difference – has, in the 20th century, replaced religion as the opium of the people.

But it's the dream that continues to speak most deeply to us. And maybe the superstition of love is our last reservoir of spirituality in the face of those "specialists of the soul" who would seek to *reform* relationships in accordance with their ghastly notions of "negotiation", "support", "partnership".

I ALWAYS come back to the Stones when I think of the Smiths, because of the camp, but mainly because of the way each band illuminates their era for us. For the Stones, satisfaction was the goal: everything would be *alright* if we shed the inhibitions that held us back and down. Revolution meant good sex on the 'morrow.

But the Stones were the product of expansive times, the Smiths the product of contracted and beleaguered times. With the Smiths it was a question not of desire but of *longing* – the yearning to belong to or with someone, to belong somewhere. The dream that two half-a-persons can make a whole, fit hand-in-glove. The Stones and their time were all about leaving home; the Smiths and our time are about pining for a home.

It's a sign of the times, maybe, that pop-as-reinvention-of-the-self is something that resonates for fewer and fewer people in the little world that is the music press readership; that the pollwinner, the figure you most identify with is Morrissey, victim of his past, chained to his memories. And as he says, artists don't really "develop", they have their act, gift, whatever, and stick with it.

That peal of exile first heard in "Hand In Glove" still rings true in moments on "Viva Hate", and no doubt always will, no matter what follows, in the same way that traces of wantonness persist in Jagger's voice beneath all the mannered overlay of time.

AS I neurotically double-check if the tape is running, I mutter by way of apology, "I've had some bad experiences with tape recorders."

"Oh, I've had some bad experiences with *people* actually . . . you're very lucky."

Simon Reynolds

19

Black power

PUBLIC ENEMY

May 28 1988

I WAS GOIN' OVER A HISTORY THAT WAS taught by the Honourable Elijah Mohammed which we feel is the true history of the two races, both black and white. That's the true history. Do ya understand what I'm sayin'?"

It was an elegant room, typically European, elegant but sedate. And we were feeling almost comfortable, sitting near the window, sipping grapefruit juice and watching the pretty little fishing-boats bob up and down in a quaintly picturesque harbour.

We were certainly more comfortable than we had been earlier when, uninvited, we'd attended a black consciousness lecture. The man giving it had worn a red "Che" beret, black tunic, black trousers, polished black Oxfords and a patient, almost condescending smile. His students, dressed similarly, had listened attentively as he spoke, as he sketched maps and inscribed slogans on a giant paper block, resting like one of Moses' tablets of stone on a sturdy wooden easel.

Occasionally one or other of the students had raised his hand to ask or answer questions that demanded or provoked descriptions of a cruel world dominated by Caucasians, a world which, like some huge over-ripe plum would eventually collapse in on itself, a world which would literally give way beneath the weight of its own hypocrisy.

We'd listened, either unnoticed or ignored, as images of fire, blood, rape and splendid revolution were conjured then replaced by even more splendid visions of an attainable earthly paradise. This, the lecturer had said, was the truth.

The lecture had not, as you might have expected, taken place in a dank Chicago cellar lit by a single flickering light-bulb or on some street-corner in Alphabet City. No, they'd gathered, in the unlikely way this industry allows for, in a hotel dining-room, its bay window overlooking Lake Geneva, its thick floral cornicing and crystal chandeliers undoubtedly more used to entertaining elderly millionaires and diplomats' wives. *This*, though, had probably been more ominously polite, more terribly dignified than any meeting of ageing ex-patriates and we had stood uneasily in the doorway watching and listening as Public Enemy prepared themselves, *drilled* themselves as they have done every day for the last two years, for the final conflict.

NOW sitting in the rapper Chuck D's hotel room, with the fishing-boats still bobbing in the harbour, we listen again to the lecturer and leader of Public Enemy's Security Of The First World, Professor Griff. Chuck watches quietly from a corner. Griff talks amiably and we, having this time been invited, feel like confidants, party to secrets none of us Caucasians should really share.

"The question that we raise," says Griff, "is, if America is named 'America', why did they give Christopher Columbus the credit when the Indians were there 6,000 years before he was and there was also a man by the name of Americus Vaspucci who was also there before him. Why do they give Columbus the credit for discovering America? These questions need to be raised if we're to stay in the education system we're presently under. Black people around the world need to be re-educated from the very beginning and taught the *truth*."

And whites, we inquire.

"Of *course*. See, we have a message, toward raising the consciousness of our people, but the message is for *all* people because white people need to be taught the knowledge of themselves also. You understand what I'm sayin'? And that's one thing that Moses came to teach white people when they lived in the Caucus mountains."

Could you, um, go over that for us?

"Well you see," expands Griff, "it may be something that you may not readily understand, you'd probably have to do research but, um, we know and understand that the race today called the White Race or the Caucasian Race came from the Caucus mountains. Now this is where the white race lived for approximately 2,000 years. Now, the things that went on up in the caves and the mountains of Europe, white people are not taught.

"You're not taught that it was not black people who made it with monkeys, animals and dogs, but it was white people who did these things. It was not us who ate our meat raw, uncooked with blood dripping out of it, it was white people who did these things. When they mention a caveman walking around a cave with leopard and lamb and bear skins on, carrying a club, they're not talking about black people. What society, what people get confused about is when white people start to talk about dinosaurs. Y'all wasn't *there* then. Do you understand what I'm sayin'?"

Mmm.

"You know nothing about that, nothing. What . . . what's that character's name that came up with the evolutionary theory?"

Charles Darwin.

"Yeah, Darwin. Came up with the theory about man evolving from apes. That's a *lie*. There is a sayin' that 'I'm a monkey's uncle.' Where did that sayin' come from? It came from the Caucasian mountains because it's actually true. White people are actually monkeys' uncles because that's who they made it with in the Caucasian hills."

We ponder our place as monkeys' uncles having, only seconds before, believed ourselves to be monkeys' nephews.

"Yeah, the type of *sound* y'all like, the acid rock and the rock-type stuff, came from conversations that you *tried* to have in the caves and, being that the caves were so hollow, you had a confused conversation and that's the type of sound that it created. You may not believe this but it's *true*. Do ya know what I'm sayin'?"

Mmm. A lot of white people might consider the view that they're monkeys' uncles offensive, not to say racist.

"True. But, listen, why can't we deal with the *truth*. It was white people who were all around the world sayin' that black people had tails, sayin' that we were just no-good, downright ignorant, half human, not even *half* human. *We* didn't do this. All we did was tell the truth. And that's the truth. You may not be able to swallow that. *We've* been taught that we've been made other than our own selves. We haven't been taught we was black, we been taught that we was niggers, coons, shines, hambones, the nothings of the earth. So, when the truth exists in their faces, a lot of *black* people don't even believe it. We was talking to a journalist today. She didn't wanna be called black, she wanna be called an English woman. *English*. But she's *black*."

CAN'T you understand that many people want to be judged purely by their character?

"You know, in no society do people accept you for your character. They give less than a damn about your character. Did white people wanna know about our character when they put us on slave-ships? Did they? You think Nazi Germany cared about the Jews' character when they put them in gas ovens? They give less than a damn about our character."

Of course, of course, but things have improved somewhat since then.

"Prove to me that things have improved."

Well, there aren't any slave-ships anymore and certain politicians, especially in the West, have made reasonably successful legislative efforts to curb bigotry.

"Listen, when white people came to America and they took the Indians' land from them and they made treaties with them, then broke the treaties and put the Indians out on reservations, do you think that was fair?"

No, it was dreadful.

"So what do you mean that they're makin' *efforts*. They said when they freed black people that we were supposed to get 40 acres and a mule. We didn't catch nothing but hard time, nekkidness and out-of-doors and we were beat and killed by the same one who freed us. So we had no other choice but to turn right back around and say 'Look, massa, we ain't got nowhere to go 'cause you ain't taught us how to do anything but pick cotton and we ain't got no cotton fields of our own to pick so we gotta go right back to the plantation and work.'

"And you know what massa say? He say, 'Well, listen, I can't pay you', so we end up doin' more free labour. They didn't give us 40 acres and a mule. So imagine now if we was to say to America 'We want retribution, we want everything you owe us from the time we worked for you. And interest.' You know what America would have to give us, all of us, 30 to 60 million of us? America would *crumble*."

Our obviously naive demeanour finally stirs Chuck to speak.

"The only way for equality in America is for black people to be treated superior. That's what you call compensation for the inferior treatment over four hundred years. That's only commonsense. Minus 400 – you must add 400 to get equality."

Can you give us a practical example of how that might work?

"Black people shouldn't have to pay taxes," states Chuck. "Number one, alright? Also black people should be paid . . . I . . . can't put into monetary terms. . . 250 billion's a *nice* figure. *And* some."

"More than that," says Griff.

"*And* be given a big part of their country," continues Chuck, "and then they can pay for us for f***in' *mental* damage that we have to rebuild. It's a long process. Now you wanna talk about places like England and you wanna say how it's *liberal* and more *equal* there. No, you can't say *anything* 'cause the f***in' foundations of the UK have created hell in the world. They planted seeds in damn near four-fifths of the planet if not more. It's created hell in Asia, South

America, Central America, North America, Australia, Africa . . . am I missing anything?

"You see the relationship – England, Israel, America and South Africa." Chuck laughs adding, "Are the four countries that Griff *loves* . . . You see, what I'm sayin' is you can't change people's attitudes without changin' the structure they live in. You have to destroy the system, destroy whatever exists today in order for things to get better."

IS VIOLENCE justifiable?

"When God destroyed Sodom and Gomorrah," demands Griff, "was that justifiable?"

Um, we tend to be a little atheistic.

"Listen, we're not takin' orders from anyone but God. God gives the orders man. Understand what I'm sayin'?"

Well, no, because it seems to us that religion only reinforces our worst habits. Religion, because it's morally based, is as capable if not more capable of oppression than any other system.

"Well, if you're talkin' about this religion called Christianity and the way a lot of these white Arabs practice Islam, yes. Very much so."

So, when you're talking about God, you don't mean a Christian god.

"A Christian god? No, see, 'cause the Christian god is a *white* god, that god we ain't got nothin' to do with. *You* made your god white, *you* painted Jesus as a white man, *you* made us look up into the sky for a pie-in-the-sky type religion, to make us think that once we died we was gonna go up to heaven and eat milk and honey. No, we don't believe in that type of god."

But doesn't that "type of god", that Baptist, Mormo Evangelical, Born Again stuff, hold sway with a great many American blacks?

"Yes, yes," agrees Griff.

"Well, there you go," says Chuck, "you were talkin' about changin' attitudes. Doesn't that have to be changed?"

WE are reminded for a moment of a speech, a transcript of which came to our attention some months ago. In it, Malcolm X, a militant black American speaker, told a worrying little story. It went something like this:

A group of people were asked how many of them wanted freedom. They all put up their hands. There were about 300 of them. Then the person said, "Well how many of you are ready to kill anybody who gets in your way for freedom?" About 50 put up their hands. And he told those 50 "You stand over here." That left 250 sitting who wanted freedom but weren't ready to kill for it. So he told the 50 "Now, you wanted freedom and you said you'd kill anybody who'd get in your way. You see those 250? You get them first. Some of them are your brothers and sisters and mothers and fathers but they're the ones who stand in the way of your freedom. They're afraid to do whatever is necessary to get it and they'll stop you from doin' it. Get rid of them and freedom will come naturally."

So, Chuck, those Baptists, those Mormons, those Evangelical Christians, those who, because of all that, are too squeamish to do anything other than stand in your way, what do you do about *them?*

"Look, what I'm sayin' is that, in America, two wrongs are gonna have to make a right."

Should we be shocked? Should we be horrified? Should we at this point leave our grapefruit juice to turn sour on the coffee table and abandon the seductive panorama to two people too far gone to appreciate it? Well, we might . . . we might if we were thick.

INEVITABLY there are those critics who do, that English woman for instance, so English she's "forgotten" she was black. She went. Because inevitably there are those critics who regard Public Enemy's work as a "statement", who choose to separate style and "content" and concentrate only on "content" even as they pay lip-service to Public Enemy's "imagination". Because, for them, all imagination really means is a sort of super-sensitive rendering of "reality". And inevitably these people – the socialists, the liberals, the humanists – continue to focus on this "reality" rather than on the extent to which Public Enemy's noise, the noise as a thing itself, engages the mind in certain transformations.

For many, Public Enemy's increasingly outspoken statements, normally reserved for interviews, are becoming a tenet by which to judge their work. This is the sort of filthy habit common to socialists, humanists and liberals who, rooted in a passion to protect and defend values traditionally considered to lie outside of rock, namely truth and morality, and believing rightly that these values are compromised by rock, condemn not only Public Enemy the politicians but also Public Enemy the noise.

But Public Enemy's work, whether they or their critics like it or not, is *not* a statement. Their interviews *are* a statement, their work is *not*. We cannot, with them, separate style from content, to attempt to do so is to engage in a pseudo-problem. Their noise, encountered as noise, is an experience, not a statement or an answer to a question. Their noise, and we must stress here their noise – rap, rhythm and sonics – is not *about* something, it *is* something. Their noise is a thing *in* the world, not just a text or commentary *on* the world.

THEY, the people, well . . . they're different.

"You're talking about a total brain-washing," says Chuck, "a devious f***in' plan that's worked. Those mothers that spent money and built those ships or planted their seeds in those other lands, they put together a mother, they put together a hell of a game-plan.

"It's still in effect. It's starting to backfire but we might not see it totally backfire for another 500 years. But *this*, yo, the people who put this together knew what they was doin'. And our whole thing is, if you're gonna believe in the system, though you might've been born in 1965 or '66 or whatever, if you gonna believe in the systems that are takin' place and you gonna believe in the way life *was*, or if you gonna ignore what happened back then and wanna lead life from this point on, then *you're* not talkin' about repairin' the situation."

But this *was* all a terribly long time ago.

"A lot of whites say, 'Well, that was then, this is now. Don't worry about what was then.' And, meanwhile, you can't tell that to a Jew."

"Nope," confirms Griff, "can't tell that to a Jew."

"You can't tell that to a Jew," repeats Chuck with a certain amount of satisfaction.

Are you insulted when we say we don't feel responsible?

"Hell, yeah. Shit yeah. How the f*** you gonna repair something without knowing the problem? Do you know what I'm sayin'? How you gonna repair something without fully diagnosing the problem? You can't fix *shit*, you can't say, 'Well, I'll just *fix* it. F*** it, I don't know *what* the problem is, I'll just *fix* it.' "

Can't we do it together? Can't the black man and the white man sit together at the same table and attempt to "fix it" together?

"Never happen," says Griff, "that will never happen."

Can't we even *hope* for it?

"No, it's not the nature of white people to be equal with black people. Imagine the slave-trader wantin' to be equal with the slave now. That will never ever happen, it's never happened in history. Name someplace where that ever happened."

DON'T you trust any white people?

"Naturally there are white people that we trust. Come on, I mean, that's *ridiculous*. We couldn't fly in no planes, 'cause black people don't fly planes. You got to say 'Okay, this sort of thing we got to place in the hand of God.' "

"It's a working relationship," adds Chuck philosophically, stressing the word "working".

Still sounds a bit racist to us.

"It's not racism, it's the truth. We tell the truth. People think it's racist just 'cause the media says so. Like Louis Farrakhan is anti-semitic. People read . . . believe. They don't go into it, they don't even know what anti-semitic is."

"Tell 'em what anti-semitic is, Griff."

"Okay, listen," Griff tells us. "If you got the Jews and they say that anything that is said against a Jew, if you don't believe what the Jews believe, then you anti-semitic. Not only a belief, but if you're not in their favour you anti-semitic. What does that have to do with Minister Farrakhan when he's tellin' the truth about Jews? The Jews set up the slave-trade – he said that. That's the truth, that's not bein' anti-semitic. Am I right or wrong?"

Um.

"Palestine," continues Griff, poking one of us in the arm, "that's the after-effect of slavery 'cause they did the same thing to us. They tried to sneak into Uganda to take the land from the Ugandan people. Idi Amin didn't go for it, he said no. He rounded up all these Jews and murdered them, all the black people that sympathised with them, he murdered them too. He ran all of the Jews out, took the business back from the Jews and gave them to his own people. Do you know what I'm sayin'? That's not bein' anti-semitic."

You don't think that's being anti-semitic?

"Let me tell you something right now. If the Palestinians took up arms, went into Israel and killed all the Jews, it'd be alright. 'Cause they shouldn't be there."

"Listen Griff," interrupts Chuck, posing as the voice of reason, "let's not even talk about this. I'm sayin' let's look at this realistically."

Yeah, please, yeah. Let's look at it realistically.

"And South Africa," adds Chuck. "Look at South Africa. Who belongs there? I tell you, man, they're all in it together. Who do you think backed Israel when they declared the State of Israel? I'll tell you. Britain, America, South Africa . . . and Germany. Nazi Germany. Nazi Germany financed it. Do you know what I'm sayin'?"

No, not anymore, no. This really does sound racist.

"Listen, to be a racist you must prevent people of a certain race from doin' certain things. We can't prevent nobody from doin' jack *shit*."

But you want that power.

"If we had the power we couldn't do the devilish things that they've done. And that's the only way we could get equality, which is sayin' that we have to in turn become devils in order to balance this shit out. We have to do devilish deeds. How do you compensate for the Holocaust? You *can't*."

Exactly. You *can't*.

"Chuck," offers Griff, "do you know what they're doin'? They're goin' all around the world diggin' up graves and they're findin' everybody who had anything to do with the Holocaust and they're *killin'* them. Imagine if we did that. White folks would be dyin' every day."

"See, as a black person," explains Chuck, "you gotta ask yourself, what do I need to gain equality? Tell Rockefeller to give up some of them dollars. Tell the Kennedys, tell these mothers to give up some of their *seats*. Destroy this f***in' *system*. Black people shouldn't have to pay taxes. And people say 'Well, talk realistically.' *That's* real. That's as real as we can get, you can't get no more real than that. So if you say 'That's unrealistic, that can't be done' and I say, 'If that can't be done then that can't be done' then you'll find a situation where, when people find out about the truth, then they're gonna resort to violence."

"Yeah," continues Griff, "that's where it's headin' to. Armageddon. I'm tellin' you.

"Some day people are gonna wake up to the truth. But they lie to us. Imagine me comin' into my church every Sunday and seeing a picture on the wall and they tell me this is Jesus. And I'm supposed to *believe* this. And I turn round and say, 'Wait a minute, let me read this in the Scripture', and I open the Bible and I see that he had hair like lamb's wool and his skin was a bronze colour. No, somebody's lyin'. And then I walk into Chuck's father's church and I see Jesus with blond hair now and I may see him as a brunette. No I can't go for that. I got to ask. Human nature calls for that.

"You have to see *you* in religion, you have to see *you* in education. They say we're part of society, but you have to see *you* and we don't see ourselves. They *lie* to us when they say Christopher Columbus discovered America. A black man was on the ship *with him* showing him how to *get* here. But *they* don't teach that. They don't teach you that the first Chinese was black. They don't teach you that the first Europeans were black. Do they? They don't teach you that we built the pyramids, they say that some Jews in slavery built them which is a *damn* lie. They don't teach these things. We got to tell the *truth*. Nothing else. And if to tell the truth is being radical then we're radical."

"And this," explains Chuck, "is how things are learned. You tell the truth and you give examples. You weigh logic."

"Let me give you an example," says Griff. "They say that the white Jews built the pyramids. Shit. The Jews can't even build *houses* that stand up nowadays. How the hell did they build the pyramids? Do you understand what I'm sayin'? They can't build a building, man, that's standing up too well. They got to rebuild cars every day of the year. No, man, a black man with high mathematics built the pyramids. And that's proof. *That's* the example."

SILENCE engulfs the room, obliterating the view, drowning any possible retort, rendering us utterly speechless, capable only of contemplating this alternative history, this gallows of everpresent crimes that has us, the Jews, everyone, *everyone* other than Public Enemy and Louis Farrakhan sitting guiltily in the dock awaiting sentence for a catalogue of incalculable crimes.

Griff's genial tone, pitched despite the verbiage, in a conciliatory tenor, might be the tone of an executioner, who, having nothing personal against the condemned, is happy to offer him some last request. The situation is at once real and surreal. So real, in fact, it's unbelievable.

We brace ourselves for what comes next . . .

"I'm a firm believer in separation," says Chuck. "You *cannot* have whites take care of your situation. You have to do it yourself. And the thing about it is it's *unfair* for us to have to do it ourselves because we didn't create this hell. But we got to do it ourselves because it's come to the point where we say 'No, no, we don't *need* your help. You don't f*** *shit* up now. Just stay there and leave us the f*** alone and *we'll* do this. Just give us these things and we'll be alright.' "

"That's what that lady said to me today," remembers Griff. "She said the South Africans were afraid of Margaret Thatcher calling for economic sanctions. I said, 'Bullshit. Tell that bulldog-faced woman to get the f*** out of South Africa, and black people will . . .' "

"It's true," interrupts Chuck, "for example, you're gonna come to a point where people get to a stage of organisation where if Thatcher can't do anything for the South African situation, somebody's just gonna come up and blow Thatcher away. And you know something? It won't be a black person. It'll be a white person sayin' 'This is *wrong*.' "

Because whites are more violent, more capable of devilish deeds.

It's difficult. No, not difficult, impossible. Impossible even sitting in the luxury afforded by Swiss hotels beneath the silent majesty of the Alps, to remain detached, restful, contemplative, emotionally free to be beyond indignation and approval. Yet that kind of dynamic contemplation is precisely what their noise requires.

WITH Public Enemy the "content" is only the pretext, the lure which engaged us with the noise. At this point "content" is annihilated and we're left with something purely formal, formal as in form, style.

This is how we can, in good conscience, endorse Public Enemy, who, in terms of "content", in terms of what they gob out during interviews, in terms of what they've said and are about to say, are morally abhorrent to us. We cannot only endorse Public Enemy but lose ourselves in Public Enemy, devote ourselves to Public Enemy in the same way that we can say that Leni Riefenstahl's "Triumph Of The Will" is a masterpiece. It's not that we're glossing over Public Enemy's violent black extremism or Riefenstahl's Nazi propaganda with aesthetic leniency. Public Enemy's extraordinary historical perspective is there, Riefenstahl's Nazi propaganda is there. But something else is there too, which is rejected at our loss.

What we also cannot afford to reject, and this may be difficult for some of you, is that what there is attains its transcendendant qualities not in spite of the opinions that caused it to be, but *because* of them. As with Megadeth, Swans, Easterhouse, Young Gods, Nick Cave, Anthrax and the Butthole Surfers, it's impossible to imagine Public Enemy existing at all were it not for the peculiarly obtuse angle from which they approach their "content", the world even.

In other words, their "content" is their style, their opinions *are* their form. And when it comes to style, when it comes to form, Public Enemy are faultless. Chuck finishes the last of the grapefruit juice, sets his glass down on the coffee table and, with considerable exasperation, explains why he's not a patriot. "I give less than a f*** about America and I ain't movin' because I know for a fact that my people have invested time, labour, effort and blood in that piece of rock and I ain't leavin'. I don't have that Garvey thinkin' where I'm goin' back to Africa – another f***ed with land. Where's there for me to go? I'm going to stay where I am and create *hell* if things don't come my way. The brothers and sisters are starting to wake up and there's gonna be *hell* on America's hands."

And we'd been feeling almost comfortable.

Stud Brothers

20

Songs of love and hate

ELVIS COSTELLO
May 20 1989

THE BELOVED ENTERTAINER ANSWERS MY call to his room
with a croak. He's not up yet. I'm not surprised. We've been up
most of the night, drinking our fool heads off at a party celebrating
the Irish Music Awards. We'd driven back to Dublin in the haunted hours before
dawn, drunk and rowdy, no doubt convinced we were having the time of our
lives. This morning we feel like death, of course, bones growing out of our heads,
tongues turning to chalk, hoarse-voiced and delirious.

On the phone now, to Costello, in the lobby of his hotel, I'm shaking,
wracked by nausea, chills and fever. Costello sounds as bad as I feel, which is as
bad as it gets. He asks for 15 minutes to pull himself together. I tell him we'll
give him 30 and meet him in the bar, where Sheehan and I have beers for
breakfast. Costello joins us, looking like he's been dragged all night across
scrubland, naked, by his heels. We all proceed to feel very sorry for ourselves,
and then we go up to Costello's room, heads still pounding, every nerve end
flayed and twitching.

We talk late into the afternoon, too tired almost to quit. Drinks keep arriving. Pretty soon, I'm getting drunk again. We try to remember when either of us last felt quite so bad, and Costello remembers when it was always like this for him – endless tours, fuelled by drugs and too much booze, every day a hangover, a stumbling through entire seasons, strung out on alcohol and narcotics; hell, after the novelty had worn off, leaving only the habit and the debris.

"I really thought all that nonsense had reached a kind of peak when we were in Holland doing 'Get Happy!!', " Costello says, his voice chipped at the edges with exhaustion, "when we were literally writing songs on the way to the studio from the bar. But later, it was just as bad. Probably worse. When we were in Nashville for 'Almost Blue', there was a film crew with us, making that 'South Bank Show' documentary. While they were filming, it was all very serious, and I'd be making all these ponderous statements about why I was making this country album, which everyone seemed to think was a completely lunatic thing to be doing. But as soon as the cameras stopped rolling, it was 'Right – *more drugs*, where's the f***in' drinks?' Screaming our bloody heads off, because we were just so completely f***in' *out* of it.

"A lot of people think that album sounds so depressed because I was drinking so much at the time. But there were other things that contributed to that, things were happening in my private life that I don't really want to talk about. It wasn't just drinking. I mean, I was drinking a lot in f*** in' '78. But I was having a better time then. It's when you're drinking and you're *not* happy, that's when you've got to worry. That's when it's gonna affect the way you look at things, because you're probably drinking for the wrong reasons. And *that's* when things start to get warped and you don't think anything through.

"I remember Nick Lowe once said to me, he said, 'You know, I just don't understand you. You *fight* every drink or any drugs you take. You fight them all the time. You're trying to stay straight all the way through it.' And I still do it. I'll never admit that I'm drunk. But we all drink. And sometimes it's for the right reasons . . . to let your mind off the leash for a while, and have a bit of fun, and then you don't mind if you make a bit of a prat of yourself, like last night. And it doesn't matter if you end up shouting at people, or have a punch up or whatever, as long as you wake up the same person. It's when you *don't want* to wake up the same person that you've got a problem.

"And I think I maybe went through that for a while. There were times when I'd feel every moment as bad as I do this morning. Times when you'd wake up, feeling like you were knocking on heaven's f***in' door and there'd be nobody there to f***in' answer you. Those were the worst times . . ."

THERE was a general feeling back then that you were purposely f***ing up your life to give you material for your songs.

"I think I did that for about a year," Costello says, tired now and showing it. "At the very most. And then I began to mistrust the results. Because if you do that, it's like when they pour acid in rabbits' eyes or something. What does it prove? It proves that it hurts the animal. Very smart. It's unnecessary research. And I guess I did some unnecessary research for a while. And then I'd write something that would scare the hell out of me . . . Like, there's a couple of things on 'Get Happy!!', that when I read them back, I just scared the hell out of myself. And I thought, 'Uh-uh . . . better not think any more about *this* . . . it's going too far . . .' Because you can think *too f***in' much*, you know, and it gets a bit f***in' *evil*."

Did you ever during this period think you were going too far, becoming *too* personal, too explicit, pouring too much venom, rage and spite into your songs?

"Maybe in retrospect . . . I can recognise sometimes where I maybe went over the line. But then again, I was never really that specific. I mean, people who really do pay too much attention for their own good have tried to peg certain songs to certain people. It's like a game, isn't it, that started in the early Seventies with people like Joni Mitchell. People always wanted to know who those songs were about. And people have tried that with me, and it's always been wrong.

"The fact is, those songs were never merely *confessional* . . . Even if you're satisfying your own selfish desire to put somebody down in a song or praise them, it isn't important that everybody knows who you're writing about or the specific emotional situation that provoked it. The song should have a universal appeal, otherwise it doesn't serve any purpose. It becomes merely self-indulgent. Like, 'Let me tell you some more secrets about myself . . .' It's all me me me. And that just gets really f***in' painful after a while. But then you get people saying, 'Well at least it's honest.' But *is* it? Is it honest to go around going, 'Look at my open sores.' I don't think it is. I think it's just f***in' indulgent."

DO you feel resentful, then, that people still dig through the bones of your songs, looking for the explicitly autobiographical in your writing?

"No, I don't *resent* it," Costello laughs, setting off a bout of wheezing. "I just blame John Lennon. It's the 'Plastic Ono Band', that album started it all. After that *everything* was supposed to be f***in' confessional. The early Seventies were full of all these people baring their f***in' *souls* for public scrutiny. There were records whose authenticity depended on the confessional aspect, and if you read certain magazines and the background interviews, you knew who these songs were about.

"And that for me always used to spoil it. Particularly when you found out what *dickheads* some of the people were that they were writing about. I'd rather have them be like Smokey Robinson songs, which could be about anyone. I don't think it's important that people know who 'Alison' was actually about. It's none of their f***in' business. It's a *song*. 'I Want You' is a *song*. It doesn't matter who it's about . . ."

People still automatically assume it's addressed to Cait . . .

"Yeah," he says wearily. "But it's just nonsense. It's just a song. It's a *really well written song*. It's also very personal, but you don't have to know the whole story to be touched by it . . . It's like people might say this new record is *less* personal because most of it's written in the third person. That's just as misguided. It all came out of *my* head, so how can it *not* be personal, you know . . . But there are still people, yeah, who want everything I've done documented and explained . . . but we're really getting into something else here.

"Like I say, it's all in the past . . . none of it means a damn. You can't go digging around for ever in the past. It's history. Let it go. It's what I'm doing *now* that counts. *That's* what I want people to realise."

WE were in Dublin to talk about "Spike", as if it hadn't been talked about enough already. The album arrived in February, in a blizzard of promotional activity unprecedented in Costello's career. For the first couple of weeks of the album's release, he was everywhere. You couldn't pick up a magazine, turn on the radio or television without finding Costello waxing lyrical about the record.

It got to the point eventually where all this public salesmanship seemed evidence almost of a desperate attempt by Costello to revive an interest in himself and his work, increasingly marginalised in the Eighties, and to recapture the commercial ground he'd lost after the enormous commercial success of "Armed Forces" in 1979. There were times, though, when his cheerful bluster seemed positively ingratiating.

"I certainly didn't feel that way," Costello bristles when this is brought up. "I think it's important to remember that the last 10 years with Columbia in America were often really frustrating. They just didn't know how to promote us. They'd run out of ideas. And by the end, I think they'd just given up, especially after 'King Of America', which they didn't have a f***in' clue what to do with, and 'Blood And Chocolate', which they hated and subsequently just f***in' *buried*.

"So this was our first one with Warner Brothers, and obviously you've got to accept the fact that the record company has nothing but horror stories from the past about you, and I simply didn't want to get off on the wrong foot with them and end up having to go through the same old f***in' battles just to get a f***in' record in the shops.

"So when the impetus came from America for me to promote the album, I said I'd do it. There was nothing *ingratiating* about it. As for being desperate – you can't *force* people to put you on the covers of magazines or on the television or the radio or whatever. That was *their* choice. And it just proves to me how f***in' *dull* everything must be right now, if someone with my tenure in the business can just reappear after three years and get that kind of attention. I mean, it's no big f***in' deal.

"But it amazed me, the ease which on the one hand you can come back and command the centre stage, just by saying you're there, and secondly still be regarded as somewhat outrageous. But what else is happening? In England, there's a cult a week for some band that's gonna save us all, and then you never f***in' hear of them again. It's very easy and I suppose attractive to get excited and emotional about the Darling Buds or somebody. But after a while, you can't keep up with who's the latest flame.

"And who's outrageous anymore? Like I was just in a radio station some-where in America, in the south, quite a mainstream station. And this guy said, 'Sometimes I just have to let my hair down and get outta here, go over to my old college station and play as much Nick Heyward as I like!' And with all due respect to Nick, he's *not* Jimmy Reed. I mean, I think Nick Heyward's made a couple of nice records, but he's not the wild man of rock 'n' roll. But he was this guy's definition of outrageous . . . And if that's indicative of the present climate, it's maybe not so curious that I still get some attention. And it's maybe why anything I do, not so much in England, but particularly in the States, seems to them to be effortlessly weird.

"So to get over to *them* the fact that the record isn't all *that* strange, you sometimes have to fill in a little of the background. You know, I've run into this a lot. People build up such preconceptions or they just associate you with one thing and they can't hear anything else you do. It's like they're looking at a painting you've done, upside down. Unless you can change their point of view, they're *never* gonna see.

THE last time I was in Dublin with Costello, we ended up drinking in some gaudy nightclub where the fluorescent throb and gash of neon lit us in garish hues and strobes flashed, epileptic and deranged. Bono arrived just after us. His appearance among the heathen throng was almost papal. First, the crowd parted in front of him, then gathered around him, reverent, adoring, as he advanced across the club. He settled at a table opposite us and looked around the room with the empty, dead stare of someone who'd long since lost the plot; a distant, cold glare that saw very little and understood even less. He could have been on another planet, and probably was. He was quickly surrounded by a sea of smothering supplicants, eager to pay their respects, kiss the hem of his coat, be touched by his presence, blessed by his righteousness.

"F***in' place," Costello muttered into his beer, "is turning into Lourdes."

We were at a table on a corner of the dancefloor, trying to make ourselves heard to each other above the infernal thud of the disco. Now that you're closer to us, you can hear that we're talking about "Blood And Chocolate". Costello is telling me that he had been convinced that this was the record that people had been waiting for him to make since "Get Happy!!", a return to the classic Attractions' sound, the record that at a stroke would revive his faltering commercial ambitions, thoroughly thwarted for most of the decade. This was outrageous. "Blood And Chocolate" is the most extreme and brutal of all Costello's albums. It sounds like it's been ripped screaming from the clefts of bedlam. In the bland, conservative climate of late-Eighties pop, it was a howl from an outer darkness. It stood no chance of being a hit. So when Costello tells me that he thought it would return him to the mainstream, I don't believe a word. A year later, though, in Dublin again, Costello is sticking to the same story.

"I honestly wasn't being ingenuous," he says. "I knew in America, especially, they took a huge gasp of breath when we did 'Almost Blue', and although 'King Of America' was one of those records that got me great reviews, Columbia just couldn't sell the f***in' thing . . . So I did have the notion when we came to do 'Blood And Chocolate' that in the States at least, they'd throw their hats in the air and cheer. I really did think it was the album they'd been wanting me to deliver. Because there were elements of it that I thought were stereotypical. It was like an older, grumpier version of 'This Year's Model', which I was pretty sure they'd go for. As it turned out, they did to it what they'd done to the two or three records before it. They buried the f***in' thing.

"In retrospect, I think we underestimated how f***in' *harsh* it sounded. But that was the mood we were in. We wanted it live and we wanted it loud, and we achieved that at the expense of everything else. I mean, we tried to do a ballad on that record, a really pretty song called 'Forgive Her Anything', but we physically couldn't play it. It sounded like we were playing with boxing gloves on. It needed too delicate an arrangement for the sound we'd contrived. And we got to really fighting about it. Like, 'It's your f***in' fault, you're playing too f***in' loud.' 'No, I'm not. You're playing too f***in' *fast*.' It was like the f***in' Troggs. But there was nothing we could do with it. That sound we had, there was just too much barbed wire in it. It was just too f***in' *ferocious*."

Given the subsequent split with the Attractions, was "Blood And Chocolate" meant to be a kind of last hurrah?

"Not intentionally. The idea was just to get together again and make a record. Originally it was gonna be an EP, a one-off thing, a bit of an undercover job, just to put the fun back into playing together. Because by then everything had got a bit askew. There was a lot of bad feeling that because of the way things turned out, the Attractions ended up playing on only one track on 'King Of America'. And the internal politics surrounding that record weren't too pleasant. And I don't think I handled it very well. But neither did a couple of the group. It just got unnecessarily ugly, you know. Like you were there that night at the Duke Of York's when I had that row with Steve. That's the sort of thing that was happening. People were being set up against each other. And I hate all that shit, and I didn't want everything to fall apart in acrimony, so the main thing was just to get back together instead of bickering. The thing was, I had no idea it was gonna turn out to be so extreme. But I love it. I think it's one of the two or three best records we made together."

Releasing two six-minute singles from it, "Tokyo Storm Warning" and "I Want You", didn't seem to be the most thoughtful commercial strategy. Were you just being perverse?

"No . . . I really thought they were the best two songs on the record. There were maybe a couple of others that could've been singles. 'I Hope You're Happy Now' might've been a hit, or 'Blue Chair'. But I couldn't see the wood for the trees over that one. You know, I sometimes tend to get too self-conscious about pop music. When I've got a good pop song, I have difficulty actually doing it properly. I somehow want to f*** it up. And I think the idea sometimes of releasing the obvious poppy track from an album as a single is patronising . . ."

Doesn't "Veronica" fall into that category?

"No," Costello says firmly, prepared to defend this one to the hilt, whatever the damage. "That's *unashamedly pop music*. You know, with that, I've come back to the way I was thinking when we did things like 'Oliver's Army'. I'm loathe to say the word, because the minute you say something's subversive, it's not subversive any more . . . But there is a trick to it, you know, where you can slip something out that takes people a while to figure out what it is you're actually singing about. With 'Veronica', if people had realized straight off that it was about an old woman, they might have thought it was too maudlin and just shut it off. Whereas the whole point of the song is that there is some hope and defiance in the character. So I think it's really good that it sounds like it's about a *young* girl, instead of it being a ponderous thing about an old woman, or something self-consciously dramatic like 'Eleanor Rigby'. Which is a great record, but you immediately know it's about this strange person. Whereas the idea with 'Veronica' isn't to patronise the character. It's said with love. So I like the idea that the music is really kind of bright and pretty. It's the prettiest record I've made in ages."

"VERONICA" is one of two tracks on "Spike" written with Paul McCartney. Another of their collaborations, "My Brave Face", has just been released as the ex-Beatles' new single; more are to follow on McCartney's forthcoming LP, "Flowers In The Dirt". We had talked the previous evening about the collaboration, and Costello, getting drunk, had worked himself into a rare old fit about the jaundiced view some people have of McCartney: he'd even been told that working with him had somehow devalued his own critical standing.

"That's true," Costello says the morning after, nursing a hangover, feeling fragile but feisty. "People have actually told me that. But f*** 'em. They're people who wouldn't know a good piece of music if it boned 'em up the arse."

So what was your immediate response when the call came from the McCartney Empire? Did you think you were on to an easy earner? Were you flattered? Suspicious?

"It might sound facile," Costello says, "but I didn't think about it in any of those terms. I just thought, 'Let's give it a go.' And it was all very unselfconscious – no big deal. We just got on with it. Occasionally, I'd look up and think, 'Oh, hell, it's *him*.' Because he really – don't laugh – he really does look *frighteningly like him*. The same was true of Orbison. He's one of those people who look exactly like you expect them to look. You know, I think of him like a Buzz Aldrin or somebody. Somebody who's been to the moon and back. Nobody – none of us in whatever part of the business we're in – none of us can conceive what it must be like to have been through what he's experienced. It's a unique experience, probably, in the 20th century to be him. And that's not making too big a thing of it.

"And the fact that he's so easy going about it all just seems to rile people. I mean, he could be a mad person, he could have reacted to what he went through in any number of ways that could prevent him now from being as straightforward and normal as he apparently is. The very fact that this guy has sort of *glided* through life and been very well rewarded is the cause, I think, of most of the flak he gets. It's just f***in' envy, that's what it is when you get right down to it . . ."

And he hasn't been shot, so he's not a legend.

"Absolutely," Costello says, heaving forward. "And he's uncomfortably undramatic about this thing he's been through. But, you know, he has been through it all, through more things than you could probably imagine. So why does he have to live up to somebody else's fantasy of who he is? I think that's a completely unreasonable demand to make of anyone.

"It's like these people who criticise him for being too rich or too famous. What the f*** has it got to do with them? It's just crap, you know. Why don't they just shut the f*** up and let him get on with his music. I also think that people who criticise him for being sentimental are talking a lot of shit as well. Because in any other line of work, if a man of 46 wasn't sentimental about his kids, they'd think he was a f***in' *sociopath*, you know. He's a married man, he has a nice life. What's the f***in' matter with that? F***in' hell, just because he's famous they want him to be at the barricades all the f***in' time. It's just stupid. He's just a really good musician, probably one of the best there has been in a long time . . . it's absolutely coming out of his fingers, you know . . . and if he doesn't want to use that musical talent to say world-changing things, that's *his* f***in' business."

"Blood And Chocolate" struck more than one commentator as a protracted musical identification with the troubled genius of John Lennon. When the invitation came to work with McCartney, was there maybe a feeling that you were being cast in the role that Lennon once played?

"No," Costello says quickly. "Lennon's obviously not around to be fallible or great or whatever – some bastard shot him – so in America, I think they're sometimes obviously fitting up a lot of people for the role. And I think it's a dangerous thing. In America, some really neurotic critics are trying to fit me in those shoes. And I think it's f***in' irresponsible. You know, COME ON. DRAW A F***IN' TARGET ON MY BACK . . ."

Costello has been through all this before, after the notorious Columbus incident he received nearly 200 death threats in a week.

"Don't remind me," he shudders. "Don't remind me."

THE afternoon draws on. We are both feeling as parched as f***. Costello orders another round of drinks. We talk about some of his other recent collaborations, most notably with Roy Orbison, whose version of the radically re-written "The Comedians" was the undisputed highspot of Orbison's posthumous "Mystery Girl" LP. Before flying out to Dublin, I had belatedly caught up with the "Roy Orbison And Friends: A Black And White Night" video of the commemorative concert in Los Angeles, at which Orbison was backed by an all star cast including Elvis Presley's Taking Care Of Business band (the TCBs, featuring Glen D Hardin, Ron Tutt, Jerry Scheff and legendary guitarist James Burton, who appeared on "King Of America"). Also on the show were Costello, Tom

Waits, Jackson Browne, KD Lang, Bonnie Raitt and Bruce Springsteen.

So what was it like, Elvis, clocking in behind the Big O?

"Well, it was very hard to be in *awe* of him," Costello says. "He was just very gentle, a little removed, perhaps a bit bemused by all the attention, but quite moved by everyone's enthusiasm. Because basically it was a big pain in the arse doing the show. I mean, it looked a lot of fun when they cut it together, but I have to say the production people had very little consideration for the musicians, including Roy.

"Basically, they didn't have a f***in' clue. In the end, T-Bone took a lot of the heat and he ended up telling them what to do, otherwise they would've had the musicians leaving in droves. Because there was one point where there was nearly a rebellion. Even with all deference to Roy, I think there was a point where some of the musicians were ready to walk, because there were a lot of ugly political things going down that could've been avoided if they'd been a bit more sensible. And what you see is this really good-natured show, so it really goes to show how much people dug him, because they all put that behind them. And a lot of the credit for that has to go to the TCBs, particularly, even though they were the ones most taken advantage of.

"Like, Rolling Stone came to take pictures and they didn't even ask James Burton to be in the shot. The guy from Rolling Stone didn't even recognise him. It was sort of, 'Right, we'll have Roy in the middle, and Bruce, you sit this side of Roy, and Elvis, you sit on the other side . . .' I said, 'What does this make me? The Holy Ghost or God the Son?' Because that's what it looked like . . . the f***in' Holy Trinity, with Roy as God the Father, you know . . ."

The show brought you into immediate contact with some people like Springsteen, about whom you've often been less than flattering . . .

"Let's be frank," Costello laughs. "They were people I've often been downright f***in' *rude* about. In fact, I've usually slagged them off, which I think is fair enough. I have my opinions about them and they probably know what they think about me. They might get a little outraged sometimes, but I don't give a flying f***, you know."

So how did you hit it off with old Bruce?

"I thought Bruce wasn't too bad," Costello says, and I can only think the drinks are having an effect. "I mean, he didn't come until the day of the show. But he turned up, no entourage, no bodyguards, no manager, no roadie. Carrying his own guitar as far as I could see. And I assumed he knew the songs so well he could just busk it. But I have this nice little image of him . . . Where we did the show was at the Coconut Grove, in the Ambassador Hotel, where Robert Kennedy was shot. The Grove is in a kind of basement at the back, and the kitchen just behind the stage is where he got shot. Place was like something out of the f***in' 'Shining' . . . Anyway, all the boys were crammed into one dressing room. And you couldn't move for all these baskets of fruit. It's *Hollywood*, you know, so every f***er on the show gets a basket of fruit with nuts and f***in' cheese . . . And, anyway, we're all packed in there, and it suddenly reminded me of when I was a kid and I used to go to the Joe Loss shows with my dad . . . all the guys in the band, standing around in their underwear, smoking . . . It was great. We were really like the Orchestra . . . And just before we were due on, I looked around and there's Springsteen. He's got a Walkman on, and he's got his electric guitar and he's got the chart of 'Only The Lonely', and he's looking really intense and worried. And suddenly he went, 'Oh, f*** – that's how it goes.'

"But I thought he played great on the show. He played his guitar solo, didn't he? That *one* guitar solo that he does. He plays with his *eyebrows*, have you noticed that? And there were a couple of songs where he has to trade off guitar parts with James Burton, and everybody thought he was really gonna be out of his depth. But he didn't try to outflash Burton. You can't, let's face it. So he played his one note solo and he played it very emphatically, like he really meant it. And James came back with this ridiculously fancy lick that he does and gave Springsteen this look, you know, 'Top *that*, boy.' And Bruce is going, 'Oooooh, *shit* . . . back to the one note solo . . .' I thought he was pretty cool."

COSTELLO is by now in a pretty expansive anecdotal mood. I ask him about Van Morrison, who appeared with him the last time he played the Albert Hall.

"I think what I really admire about him," Costello says, "apart from the fact that he makes the most incredible f***in' records, is his *singlemindedness*. People go on about him being difficult, but he does it *his* way and if you can't accept that, then go somewhere else. I don't think he's gonna cry. He's tougher than that. He really is tougher than the rest. He's in a class of one, and if you don't like it then f*** off, you know. There are only like two or three people with this kind of singular identity in rock 'n' roll. Like, Lou Reed, Dylan . . ."

You met Dylan once, didn't you?

"I've met Dylan a few times, yeah," Costello says. "We had a strange conversation once, I remember. I met all his kids once in a parking lot in Minneapolis. He came to this party with all his sons. Lined them up like they were on parade, and I had to shake hands with them. He said, 'This is Jesse, he knows all the words to "Pump It Up".' And I thought, 'Now there's something wrong with this statement, Bob. He knows all the words to "Subterranean Homesick Blues" is what you probably mean.' Jesse was a punk fan. I don't know how old he is now, but then he was into the Clash and people like that. I think he thought his dad was a bit old-fashioned. Maybe he's since realized that his dad was a bit more happening than Mick Jones, you know. I hope so. I mean, I love old Mick, he's great. But Bob's always been a bit more happening than Mick, let's face it."

What do you talk to someone like Dylan about? The *weather*?

"Actually," Costello says. "yeah. With somebody like Dylan or Van, they say they're unpredictable souls who can be rude to people. So I figure if they just accept you and you just talk in an ordinary conversation about the weather or something, it means they're giving you somehow more credit than they would to someone they don't really have time for. I mean, you hear all these horror stories about these people, but you've got to remember that there are plenty of people who want a piece of them and they make unreasonable demands on them. And there are a few people that have tried to make those demands of me, so I'm aware of the fact that if you start like getting in on them and it's like, 'C'mon, Bob, where ARE the Gates Of Eden?' you'd expect to be shown the door. I'm always mindful of what it's like when somebody gets on *my* case. Sometimes it's well-meaning, but you really just can't answer their questions, because you can't *think* like them. They've got their perspective on what you do and you just can't get into it."

THE night before the interview, Costello had appeared at the Irish Music Awards. He and Christy Moore had done a version of "Dark End Of The Street", an old Costello favourite. It was a moment of sober beauty in an otherwise unremarkable pantomime. The front rows of the audience were full of wriggling Brosettes who glared at Costello with furious indignation. Turns out later that they are howling mad with him for being less than kind to Bros on a recent radio show. After the show, some of them cornered him in a local pub.

"It was as funny as hell," he says. "They all wanted my blood for slandering Luke by suggesting that he might be something less than a Titan. I just felt a bit sad for them. Because this, you know, is the extent of their musical excitement, this rather dull group. And they were going, 'Tell us you really don't hate them.' And I'm going, 'I don't *hate* them, I just don't *like* 'em. I'm not *supposed* to f*** in' like 'em. *You're* supposed to like 'em . . .' It was all a bit pathetic, really, because they'll all be embarrassed in four years time that they were ever Brosettes. It's like, where do you meet Bay City Rollers' fans these days . . . And Bros will be forgotten in the long run, because they don't represent anything particularly worthwhile. It's like Michael Jackson. He'll be forgotten in 50 years. He'll be like this person who statistically was famous, like Al Jolson or Rudy Vallee, but nobody'll really remember him. He's just a facsimile of excitement.

And because there's no substance to what he does, and because he's sold his soul to a corporate identity, which is actually bigger than he is, in the long run I think he'll be swallowed by it. It's like Whitney Houston, I think it's downright sad that somebody as good as her will take a billion dollars from Pepsi to sell herself down the river. She's just turned into this cabaret singer. You look at her and it's like the light's gone from her eyes. She's just another victim of the Pepsi Vampires."

So who are the strong, Elvis, who's to be trusted? Who's *angry* any more?

"I dunno," Costello says wearily, exhaustion creeping up on him like a slow tide. "It does seem at the moment that there's no real willingness to test anything. But it's not surprising really. All the mannerisms of rebellion in music seem to have been used up. You only have to look at Guns 'N' Roses to realize that. Cait got their album, you know, and it's f***in' terrible. It's like an Outlaws record or something. 'I'm goin' down the road with my geetar and I'm a baad muthaf***er . . .' F*** *off*, you little twat. It's about as rock 'n' roll as f***in' David Nixon. The thing is, you can't keep leaping out of the cupboard going boo to people. It's not frightening anymore.

"And the funny thing is, the *real* wildmen are still unacceptable. I'm not talking about someone like Johnny Rotten. He's completely acceptable. He's just like Quentin Crisp. He's an English eccentric. But *Jerry Lee Lewis*, man. I saw Jerry Lee, and he's still f***in' unacceptable to most people. T-Bone went for a meeting with him, because he's been working on the film they're doing about him. And they went to this really chi-chi Hollywood cafe, and this little waiter comes up and goes, 'Hi, my name ith Cwithtopher and I'll be your waiter for tonight. Is there something I can get you?'

"And Jerry Lee says 'Yeah. What about something blonde, 21 years old with big f***in' tits.' Just starts straight in, you know. Brilliant. And someone like that, they're always gonna be on the outside. He's definitely the real thing. And there's really no one else around who's that unique, that singular. I don't see anyone like that around anymore. I see a few interesting eccentrics. Morrissey. Michael Stipe. Johnny Lydon. Myself, maybe. But those heavy metal bands who think they're so f***in' outrageous. I just think, 'F*** off, pal. You don't even own the territory.'

"Because I look back at some of the things *we've* done, and it's no f***in' contest. I mean, we've had our f***in' *moments*, man. And they don't even come close."

Allan Jones

21

Crucified by success

NIRVANA

July 11 1992

THE INTERVIEW WITH NIRVANA TAKES place in a dressing-room on the edge of a river in Stockholm. The day is cloudy, with occasional flashes of sunshine. People are drinking coke, and, in Chris's case, red wine. Chris and Dave are sitting on one couch, Kurt on another. A bowl of chilli-roasted peanuts and some fruit nestles on the table. Someone's smoking.

The band seem awkward in each other's presence, slightly wary of one another. When Chris speaks, his eyes are looking anywhere but in Kurt's direction. When Kurt speaks, he does so almost defensively, as if he feels a need to justify himself in front of Chris. When Dave speaks, you know he can feel the uneasiness, but he's trying to ignore it.

Apart for a brief spot on Swedish TV earlier today, this is the first interview Nirvana have given as a band for a long while. This might account for the subdued atmosphere – although many people have pointed to Nirvana's success as creating cracks, friction within the band. Certainly, Kurt seems warier than when I last met him – photographer Steve Gullick has to go through a ridiculous rigmarole of hoods and bleached hair and agreements later on before he's allowed to take any shots.

The noise you can't hear is support band, Teenage Fanclub, soundchecking for tonight's show. Nirvana's concert is lacking in any real excitement or emotion, although the encore is inspired. It seems they still have some way to go before playing arenas becomes second nature to them. It's obvious the band aren't happy with this state of affairs, but equally obvious that they aren't prepared to compromise their principles just to make people feel easier.

As you join us, Kurt is talking about Nirvana's forthcoming album.

"WE'RE going into the studio as soon as we get back to Seattle," says Kurt. "What I'd like to do is to go into Reciprocal with Jack Endino (the engineer on 'Bleach'), and rent exactly the same equipment as was there when we recorded 'Bleach'. We record the songs with Jack on an eight-track, record them somewhere else on a 24-track with Steve Albini, and then pick the best."

So you're aiming for a rawer sound on the next album?

"Definitely less produced," says Chris.

"As long as it doesn't sound like 'Nevermind', " adds Kurt.

Why? Are you fed up with it?

"No, I really like that album," Kurt replies. "And it doesn't matter what kind of production it has because the songs are good. But it would have been better rawer. It doesn't sound very original."

"We don't want to find ourselves in Slayer's situation," Dave explains, "where the same people produced their last three records and they all sound identical. That's stupid."

When you talk about how different you want your next record to sound, isn't there an element of wanting to challenge your audience about that statement? (The implication is that, because Nirvana have become fed up with their audience, they want to alienate them.) Kurt denies this.

"It's not like that," he says. "It's more like challenging ourselves, making a record exactly as we want to. Whether our audience likes it or not doesn't matter. We don't want to be writing 'In Bloom' for the next five years."

"Maybe the next record will be the one where we can judge how much impact we've actually made," Chris wonders aloud.

"Yeah, but we know that at least 50 per cent of people who like us now aren't going to like our next record if it has a lot of abrasive, inaccessible songs on it," replies Kurt, scornfully. "If they do . . . man, that proves our theory that you can shove anything down the mainstream's throat and they'll eat it up."

"But that's what I always thought of our second record as being," interrupts Dave. "Something way less produced, where we can push the sound even further and see if we can get a noisy LP on the charts."

"But do you think that would happen?" Kurt asks him. "Let's pretend we haven't released 'Endless Nameless' yet, and it's our first single off the next album – if people bought it, wouldn't it just prove that they like us just cos it's cool to?"

"No," Chris replies. "That argument just doesn't hold any water. They wouldn't be that mindless."

(NB: "Endless Nameless" is the 10-minute long noise-fest grunge track which appeared on limited quantities of "Nevermind", and on the B-side of "Come As You Are".)

Do you think you'll have another single as big as "Teen Spirit"?

"No," states Kurt, firmly. "We haven't written any songs as good – or as poor – as that. We might write one right before we finish recording the album, because 'Teen Spirit' was written just weeks before 'Nevermind', but we're not going to try."

KURT disappears momentarily to find a cigarette. Someone (the promoter? a roadie?) pokes his head round the door, looking for Alex, Nirvana's exuberant tour manager. The strains of Teenage Fanclub's "The Concept" drift in through a window, glorious in the early evening air. Dave cracks open another can.

Earlier, a bunch of us had gone for a stroll down by the river while Kurt and Courtney traversed the town, looking for Nirvana bootlegs to liberate and then give to kids wearing official Nirvana tee-shirts. One seller became freaked out and started yelling at Courtney – but there was no repeat of the ugliness in Ireland, where Kurt was reportedly punched by a bouncer after going to stop an altercation between security and a fan.

It's apparent that there are two distinct camps in Nirvana: the newly-wed couple – and everyone else. Still, that's no reason to start believing all the malicious stories that have plagued Nirvana, and, more particularly, Kurt Cobain, since the band's rapid rise to the top. Drugs? What the f*** does it have to do with you, punk?

Chris stretches his legs, and sighs. This is gonna be a long interview. Kurt comes back, and we continue.

WHEN I saw your static performance in Oslo two days ago, I kept thinking back to what Kurt told me last year: "We're not going to be proud of the fact there are a bunch of Guns'N'Roses kids who are into our music. We don't feel comfortable progressing, playing larger venues."

"We can't," Chris agrees. "We've always treated people with that mentality with a little bit of contempt and cynicism, and to have them screaming for us . . .

Why are they screaming? What do they see in us? They're exactly the same kind of people who wanted to kick our arse in high school."

"It's just boring to play outdoors," explains his singer. "I've only just gotten used to playing large venues because the sound is at least tolerable. But, outside, the wind blows the music around so much that it doesn't feel like you're playing music, it feels like you're lip-synching to a boom box recording. Plus, these festivals are very mainstream – we're playing with Extreme and Pearl Jam, you know? Ninety per cent of the kids out there are probably just as much into Extreme as they are into us.

"I try every night," he continues, "but I just can't fool myself. I'm not going to smile and pose like Eddie Van Halen, even though he's a miserable drunk. That doesn't mean it'll be that way next month (Reading), but that's how it is, right now."

Do you feel any responsibility?

"For what?" Kurt asks.

The masses. The people who bought your record. Because you've been given this power to use.

"To me," Dave begins, tentatively, "our main responsibility is to not pretend to be something we're not. I don't think pretending to be a professional rock unit really works. If we're gonna have a shitty show, then let's have a shitty show. I can see there's a lot of responsibility playing massive shows, but other kinds? I don't know."

"It's rock 'n' roll to be irresponsible," Chris adds.

I know.

"Once you start considering this to be a responsibility, it becomes a burden," muses the drummer.

Silence.

WE'VE reached a brief impasse. Kurt starts leafing through a crap metal rag and spots a picture of Melvins (his early mentors), to his delight. Courtney sticks her head round the door to ask if we've seen Siren, because Inger Lorre slags her in it. Someone throws her a copy.

Dave starts telling me about the interview that they've just done for Swedish TV.

"THEY thanked us for saving rock 'n' roll," he laughs. "For throwing a bomb into the rock 'n' roll establishment."

Do you feel you've done that?

"Maybe we blew a paper bag up and popped it," sneers Chris.

From where I'm standing, you don't seem to have changed very much. Murmurs of agreement come from the assembled.

What do you hate most about being famous?

"Kids with Bryan Adams and Bruce Springsteen tee-shirts coming up to me and asking for autographs," Kurt says. "When people in the audience hold up a sign that says 'Even Flow' (a Pearl Jam song) on one side and 'Negative Creep' (a Nirvana song) on the other."

Silence from the other two.

Okay. What's the best thing about being famous?

"You know, that's a really good question," answers Kurt, ironically.

"We might get some perks here and there," his bassist ventures. "A free drink or two, maybe."

Do you get many groupies?

"When I was about 12," replies Kurt, "I wanted to be a rock 'n' roll star, and I thought that would be my payback to all the jocks who got girlfriends all the time. But I realised way before I became a rock star that that was stupid."

"Maybe it's flattering to all these heavy metal bands, but we find it kind of disgusting," adds Dave, Nirvana's only unmarried member.

How about drink?

"I came into this tour with a fresh perspective," Chris muses. "I used to get stressed out, drink a whole lot and react to everything. Now I just go with the flow."

"I've always loved the spontaneity of being frustrated and pissed off . . ." Kurt challenges him.

" . . . and drunk," finished Chris. "Oh yeah! I've had some of my best inspirations intoxicated – it's a different reality. It's like living in a movie or a cartoon, where your subconscious takes off. That's where all the good stories come from. But it's such hell on your body."

Has the sudden fame appreciably changed your lifestyles?

"Definitely," responds Kurt, vehemently.

"It hasn't changed mine," his bassist disagrees. "I can still go down to Safeway, buy fruit and vegetables, walk around town. I don't care if people stare at me or whatever."

"You don't?" Kurt asks him. "At all?"

"No," replies Chris. "And the more they see me, especially in Seattle, the more . . ."

"Oh yeah, eventually they'll get tired of sniggering at you and talking behind your back." Kurt finishes the sentence for him. "Well, I've been confronted by people wanting to beat me up, by people heckling me and being so drunk and obnoxious because they think I'm this pissy rock star bastard who can't come to grips with his fame.

"I was in a rock club the other night," he continues, "and one guy comes up, pats me on the back and says, 'You've got a really good thing going, you know? Your band members are cool, you write great songs, you affected a lot of people, but, man, you've really got to get your personal shit together!' Then another person comes up and says, 'I hope you overcome your drug problems.' All this happens within an hour while I'm trying to watch the Melvins, minding my own business.

"There were about five or six kids sitting around, very drunk, screaming 'Rock star! Rock star! Oh, look, he's going to freak out any minute! He's going to have a tantrum! He's going to start crying!' Then this other guy comes up, puts his arm around me and says, 'You know, my girlfriend broke up with me and took my Nirvana album, so you should give me $14 to buy a new CD, cos you can afford that now you're a big rock star.' And I said, 'Gee. That's a clever thing to say. Why don't you f*** off?' "

"But you have to ignore them," Chris warns him, "or it becomes an obsession. I have dreams about being nude in public, and I interpret them as worrying about sticking out. Forget it! It can become a preoccupation. I was like that, too, when I used to see someone famous . . ."

"Yeah, but did you pitch them shit?" Kurt interrupts him.

"No," Chris replies. "I didn't, but that incident you mentioned seems to be pretty isolated."

"IT'S not isolated," snarls Kurt. "It happens to me all the time – every time I go out, every f***ing time. It's stupid. And, if it bothers me that much, I'm going to do something about it. F*** it, rock doesn't mean that much to me. I still love to be in a band and play music with Chris and Dave, but if it means that we have to resort to playing in a practice room and never touring again, then so be it."

Chris and Dave fall silent. The mood in the room has turned dark.

"I have to hear rumours about me all the time," the singer growls. "I'm totally sick of it. If I'm going to take drugs that's my own f***ing prerogative, and if I don't take drugs it's my own f***ing prerogative. It's nobody's business, and I don't care if people take drugs and I don't care if people don't take drugs.

"It all started with just one article in one of the shittiest, cock rock-orientated LA magazines," he continues, "where this guy assumed I was on heroin because he noticed that I was tired. Since then, the rumours have spread like wildfire. I can't deny that I have taken drugs and I still do, every once in a while. But I'm not a f***ing heroin addict, and I'm not going to . . ."

He trails off, momentarily wordless.

"It's impossible to be on tour and to be on heroin," he begins again. "I don't know any band that could do it, unless you're Keith Richards and you're being given blood transfusions every three days, and you have runners going out and scoring drugs for you."

Kurt glowers with anger.

"I never realised that mainstream audiences react towards mainstream rock stars in this manner, because I've never paid attention before," he rails. "I don't mean to complain as much as I do, but it's a load of shit. It's really stupid. I've had days where I've considered this to be a job, and I never thought that would happen. It makes me question the point of it all. I'm only gonna bitch about it for another year and, if I can't handle it after that, we're gonna have to make some drastic changes."

Everett True

About the writers

Geoff Brown, a former professional drummer, left in 1977 to edit *Black Music* and *Black Music & Jazz Review*. He then moved to *Time Out* where he was music, sport and, finally, senior editor. He has contributed to many newspapers and magazines and his books include *Diana Ross* (Sidgwick), *Michael Jackson: Body & Soul* (Virgin) and *Blackwell Guide to Soul Recordings*. His TV writing includes the narration to Channel 4's "Hip to the Tip: The Story of Atlantic Records".

Ray Coleman, editor-in-chief of the *Melody Maker* from 1970 to 1981, has written biographies of John Lennon, Eric Clapton, the Rolling Stones (co-authored with Bill Wyman), Gary Numan, Beatles manager Brian Epstein, Gerry Marsden and the Carpenters. He writes on music in international publications as diverse as the *Daily Telegraph* and *Billboard*.

Harry Doherty's life has been richly varied since his days at *Melody Maker*. His time at Dave Dee's well-funded, ill-fated record company was great fun. He then went on to produce a documentary series on Capital Radio before becoming founding Editor of *Metal Hammer* in 1986. After a two-year absence during which *Hard 'n' Heavy*, the video magazine, was launched, he returned to *Metal Hammer* publishers, Rockteam, as group editor-in-chief for Europe. He left in December 1993 and will head a new publishing group in 1994 that launches its first "noisy" title this spring.

Allan Jones has been on the staff of *Melody Maker* for over twenty years, ten of those as Editor. He has interviewed many of the biggest names in rock'n'roll, and is the author of *Pearl Jam: The Illustrated Story*, published in August 1994 by Hamlyn.

Simon Reynolds was *Melody Maker* staff feature writer between 1986 and 1990. He left to go freelance in 1990, and subsequently alternated between London and New York. He currently writes for the *New York Times*, *Spin*, *Artforum*, *Rolling Stone*, *iD*, the *Observer*, *The Wire*, *Mojo*, *Vibe*, *Details* – and, of course, *MM*. His books include *Blissed Out: The Raptures of Rock* (Serpent's Tail, 1990) – a collection of essays, most of which originally appeared in *MM* – and *The Sex Revolts: Gender, Rebellion & Rock 'n' Roll*, co-authored with Joy Press (Serpent's Tail, to be published in the autumn of 1994).

Mat Smith joined *Melody Maker* in 1986. He is currently Deputy News Editor. However, his career almost came to an early end when he asked a drunk and irritable Jeffrey Lee Pierce: "Do you think you're capable of murder?" Whereupon the Gun Club singer smashed the beer glass he was drinking from, leapt across the table, and attempted to slash his inquisitor's throat. Mat's never asked that question since.

The Stud Brothers are Dominic Wills and Ben Mothersole. They met in late 1985 while both attempting to seduce the lead singer at a gig by American proto-grunge band the Electric Chairs. As well as *Melody Maker*, the Stud Brothers have contributed to the *Tatler*, the *European* and numerous foreign publications, and have also appeared on Radio One, Two and Four and many youth television shows requiring a clear head and sharp tongue. The Stud Brothers are currently co-editors of the glossy anarchist fanzine *Deadline*.

Adam Sweeting left the *Melody Maker* in 1986 to pursue a freelance writing career. After writing about rock music regularly for the *Guardian*, he became the paper's rock critic, then in 1993 adopted a new role as feature writer specialising in arts and media. He also contributes to *GQ*, the *Radio Times* and *New Woman*, and can be heard on Radio 2.

Everett True, assistant editor, *Melody Maker*. In 1982 he started life as a columnist for Creation Records' Alan McGee's *Communication Blur* fanzine. Short-lived recording career began under the name "The Legend!" Joins *NME* in 1984, carrying out niche as the only unashamed virgin in rock 'n' roll. Threatened with physical violence at gigs. Joining the *Melody Maker* in 1988, he discovers sex, discovers alcohol, discovers Seattle, discovers Nirvana and invents "grunge". Resolves to write follow-up to Pamela Des Barres' seminal work, *I'm With The Band*, to be called *I'm With The Band, Too*. Or alternatively, *Nirvana: The Everett True Years*. Other future plans: none.

Michael Watts, now executive editor of *Esquire*, has edited the magazines of the *Sunday Correspondent* and *Evening Standard*, produced television programmes for BBC2 and Channel 4, and was London correspondent for the *Los Angeles Times*. He thinks the invention of the cheap synthesizer has been fatal to making original pop music, but likes Apache Indian. He says he cannot remember the Seventies.

Chris Welch joined *Melody Maker* in 1964 as feature writer and reviewer and became Features Editor in 1970. He stayed with the *MM* until 1980 when he became assistant editor of IPC title *Musicians Only*. After leaving *MO*, he concentrated on writing books and among his bestsellers was the first book on Jimi Hendrix, *Hendrix: A Biography*. He also wrote books on Paul McCartney, Marc Bolan, Led Zeppelin and the official biography of Steve Winwood. His 1985 book on Tina Turner is shortly to be republished by Virgin. In 1987 Chris became Reviews Editor of *Kerrang!* and in 1988 he became editor of *Metal Hammer*, the European hard rock magazine. In 1992 he became editor of *Rock World* magazine. He is currently writing a new book on Cream and is personal manager of 23-year-old singer songwriter Jonathan Wells.

Mark Williams: When a freelancer, his reaction to the IPC/NUJ lock-out of *MM* staffers in '78 was to start *New Music News* for what is now Dennis Publishing. Several IPC staff moonlighted for *NMN* under preposterous pseudonyms during its short but amusing life, but Williams found himself ostracised by IPC thereafter and so freelanced for various US and UK titles until going to work as PRO for LA's Slash Records in 1980. He returned to set up his own magazine publishing company in '84, but in 1990 the sleeping partner woke up and extracted all the money. After operating a consultancy, latterly trying (unsuccessfully) to re-organise *Metal Hammer*, he ended up running a weekly newspaper in the depths of rural Wales.

Richard Williams was the deputy editor of the *MM* from 1970 to 1973, and its editor from 1978 to 1980. In between times he ran Island Records' A&R department and edited *Time Out*. After spending most of the 1980s at *The Times*, he joined the *Independent on Sunday*, where he edited the Sunday Review for three years before becoming the paper's chief sports writer. His books include *Bob Dylan: A Man Called Alias* (1992) and *Miles Davis: The Man in the Green Shirt* (1993).